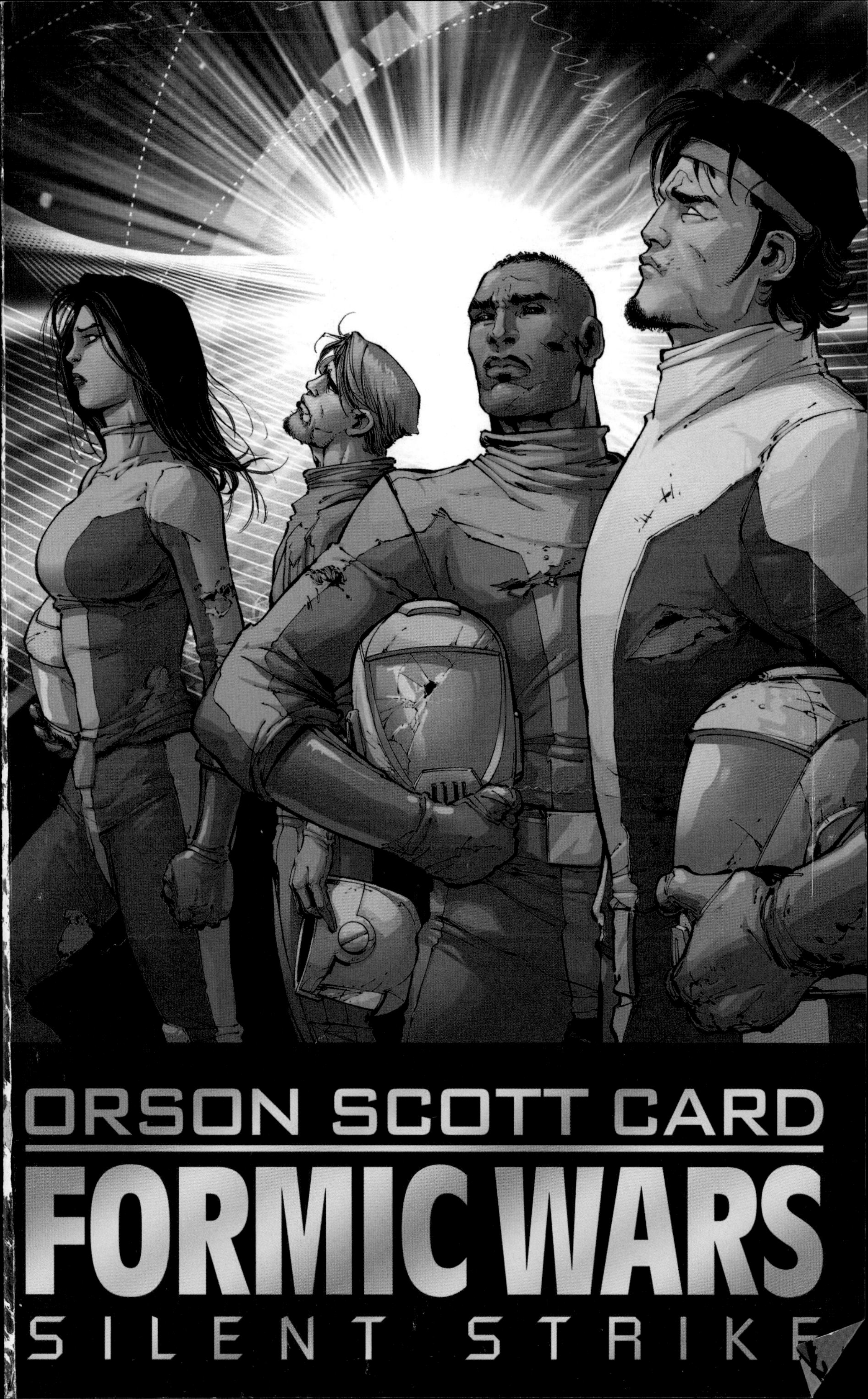

ORSON SCOTT CARD

FORMIC WARS

SILENT STRIKE

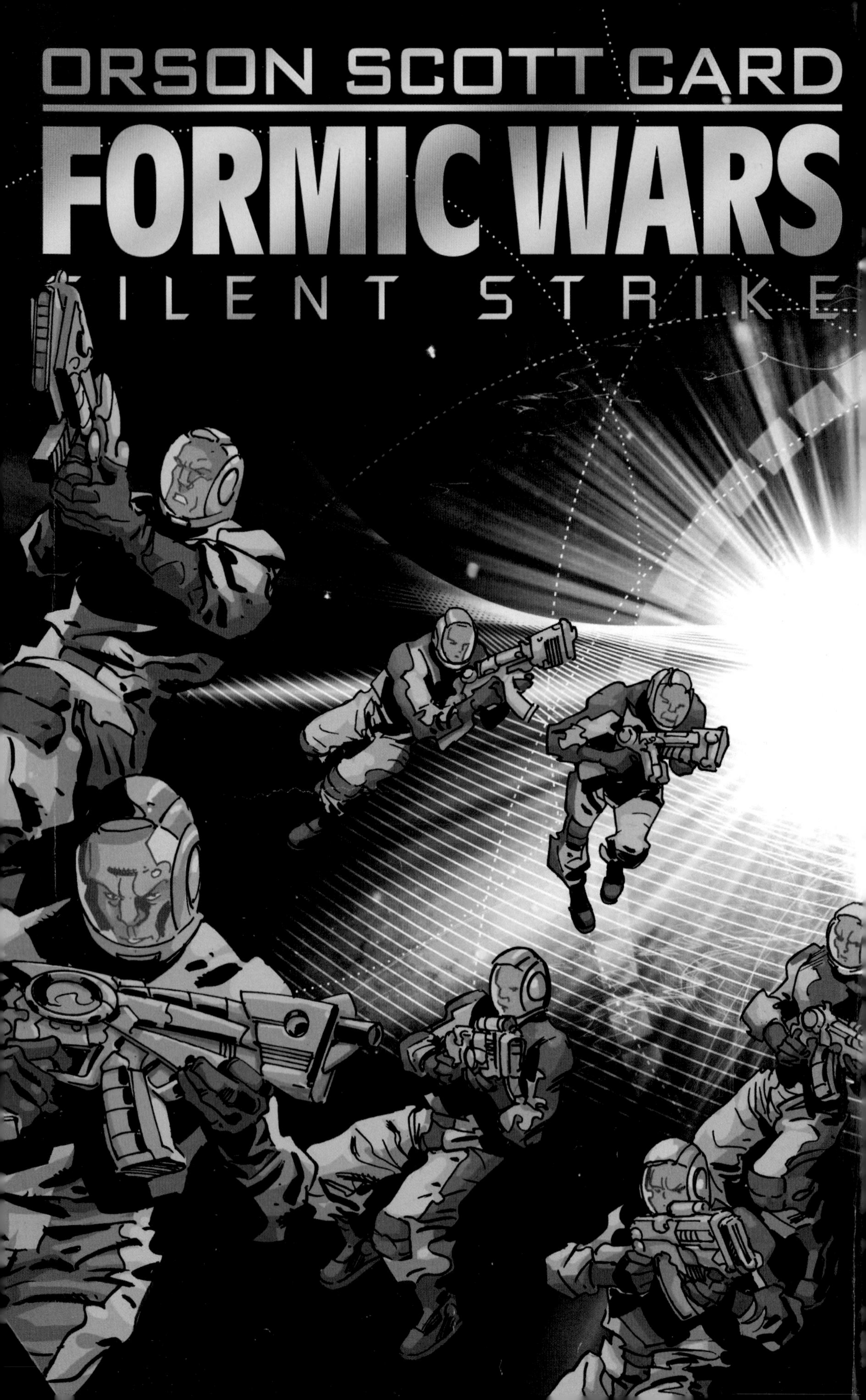
ORSON SCOTT CARD
FORMIC WARS
SILENT STRIKE

Creative Director & Executive Director:
ORSON SCOTT CARD
Plot: **ORSON SCOTT CARD**
& AARON JOHNSTON
Script: **AARON JOHNSTON**
Art: **GIANCARLO CARACUZZO**

Color Art: **JIM CHARALAMPIDIS**
Letterer: **CORY PETIT**
Cover Art: **GIUSEPPE CAMUNCOLI,**
DANNY MIKI & JIM CHARALAMPIDIS

Editor: **JORDAN D. WHITE**
Senior Editor: **NICK LOWE**

Special thanks to
KRISTINE CARD,
KATHLEEN BELLAMY,
JIM NAUSEDAS,
RUWAN JAYATILLEKE,
ARUNE SINGH
& JEFF SUTER

Collection Editor:
JENNIFER GRÜNWALD
Assistant Editors:
ALEX STARBUCK & NELSON RIBEIRO
Editor, Special Projects:
MARK D. BEAZLEY
Senior Editor, Special Projects:
JEFF YOUNGQUIST
Senior Vice President of Sales:
DAVID GABRIEL
SVP of Brand Planning & Communications:
MICHAEL PASCIULLO
Book Designer:
RODOLFO MURAGUCHI

Editor in Chief: **AXEL ALONSO**
Chief Creative Officer: **JOE QUESADA**
Publisher: **DAN BUCKLEY**
Executive Producer: **ALAN FINE**

FORMIC WARS: SILENT STRIKE. Contains material originally published in magazine form as FORMIC WARS: SILENT STRIKE #1-5. First printing 2012. ISBN# 978-0-7851-3614-9. Published by MARVEL WORLDWIDE, INC., a subsidiary of MARVEL ENTERTAINMENT, LLC. OFFICE OF PUBLICATION: 135 West 50th Street, New York, NY 10020. Copyright © 2011 and 2012 Orson Scott Card. All rights reserved. $24.99 per copy in the U.S. and $27.99 in Canada (GST #R127032852); Canadian Agreement #40668537. All characters featured in this issue and the distinctive names and likenesses thereof, and all related indicia are trademarks of Orson Scott Card. No similarity between any of the names, characters, persons, and/or institutions in this magazine with those of any living or dead person or institution is intended, and any such similarity which may exist is purely coincidental. Marvel and its logos are TM & © Marvel Characters, Inc. **Printed in the U.S.A.** ALAN FINE, EVP - Office of the President, Marvel Worldwide, Inc. and EVP & CMO Marvel Characters B.V.; DAN BUCKLEY, Publisher & President - Print, Animation & Digital Divisions; JOE QUESADA, Chief Creative Officer; TOM BREVOORT, SVP of Publishing; DAVID BOGART, SVP of Operations & Procurement, Publishing; RUWAN JAYATILLEKE, SVP & Associate Publisher, Publishing; C.B. CEBULSKI, SVP of Creator & Content Development; DAVID GABRIEL, SVP of Publishing Sales & Circulation; MICHAEL PASCIULLO, SVP of Brand Planning & Communications; JIM O'KEEFE, VP of Operations & Logistics; DAN CARR, Executive Director of Publishing Technology; SUSAN CRESPI, Editorial Operations Manager; ALEX MORALES, Publishing Operations Manager; STAN LEE, Chairman Emeritus. For information regarding advertising in Marvel Comics or on Marvel.com, please contact Niza Disla, Director of Marvel Partnerships, at ndisla@marvel.com. For Marvel subscription inquiries, please call 800-217-9158. **Manufactured between 5/28/2012 and 6/25/2012 by R.R. DONNELLEY, INC., SALEM, VA, USA.**

10 9 8 7 6 5 4 3 2 1

ORSON SCOTT CARD
FORMIC WARS
SILENT STRIKE

VICTOR DELGADO

IMALA BOOTSTAMP

UKKO JUKES

LEM JUKES

MAZER RACKHAM

WIT O'TOOLE

PREVIOUSLY IN
FORMIC WARS:
BURNING EARTH

When a family of asteroid miners detects an alien ship approaching, they send seventeen-year-old **Victor Delgado** to the moon to warn Earth. Upon arrival, Victor's story is met with skepticism, until a lunar trade official named **Imala Bootstamp** believes Victor and takes him to **Ukko Jukes**, CEO of the world's largest space-mining corporation. Ukko alerts Earth, but the warning comes too late; the ship has already destroyed a space station and killed most of Victor's family. **Lem Jukes**, Ukko's son and captain of a corporate mining ship, barely escaped with his life.

The "Formics," as the humans name the aliens, arrive on Earth and send three giant landers down to China and begin scouring the countryside, annihilating all life they encounter. Lieutenant **Mazer Rackham** leads an assault against the aliens, but he fails and is seriously wounded. A Chinese boy nurses Mazer back to health, and the two of them team up with Captain **Wit O'Toole**, leader of MOPs, an elite special forces unit.

Wit and Mazer manage to destroy one of the landers and assist the Chinese military, but the Formics attack and decimate their base. Meanwhile, with Lem Jukes' help, Imala and Victor fly unnoticed to the Formic mother ship. Unfortunately, Lem is unable to stop his father from launching an attack, and Ukko sends out a fleet of drone ships equipped with experimental weapons just as Victor manages to infiltrate the vessel. Victor is caught in the crossfire...and the Formics are just getting started.

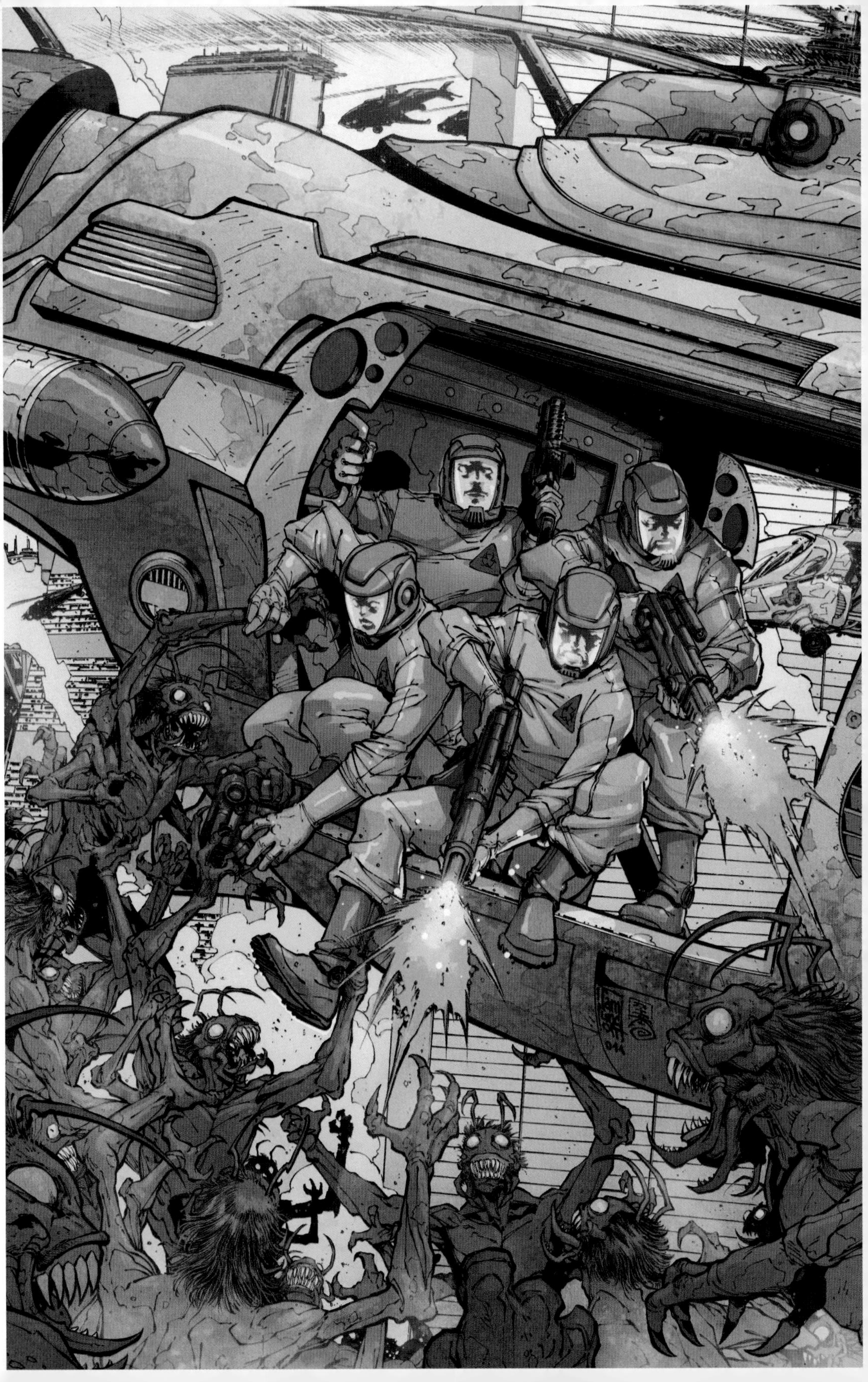

The first two months of the Formic invasion produced the greatest number of human casualties. Many were victims of what came to be known as the Scouring of China, in which Formic landers and flyers stripped the landscape of all biological life and turned much of southeast China into a scorched, barren wasteland. The Formics collected this biomass — which consisted of crops, plants, animal life, and human corpses — in the hopes of breaking it down into fuel. Those efforts were frustrated by three soldiers of the Mobile Operations Police (MOPs), who destroyed one of the Formic landers and a mountain of biomass. This first human victory of the war dramatically improved global morale. Suddenly there was hope that the human race would be preserved.

That hope was dashed four days later when thousands of Formic reinforcements came down from the mother ship and gassed China's most populated cities, killing an estimated forty-four million people.

–A History of the Formic Wars, Volume One, Demosthenes

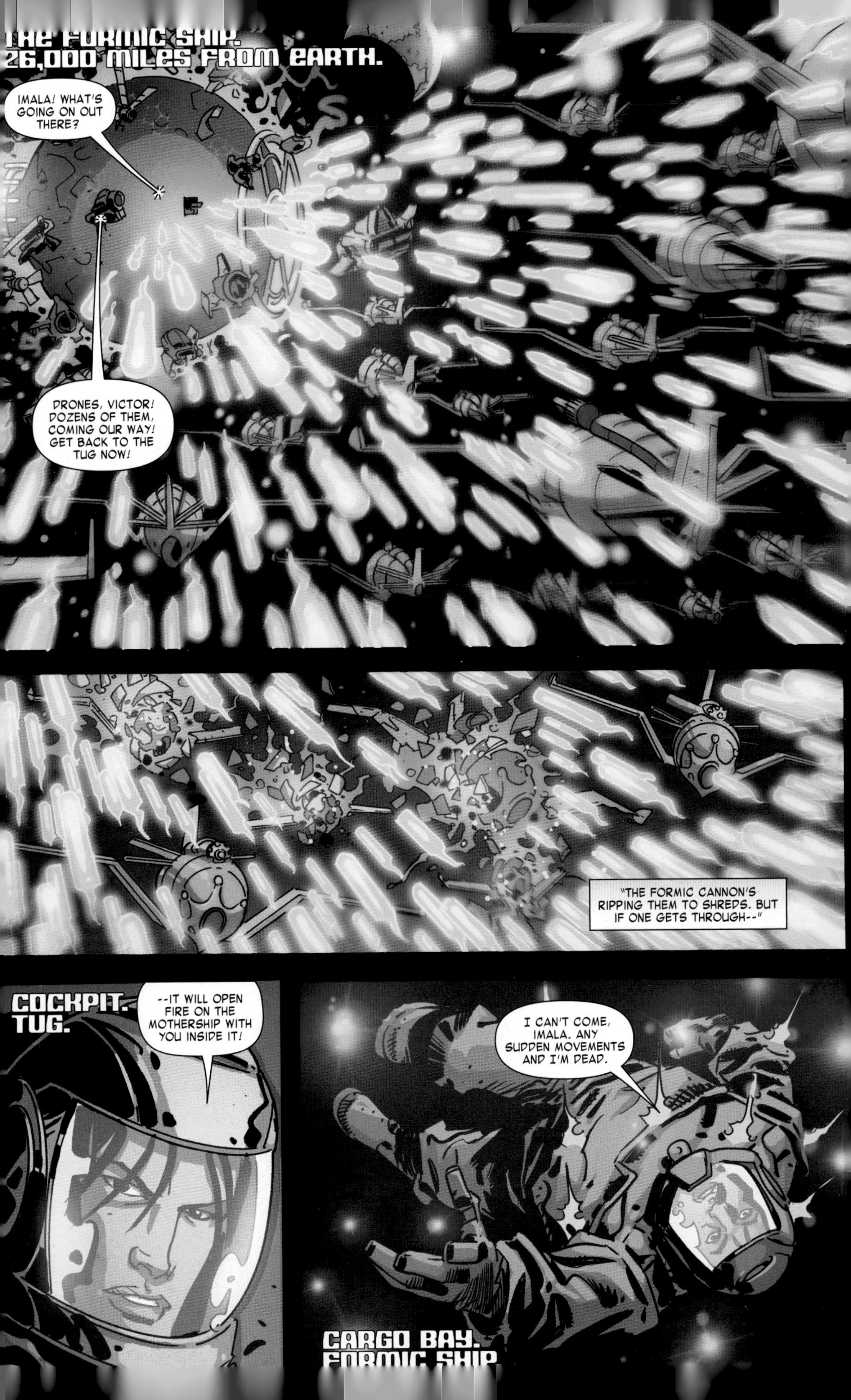
THE FORMIC SHIP. 26,000 MILES FROM EARTH.
IMALA! WHAT'S GOING ON OUT THERE?
DRONES, VICTOR! DOZENS OF THEM, COMING OUR WAY! GET BACK TO THE TUG NOW!
"THE FORMIC CANNON'S RIPPING THEM TO SHREDS. BUT IF ONE GETS THROUGH--"
COCKPIT. TUG.
--IT WILL OPEN FIRE ON THE MOTHERSHIP WITH YOU INSIDE IT!
I CAN'T COME, IMALA. ANY SUDDEN MOVEMENTS AND I'M DEAD.
CARGO BAY. FORMIC SHIP.

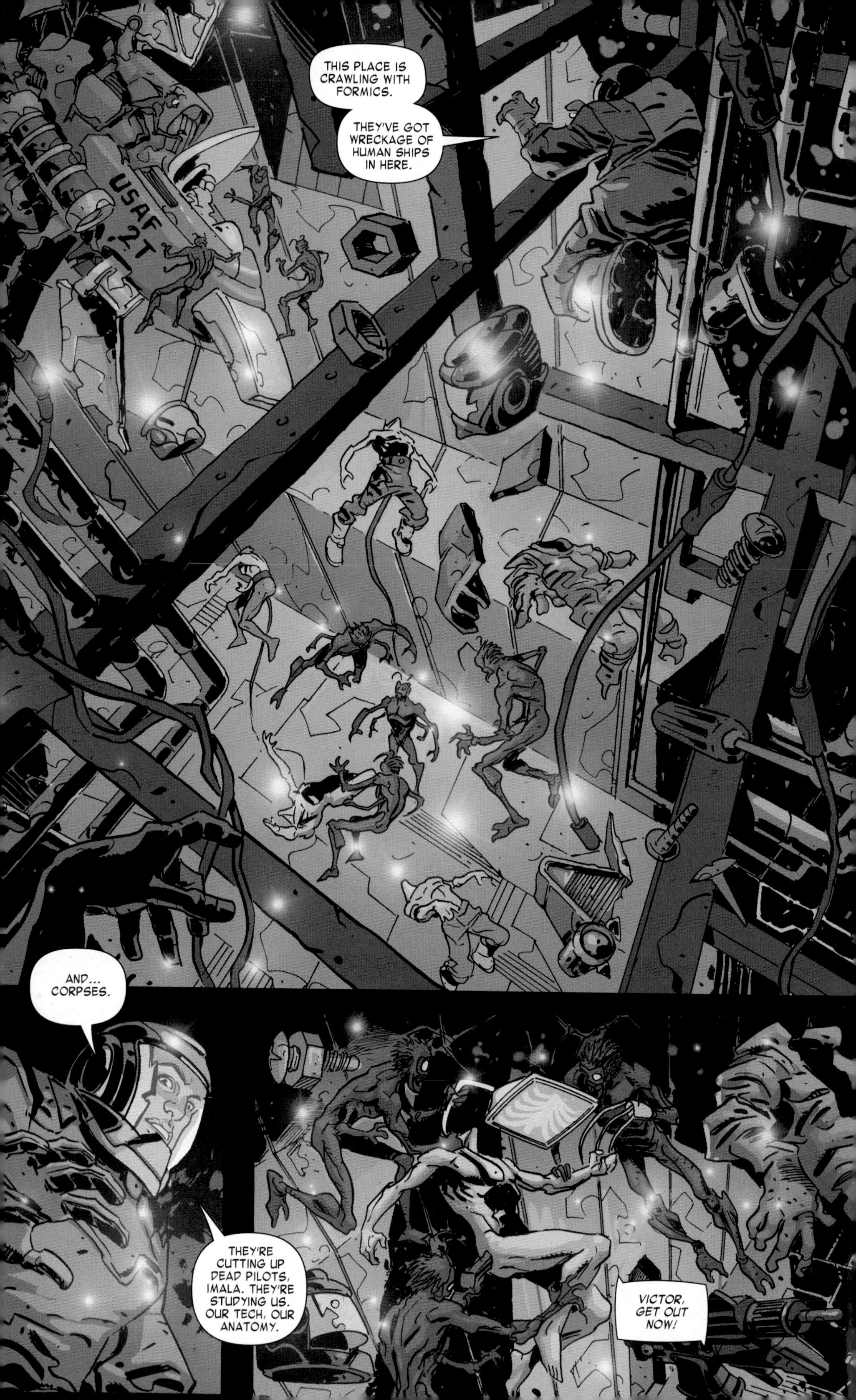
THIS PLACE IS CRAWLING WITH FORMICS.
THEY'VE GOT WRECKAGE OF HUMAN SHIPS IN HERE.
USAF
AND... CORPSES.
THEY'RE CUTTING UP DEAD PILOTS, IMALA. THEY'RE STUDYING US. OUR TECH, OUR ANATOMY.
VICTOR, GET OUT NOW!

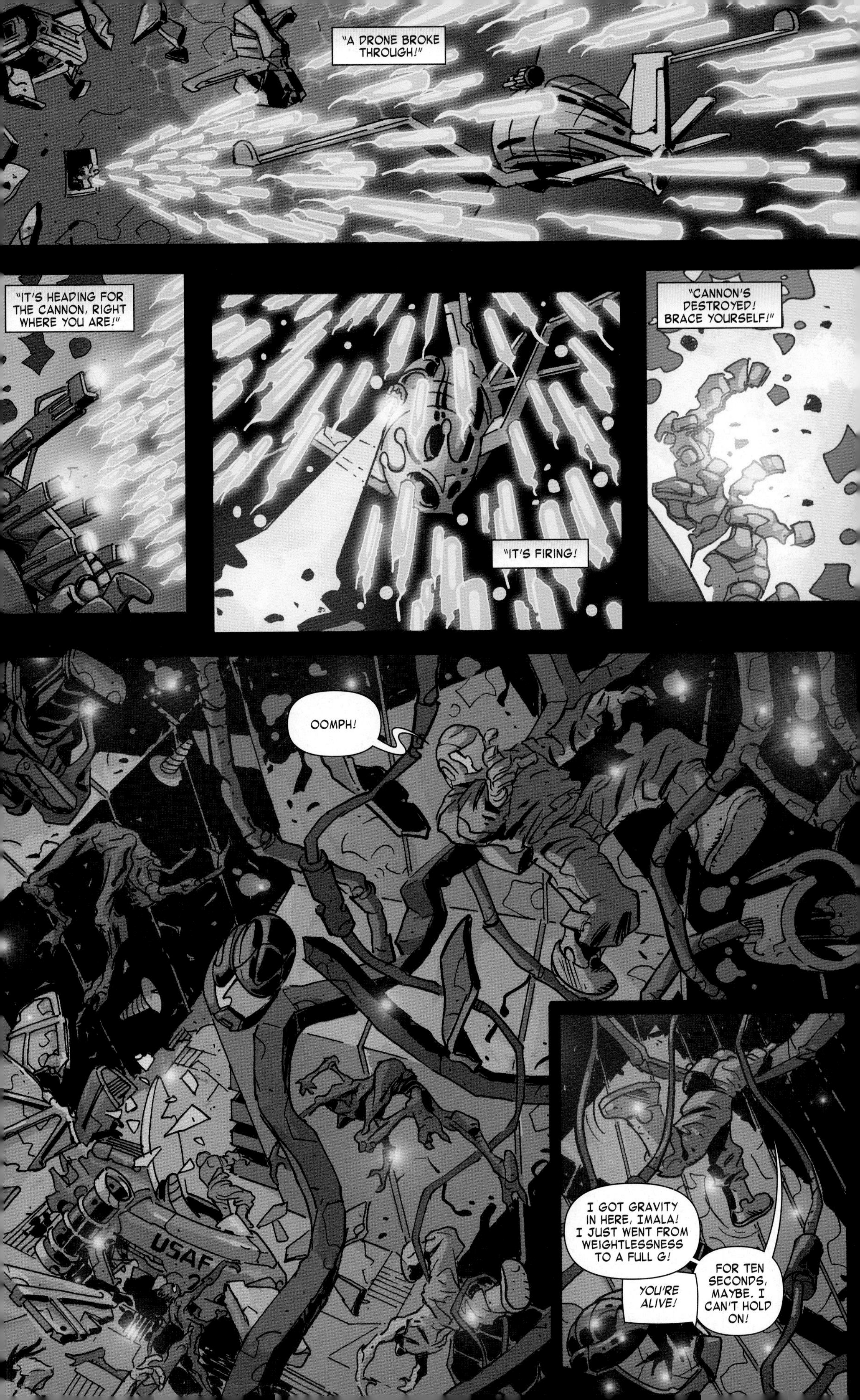
"A DRONE BROKE THROUGH!"
"IT'S HEADING FOR THE CANNON, RIGHT WHERE YOU ARE!"
"IT'S FIRING!
"CANNON'S DESTROYED! BRACE YOURSELF!"
OOMPH!
USAF
I GOT GRAVITY IN HERE, IMALA! I JUST WENT FROM WEIGHTLESSNESS TO A FULL G!
YOU'RE ALIVE!
FOR TEN SECONDS, MAYBE. I CAN'T HOLD ON!

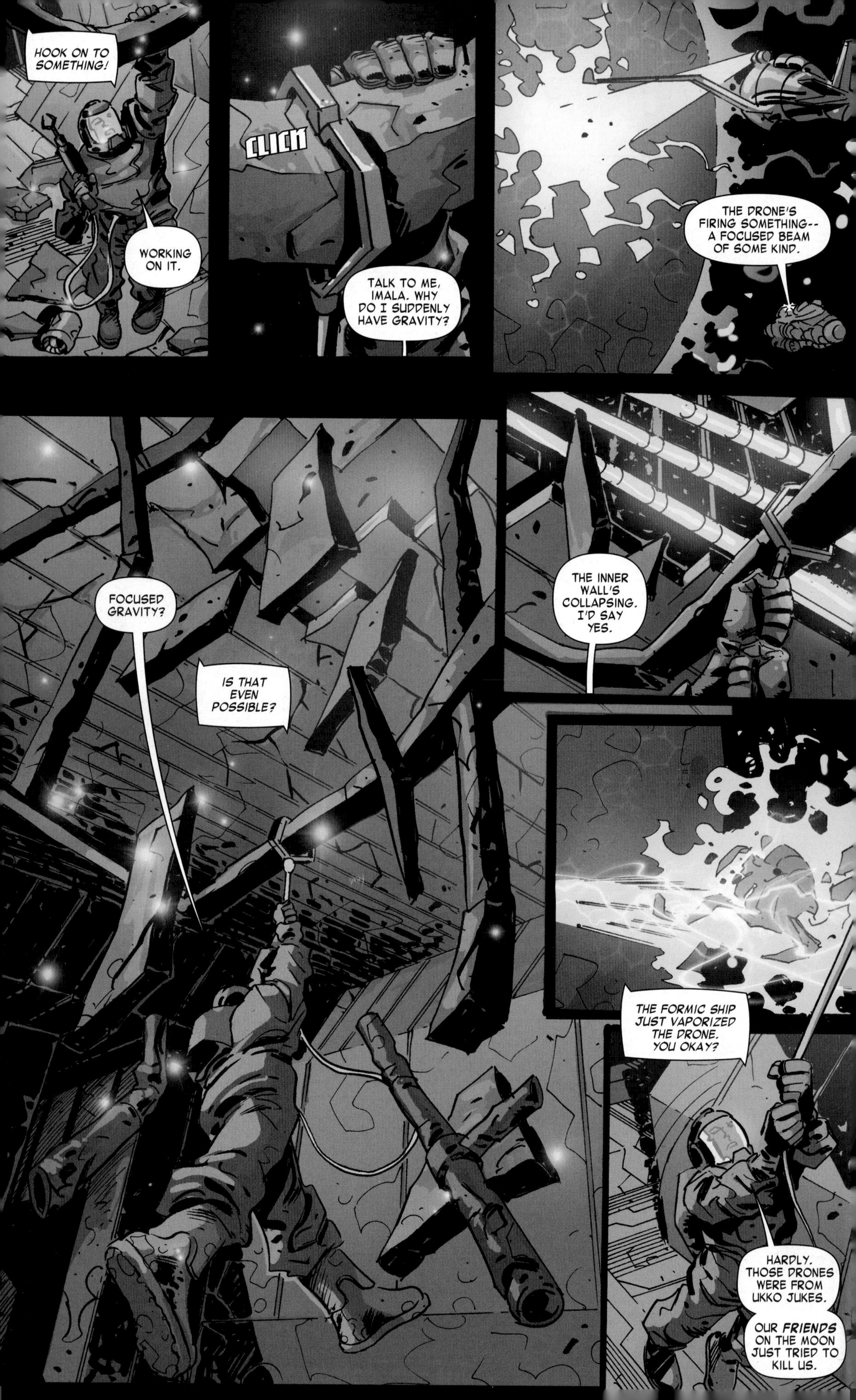
HOOK ON TO SOMETHING!
WORKING ON IT.
CLICK
TALK TO ME, IMALA. WHY DO I SUDDENLY HAVE GRAVITY?
THE DRONE'S FIRING SOMETHING-- A FOCUSED BEAM OF SOME KIND.
FOCUSED GRAVITY?
IS THAT EVEN POSSIBLE?
THE INNER WALL'S COLLAPSING. I'D SAY YES.
THE FORMIC SHIP JUST VAPORIZED THE DRONE. YOU OKAY?
HARDLY. THOSE DRONES WERE FROM UKKO JUKES.
OUR FRIENDS ON THE MOON JUST TRIED TO KILL US.

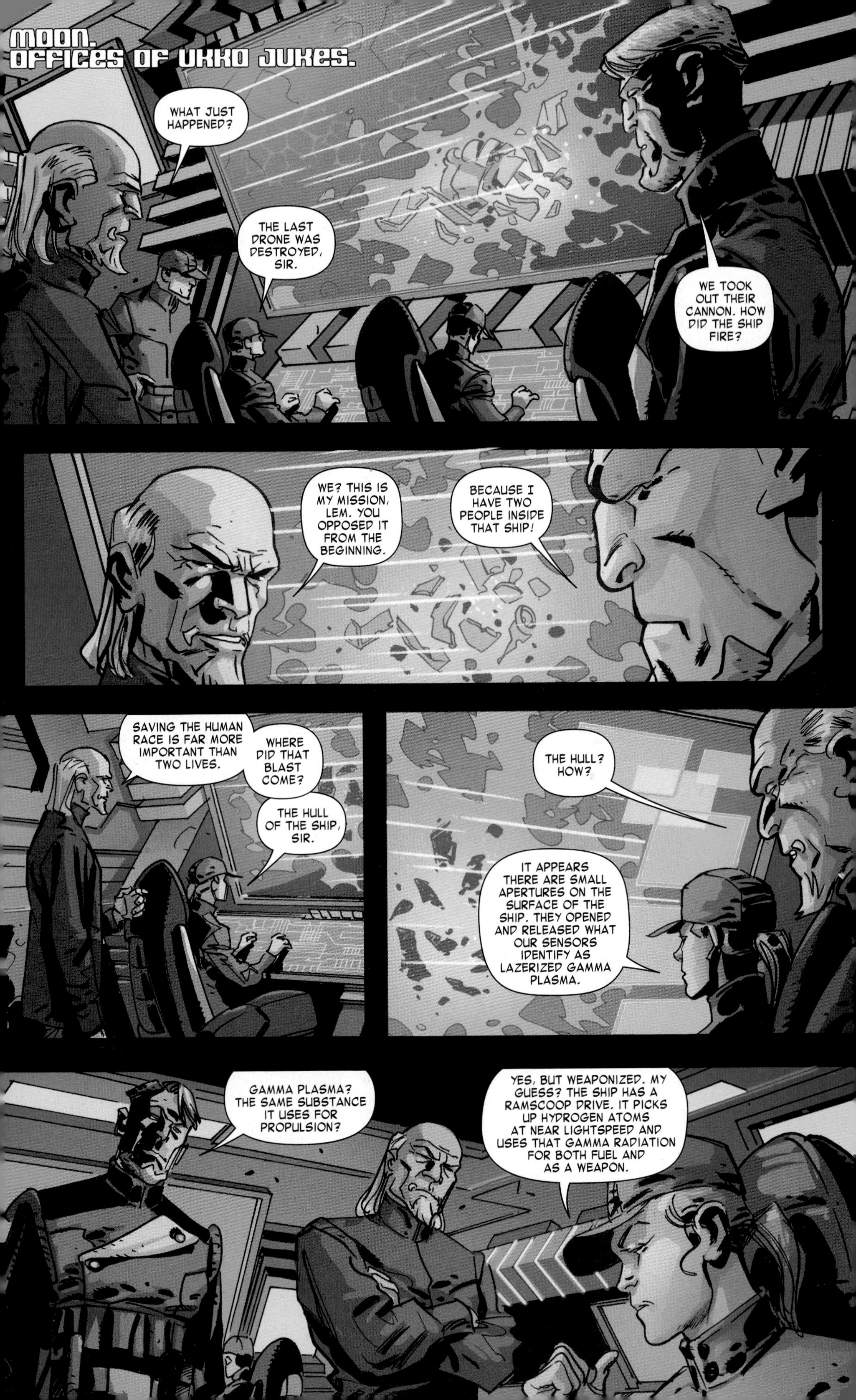
MOON.
OFFICES OF UKKO JUKES.
WHAT JUST HAPPENED?
THE LAST DRONE WAS DESTROYED, SIR.
WE TOOK OUT THEIR CANNON. HOW DID THE SHIP FIRE?
WE? THIS IS MY MISSION, LEM. YOU OPPOSED IT FROM THE BEGINNING.
BECAUSE I HAVE TWO PEOPLE INSIDE THAT SHIP!
SAVING THE HUMAN RACE IS FAR MORE IMPORTANT THAN TWO LIVES.
WHERE DID THAT BLAST COME?
THE HULL OF THE SHIP, SIR.
THE HULL? HOW?
IT APPEARS THERE ARE SMALL APERTURES ON THE SURFACE OF THE SHIP. THEY OPENED AND RELEASED WHAT OUR SENSORS IDENTIFY AS LAZERIZED GAMMA PLASMA.
GAMMA PLASMA? THE SAME SUBSTANCE IT USES FOR PROPULSION?
YES, BUT WEAPONIZED. MY GUESS? THE SHIP HAS A RAMSCOOP DRIVE. IT PICKS UP HYDROGEN ATOMS AT NEAR LIGHTSPEED AND USES THAT GAMMA RADIATION FOR BOTH FUEL AND AS A WEAPON.

AND THESE APERTURES COVER THE SURFACE?

IT APPEARS SO, SIR.

WHICH MEANS THE SHIP CAN FIRE FROM ANY ANGLE AT ANY MOMENT.

GO ON AND SAY IT, LEM. I KNOW YOU MUST BE DYING TO RUB FAILURE IN MY FACE.

THIS ISN'T OVER, FATHER. WHAT ARE OUR RESOURCES?

A FEW DOZEN FIGHTERS AND OUR FLEET OF MINING SHIPS.

ALL OF WHICH WOULD BE SLICED TO RIBBONS AGAINST THAT SHIP.

THEN WE CHANGE STRATEGIES AND STOP ATTACKING FROM THE OUTSIDE.

ELABORATE.

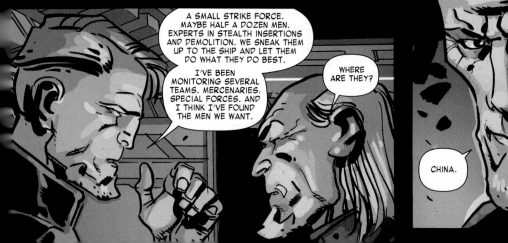

A SMALL STRIKE FORCE. MAYBE HALF A DOZEN MEN. EXPERTS IN STEALTH INSERTIONS AND DEMOLITION. WE SNEAK THEM UP TO THE SHIP AND LET THEM DO WHAT THEY DO BEST.

I'VE BEEN MONITORING SEVERAL TEAMS. MERCENARIES, SPECIAL FORCES. AND I THINK I'VE FOUND THE MEN WE WANT.

WHERE ARE THEY?

CHINA.

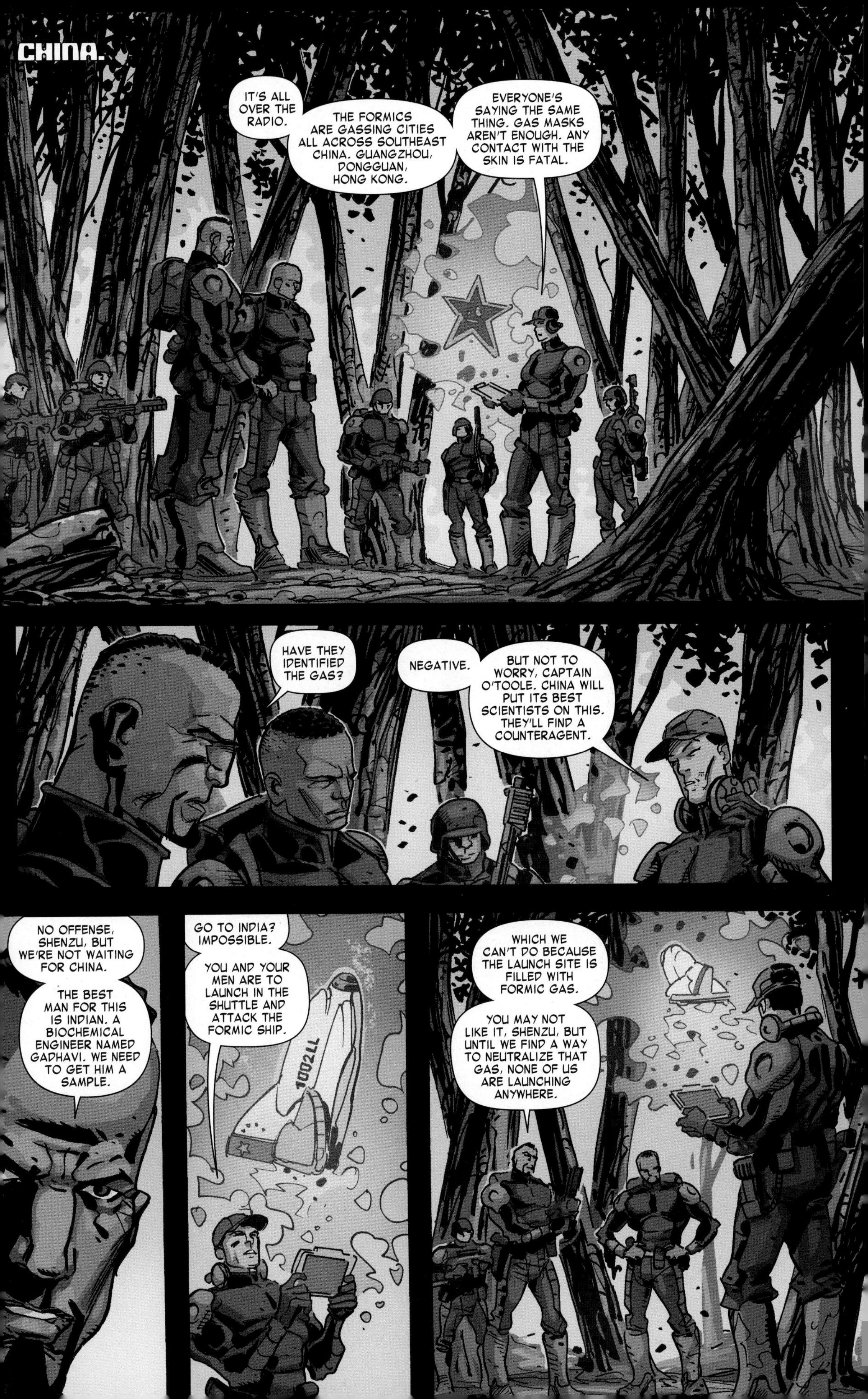
CHINA.
IT'S ALL OVER THE RADIO.
THE FORMICS ARE GASSING CITIES ALL ACROSS SOUTHEAST CHINA. GUANGZHOU, DONGGUAN, HONG KONG.
EVERYONE'S SAYING THE SAME THING. GAS MASKS AREN'T ENOUGH. ANY CONTACT WITH THE SKIN IS FATAL.
HAVE THEY IDENTIFIED THE GAS?
NEGATIVE.
BUT NOT TO WORRY, CAPTAIN O'TOOLE. CHINA WILL PUT ITS BEST SCIENTISTS ON THIS. THEY'LL FIND A COUNTERAGENT.
NO OFFENSE, SHENZU, BUT WE'RE NOT WAITING FOR CHINA.
THE BEST MAN FOR THIS IS INDIAN. A BIOCHEMICAL ENGINEER NAMED GADHAVI. WE NEED TO GET HIM A SAMPLE.
GO TO INDIA? IMPOSSIBLE.
YOU AND YOUR MEN ARE TO LAUNCH IN THE SHUTTLE AND ATTACK THE FORMIC SHIP.
1002LL
WHICH WE CAN'T DO BECAUSE THE LAUNCH SITE IS FILLED WITH FORMIC GAS.
YOU MAY NOT LIKE IT, SHENZU, BUT UNTIL WE FIND A WAY TO NEUTRALIZE THAT GAS, NONE OF US ARE LAUNCHING ANYWHERE.

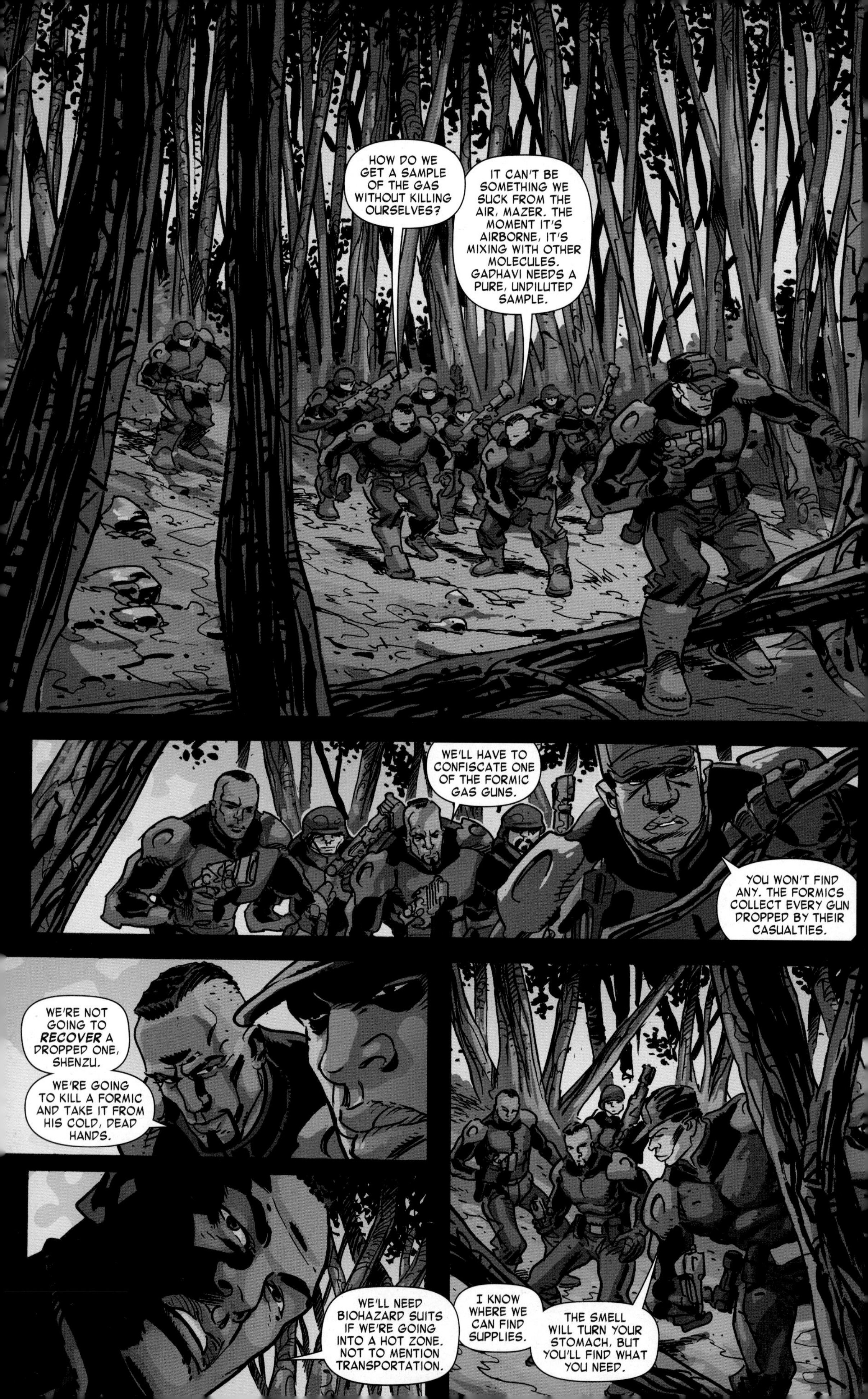
HOW DO WE GET A SAMPLE OF THE GAS WITHOUT KILLING OURSELVES?
IT CAN'T BE SOMETHING WE SUCK FROM THE AIR, MAZER. THE MOMENT IT'S AIRBORNE, IT'S MIXING WITH OTHER MOLECULES. GADHAVI NEEDS A PURE, UNDILUTED SAMPLE.
WE'LL HAVE TO CONFISCATE ONE OF THE FORMIC GAS GUNS.
YOU WON'T FIND ANY. THE FORMICS COLLECT EVERY GUN DROPPED BY THEIR CASUALTIES.
WE'RE NOT GOING TO ***RECOVER*** A DROPPED ONE, SHENZU.
WE'RE GOING TO KILL A FORMIC AND TAKE IT FROM HIS COLD, DEAD HANDS.
WE'LL NEED BIOHAZARD SUITS IF WE'RE GOING INTO A HOT ZONE. NOT TO MENTION TRANSPORTATION.
I KNOW WHERE WE CAN FIND SUPPLIES.
THE SMELL WILL TURN YOUR STOMACH, BUT YOU'LL FIND WHAT YOU NEED.

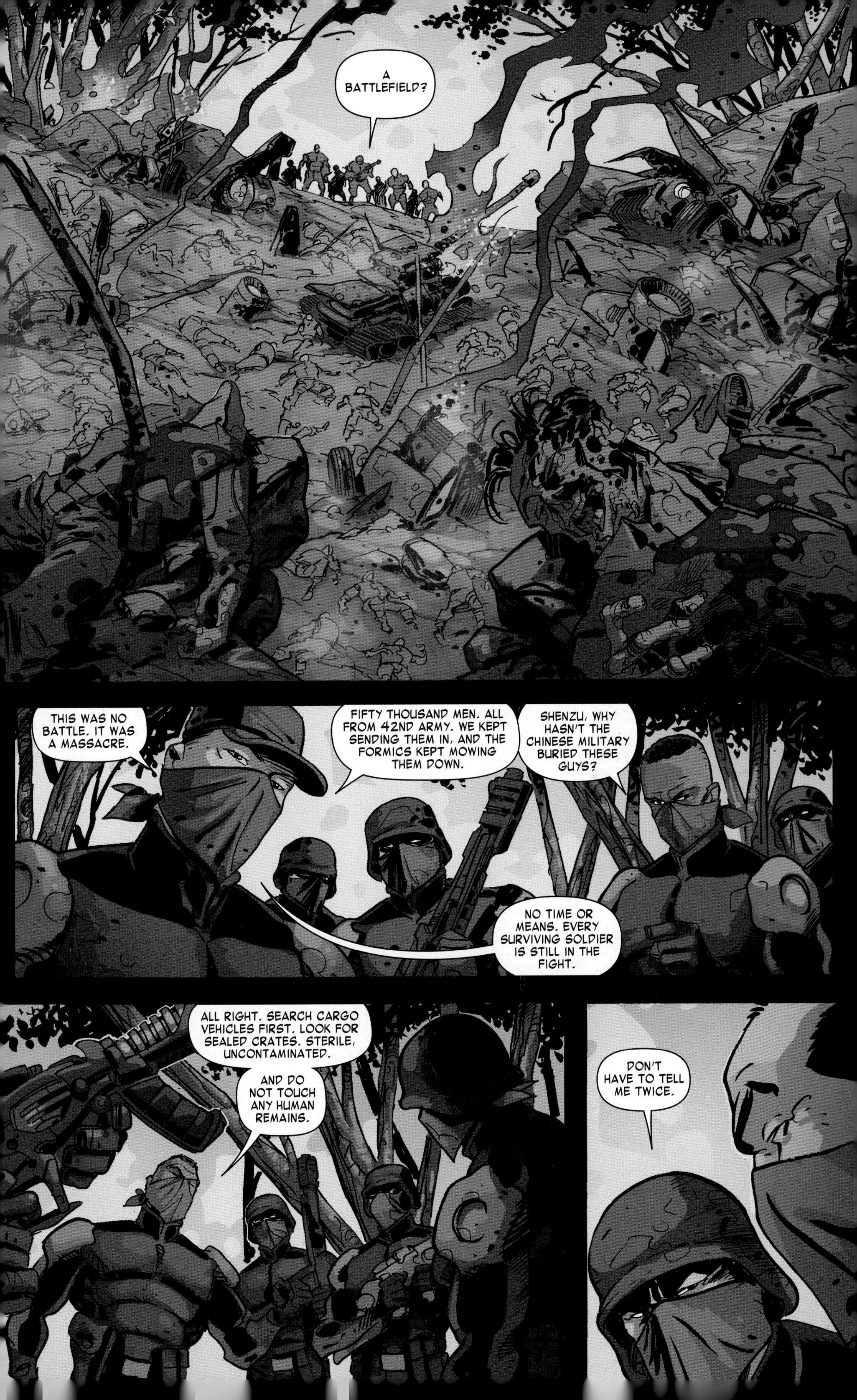
A BATTLEFIELD?
THIS WAS NO BATTLE. IT WAS A MASSACRE.
FIFTY THOUSAND MEN. ALL FROM 42ND ARMY. WE KEPT SENDING THEM IN, AND THE FORMICS KEPT MOWING THEM DOWN.
SHENZU, WHY HASN'T THE CHINESE MILITARY BURIED THESE GUYS?
NO TIME OR MEANS. EVERY SURVIVING SOLDIER IS STILL IN THE FIGHT.
ALL RIGHT. SEARCH CARGO VEHICLES FIRST. LOOK FOR SEALED CRATES. STERILE, UNCONTAMINATED.
AND DO NOT TOUCH ANY HUMAN REMAINS.
DON'T HAVE TO TELL ME TWICE.

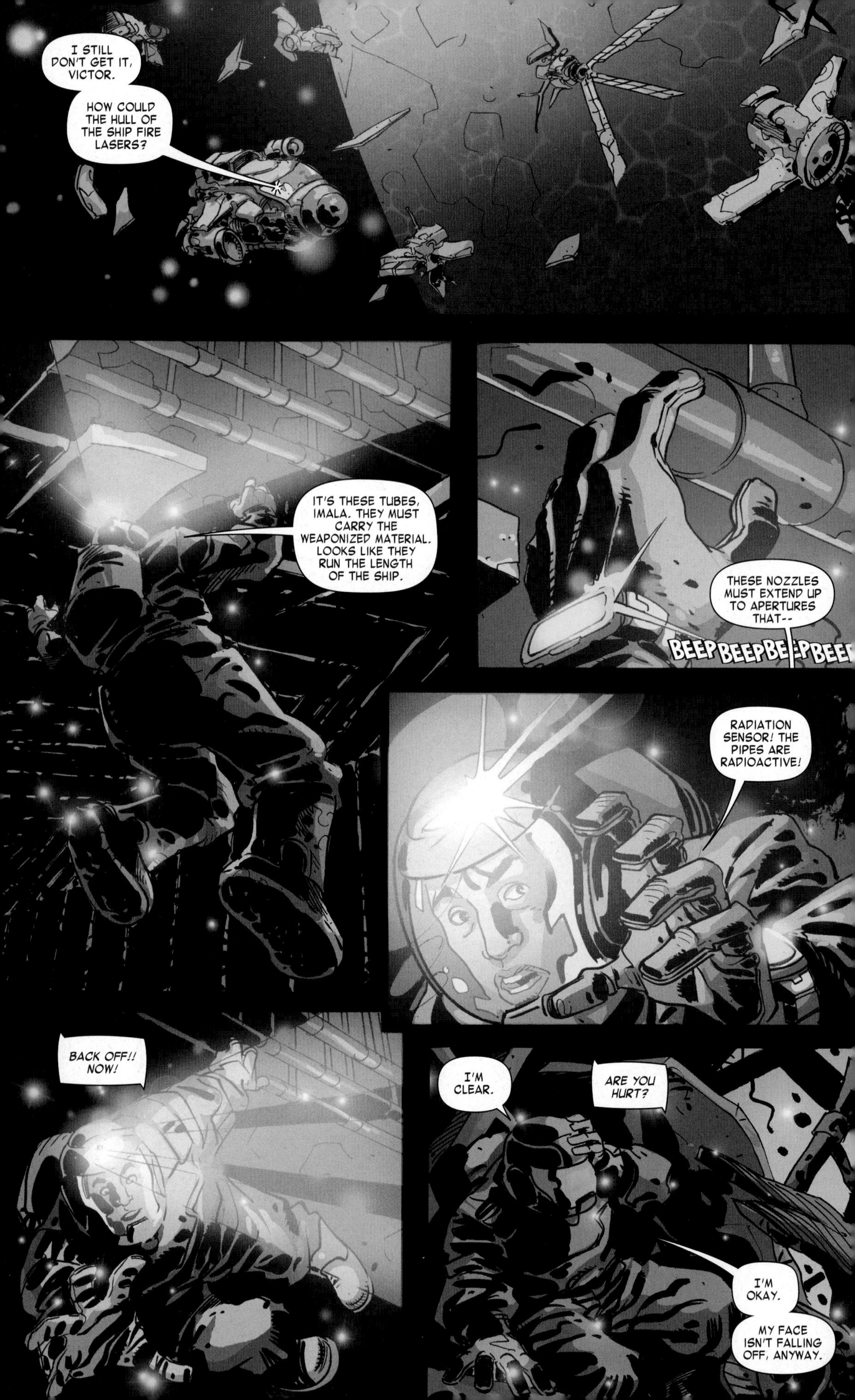
I STILL DON'T GET IT, VICTOR.
HOW COULD THE HULL OF THE SHIP FIRE LASERS?
IT'S THESE TUBES, IMALA. THEY MUST CARRY THE WEAPONIZED MATERIAL. LOOKS LIKE THEY RUN THE LENGTH OF THE SHIP.
THESE NOZZLES MUST EXTEND UP TO APERTURES THAT--
BEEP BEEPBEEPBEEP
RADIATION SENSOR! THE PIPES ARE RADIOACTIVE!
BACK OFF!! NOW!
I'M CLEAR.
ARE YOU HURT?
I'M OKAY.
MY FACE ISN'T FALLING OFF, ANYWAY.

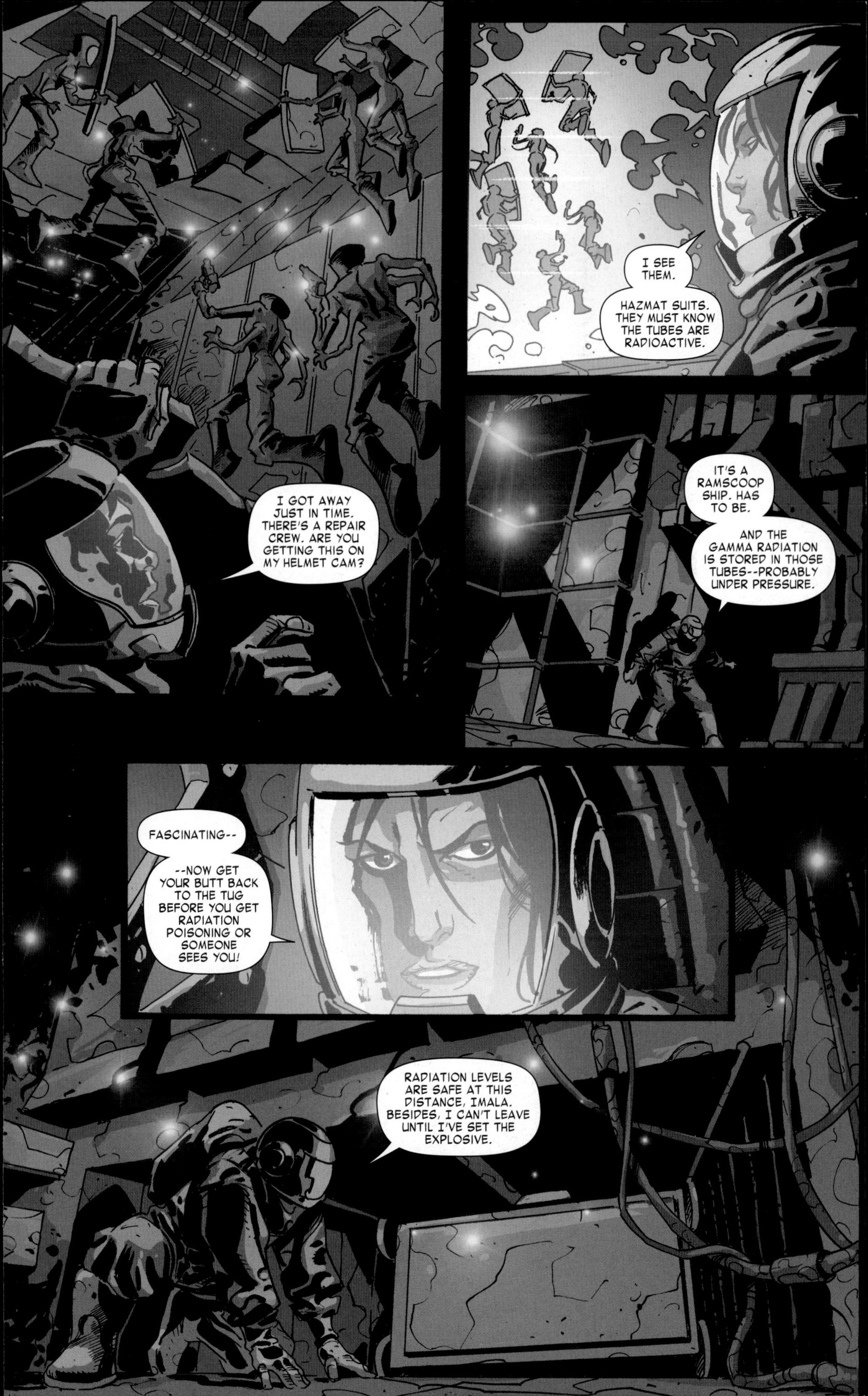
I GOT AWAY JUST IN TIME. THERE'S A REPAIR CREW. ARE YOU GETTING THIS ON MY HELMET CAM?
I SEE THEM.
HAZMAT SUITS. THEY MUST KNOW THE TUBES ARE RADIOACTIVE.
IT'S A RAMSCOOP SHIP. HAS TO BE.
AND THE GAMMA RADIATION IS STORED IN THOSE TUBES--PROBABLY UNDER PRESSURE.
FASCINATING--
--NOW GET YOUR BUTT BACK TO THE TUG BEFORE YOU GET RADIATION POISONING OR SOMEONE SEES YOU!
RADIATION LEVELS ARE SAFE AT THIS DISTANCE, IMALA. BESIDES, I CAN'T LEAVE UNTIL I'VE SET THE EXPLOSIVE.

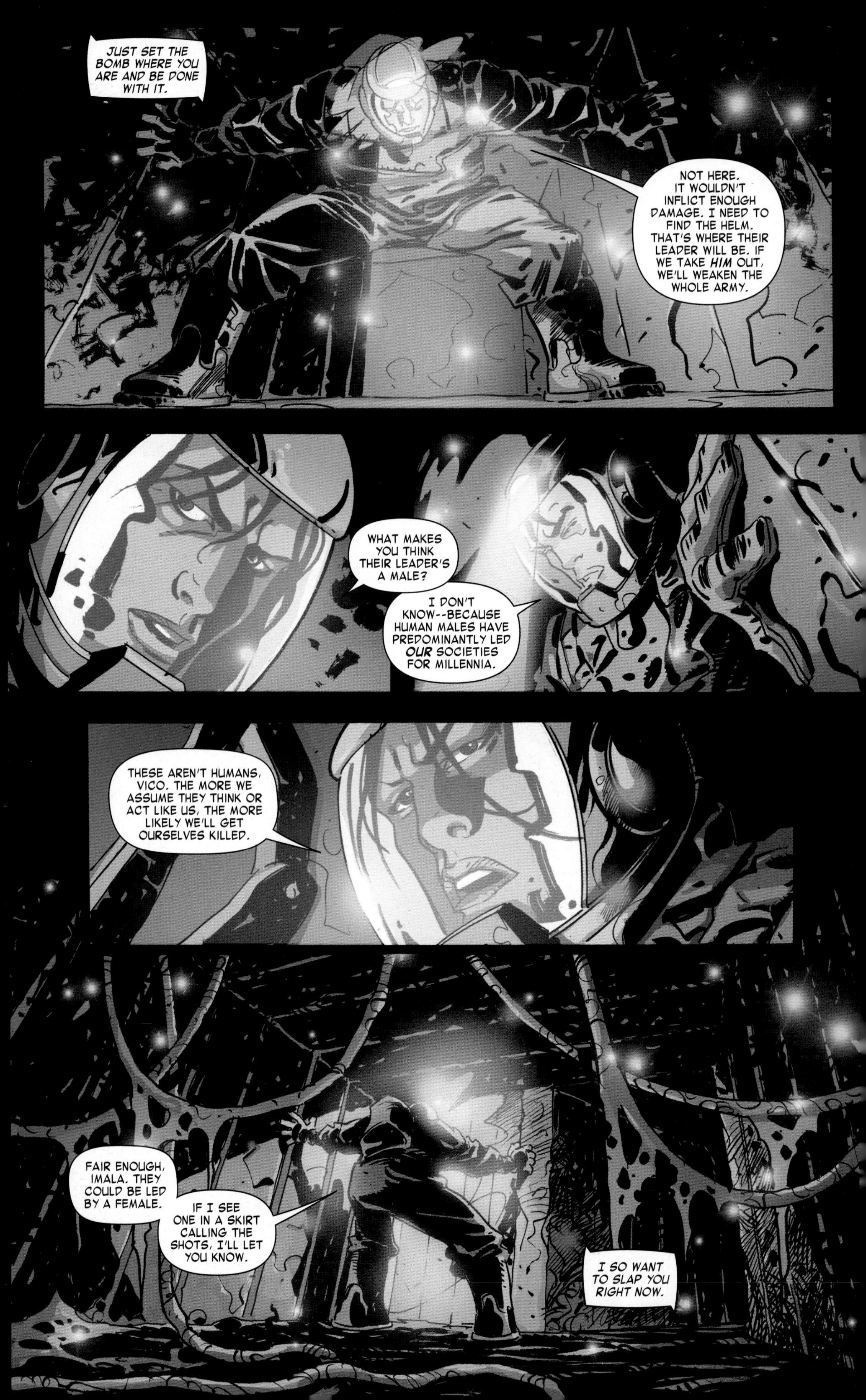
JUST SET THE BOMB WHERE YOU ARE AND BE DONE WITH IT.
NOT HERE. IT WOULDN'T INFLICT ENOUGH DAMAGE. I NEED TO FIND THE HELM. THAT'S WHERE THEIR LEADER WILL BE. IF WE TAKE HIM OUT, WE'LL WEAKEN THE WHOLE ARMY.
WHAT MAKES YOU THINK THEIR LEADER'S A MALE?
I DON'T KNOW--BECAUSE HUMAN MALES HAVE PREDOMINANTLY LED OUR SOCIETIES FOR MILLENNIA.
THESE AREN'T HUMANS, VICO. THE MORE WE ASSUME THEY THINK OR ACT LIKE US, THE MORE LIKELY WE'LL GET OURSELVES KILLED.
FAIR ENOUGH, IMALA. THEY COULD BE LED BY A FEMALE.
IF I SEE ONE IN A SKIRT CALLING THE SHOTS, I'LL LET YOU KNOW.
I SO WANT TO SLAP YOU RIGHT NOW.

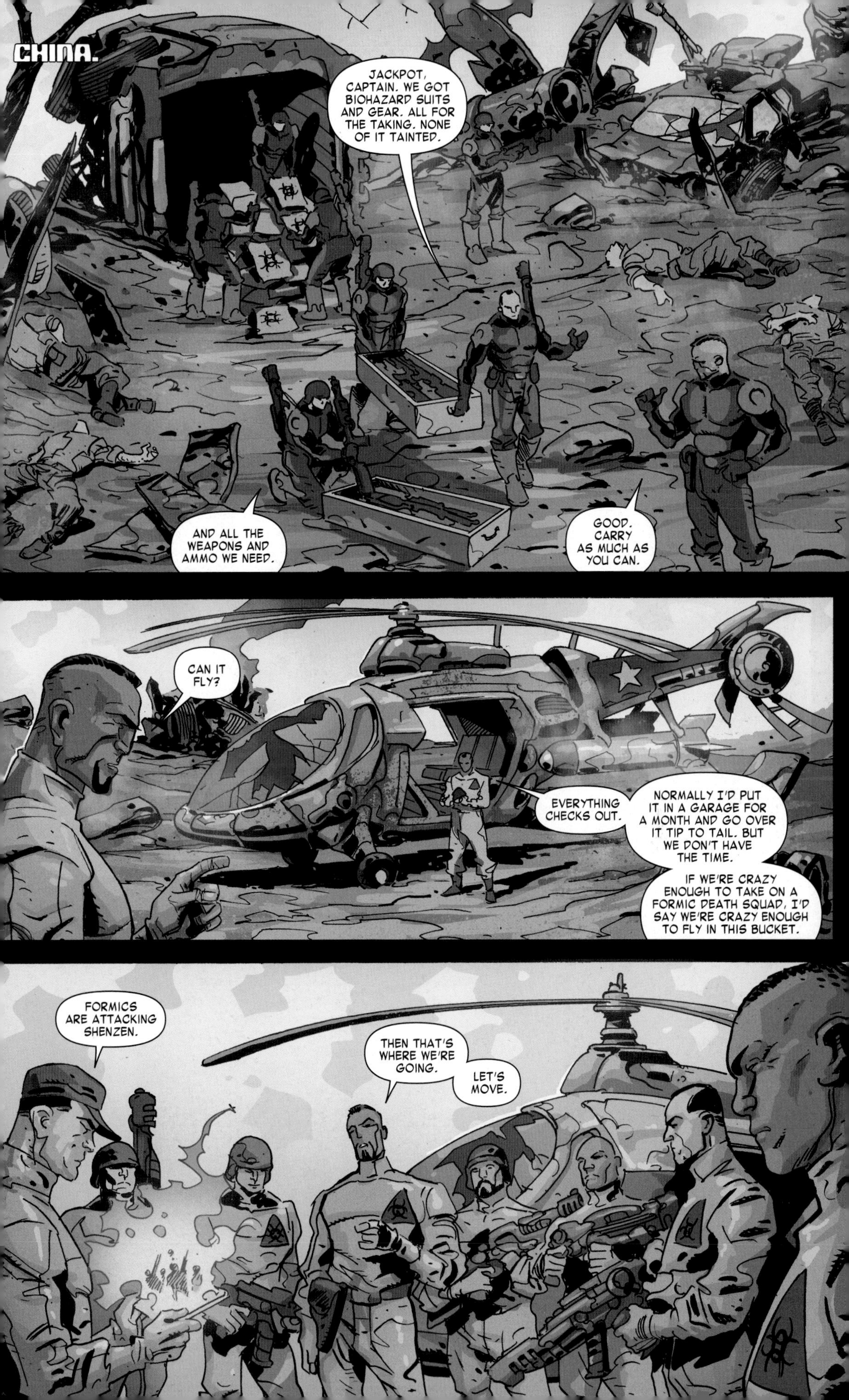
CHINA.
JACKPOT, CAPTAIN. WE GOT BIOHAZARD SUITS AND GEAR. ALL FOR THE TAKING. NONE OF IT TAINTED.
AND ALL THE WEAPONS AND AMMO WE NEED.
GOOD. CARRY AS MUCH AS YOU CAN.
CAN IT FLY?
EVERYTHING CHECKS OUT.
NORMALLY I'D PUT IT IN A GARAGE FOR A MONTH AND GO OVER IT TIP TO TAIL. BUT WE DON'T HAVE THE TIME.
IF WE'RE CRAZY ENOUGH TO TAKE ON A FORMIC DEATH SQUAD, I'D SAY WE'RE CRAZY ENOUGH TO FLY IN THIS BUCKET.
FORMICS ARE ATTACKING SHENZEN.
THEN THAT'S WHERE WE'RE GOING.
LET'S MOVE.

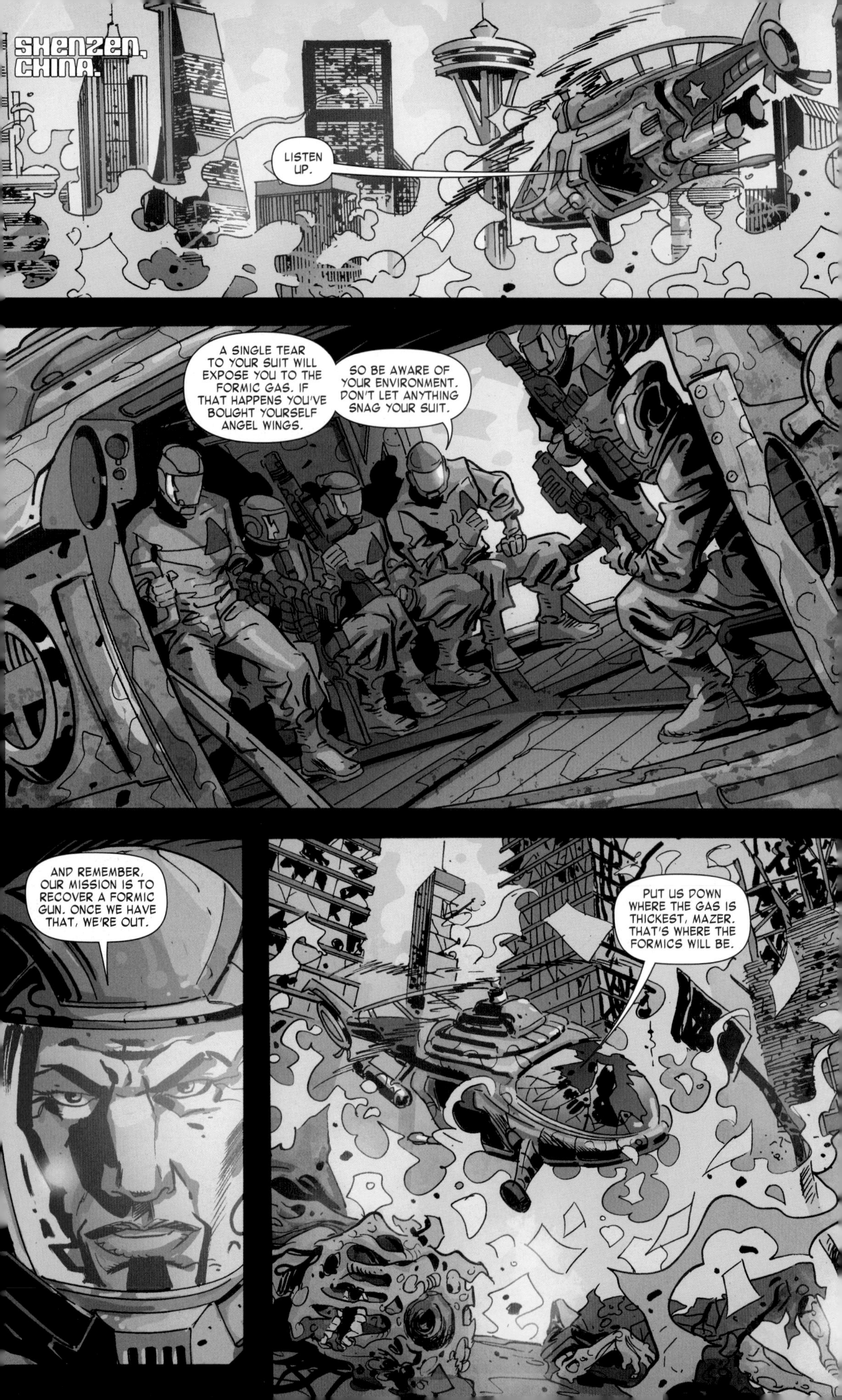
SHENZEN, CHINA.
LISTEN UP.
A SINGLE TEAR TO YOUR SUIT WILL EXPOSE YOU TO THE FORMIC GAS. IF THAT HAPPENS YOU'VE BOUGHT YOURSELF ANGEL WINGS.
SO BE AWARE OF YOUR ENVIRONMENT. DON'T LET ANYTHING SNAG YOUR SUIT.
AND REMEMBER, OUR MISSION IS TO RECOVER A FORMIC GUN. ONCE WE HAVE THAT, WE'RE OUT.
PUT US DOWN WHERE THE GAS IS THICKEST, MAZER. THAT'S WHERE THE FORMICS WILL BE.

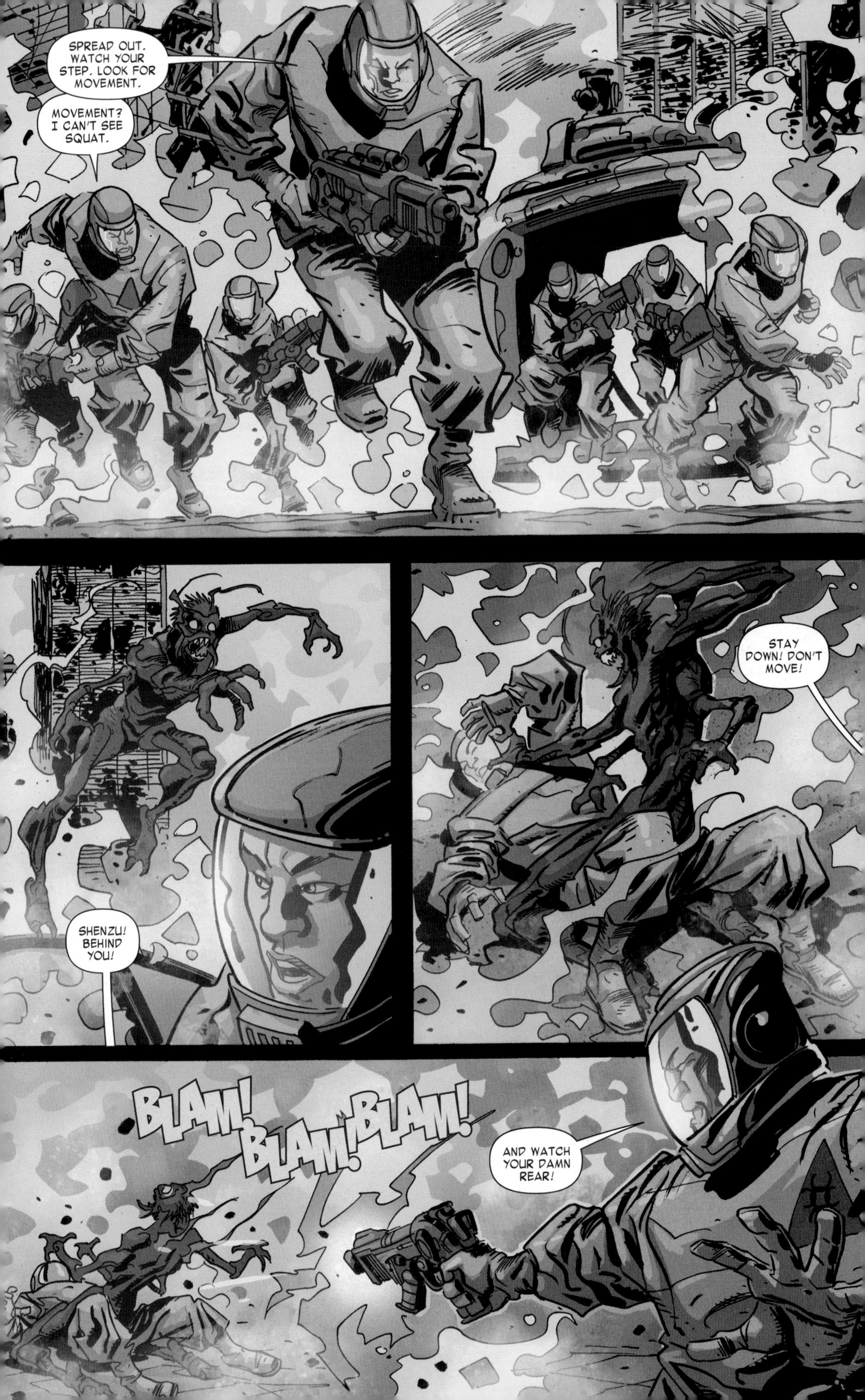
SPREAD OUT. WATCH YOUR STEP. LOOK FOR MOVEMENT.
MOVEMENT? I CAN'T SEE SQUAT.
SHENZU! BEHIND YOU!
STAY DOWN! DON'T MOVE!
BLAM! BLAM! BLAM!
AND WATCH YOUR DAMN REAR!

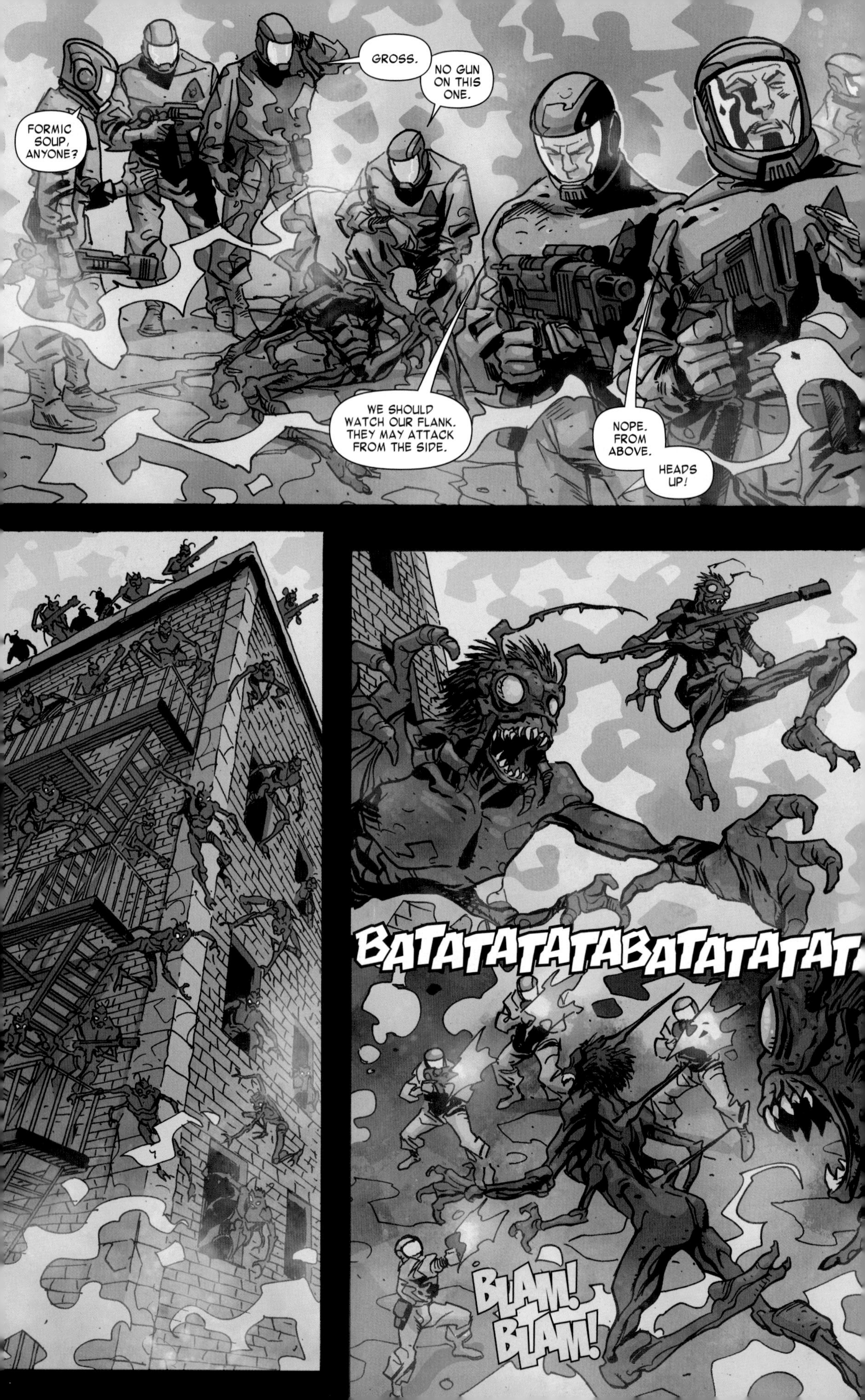
FORMIC SOUP, ANYONE?
GROSS.
NO GUN ON THIS ONE.
WE SHOULD WATCH OUR FLANK. THEY MAY ATTACK FROM THE SIDE.
NOPE. FROM ABOVE.
HEADS UP!
BATATATATATABATATATAT
BLAM! BLAM!

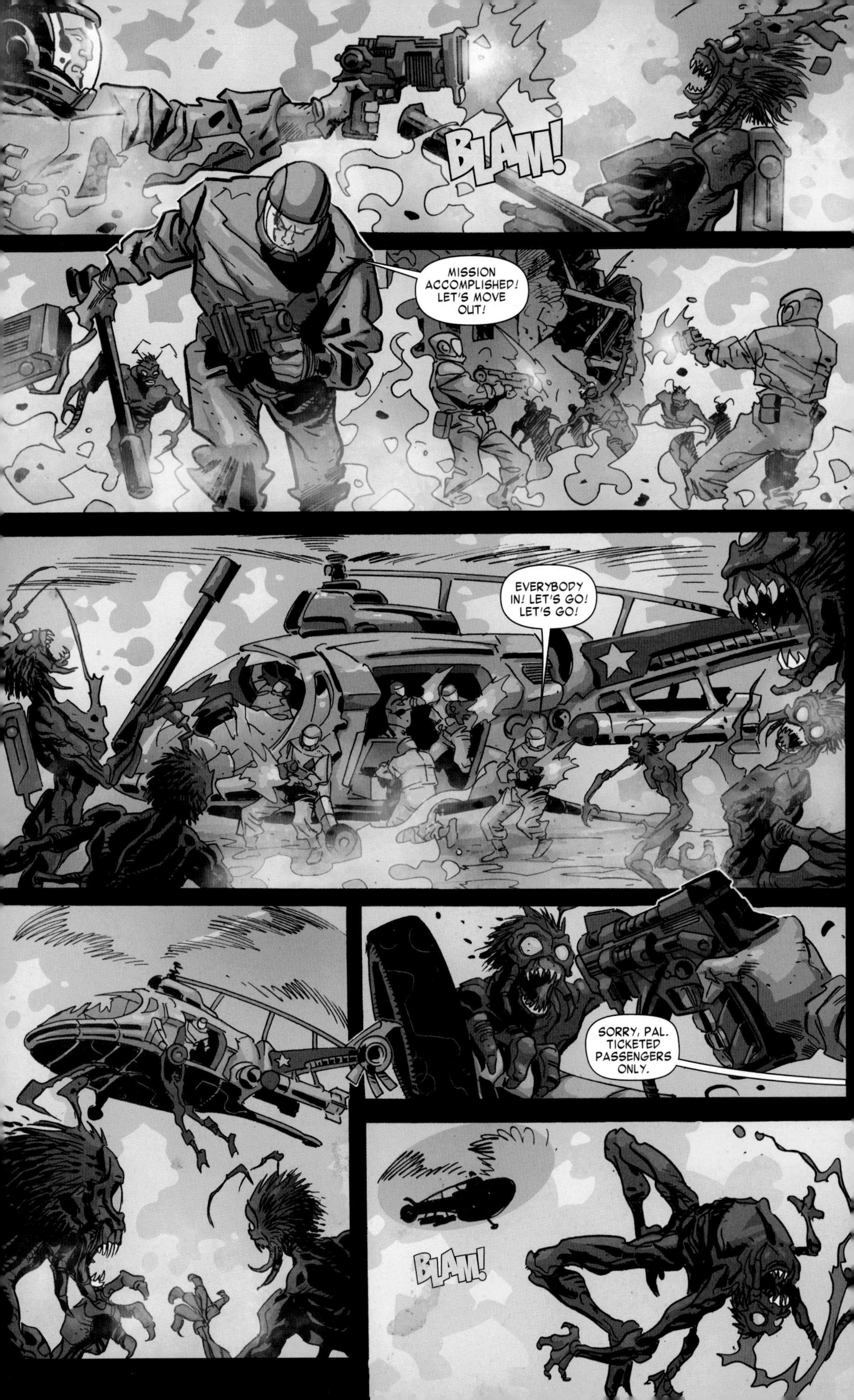
BLAM!
MISSION ACCOMPLISHED! LET'S MOVE OUT!
EVERYBODY IN! LET'S GO! LET'S GO!
SORRY, PAL. TICKETED PASSENGERS ONLY.
BLAM!

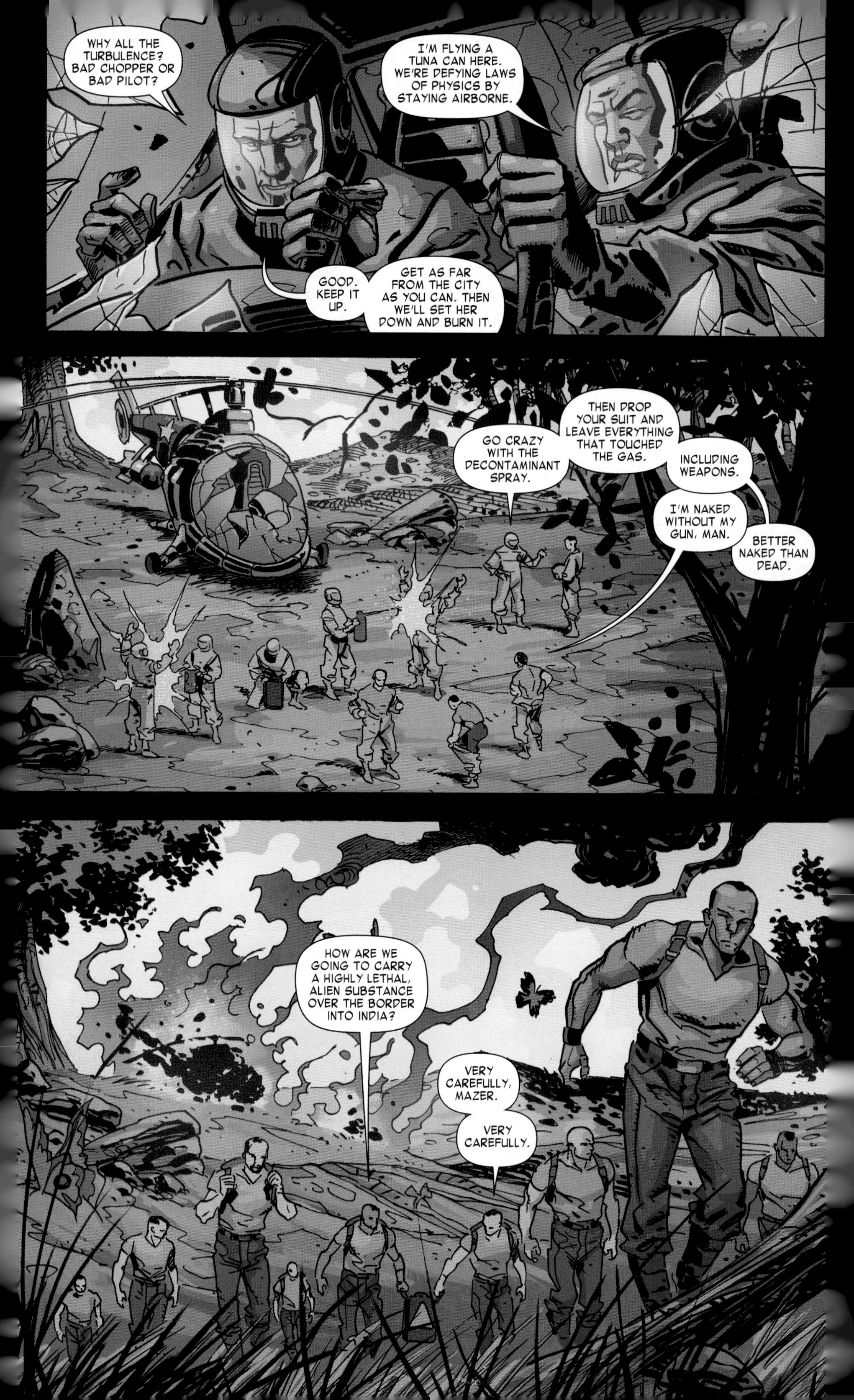
WHY ALL THE TURBULENCE? BAD CHOPPER OR BAD PILOT?
I'M FLYING A TUNA CAN HERE. WE'RE DEFYING LAWS OF PHYSICS BY STAYING AIRBORNE.
GOOD. KEEP IT UP.
GET AS FAR FROM THE CITY AS YOU CAN. THEN WE'LL SET HER DOWN AND BURN IT.
GO CRAZY WITH THE DECONTAMINANT SPRAY.
THEN DROP YOUR SUIT AND LEAVE EVERYTHING THAT TOUCHED THE GAS.
INCLUDING WEAPONS.
I'M NAKED WITHOUT MY GUN, MAN.
BETTER NAKED THAN DEAD.
HOW ARE WE GOING TO CARRY A HIGHLY LETHAL, ALIEN SUBSTANCE OVER THE BORDER INTO INDIA?
VERY CAREFULLY, MAZER.
VERY CAREFULLY.

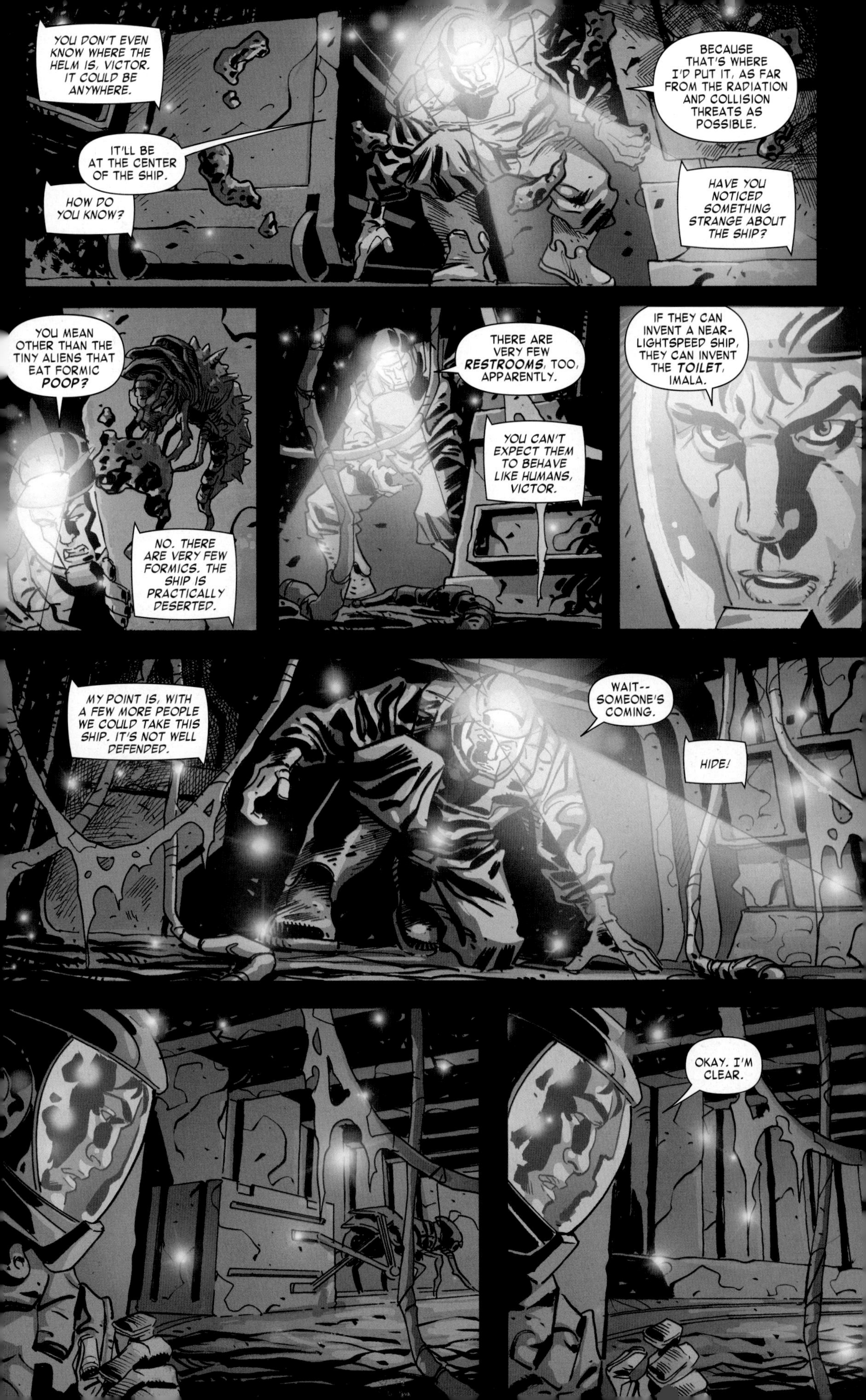
YOU DON'T EVEN KNOW WHERE THE HELM IS, VICTOR. IT COULD BE ANYWHERE.
IT'LL BE AT THE CENTER OF THE SHIP.
HOW DO YOU KNOW?
BECAUSE THAT'S WHERE I'D PUT IT, AS FAR FROM THE RADIATION AND COLLISION THREATS AS POSSIBLE.
HAVE YOU NOTICED SOMETHING STRANGE ABOUT THE SHIP?
YOU MEAN OTHER THAN THE TINY ALIENS THAT EAT FORMIC POOP?
NO. THERE ARE VERY FEW FORMICS. THE SHIP IS PRACTICALLY DESERTED.
THERE ARE VERY FEW RESTROOMS, TOO, APPARENTLY.
YOU CAN'T EXPECT THEM TO BEHAVE LIKE HUMANS, VICTOR.
IF THEY CAN INVENT A NEAR-LIGHTSPEED SHIP, THEY CAN INVENT THE TOILET, IMALA.
MY POINT IS, WITH A FEW MORE PEOPLE WE COULD TAKE THIS SHIP. IT'S NOT WELL DEFENDED.
WAIT-- SOMEONE'S COMING.
HIDE!
OKAY. I'M CLEAR.

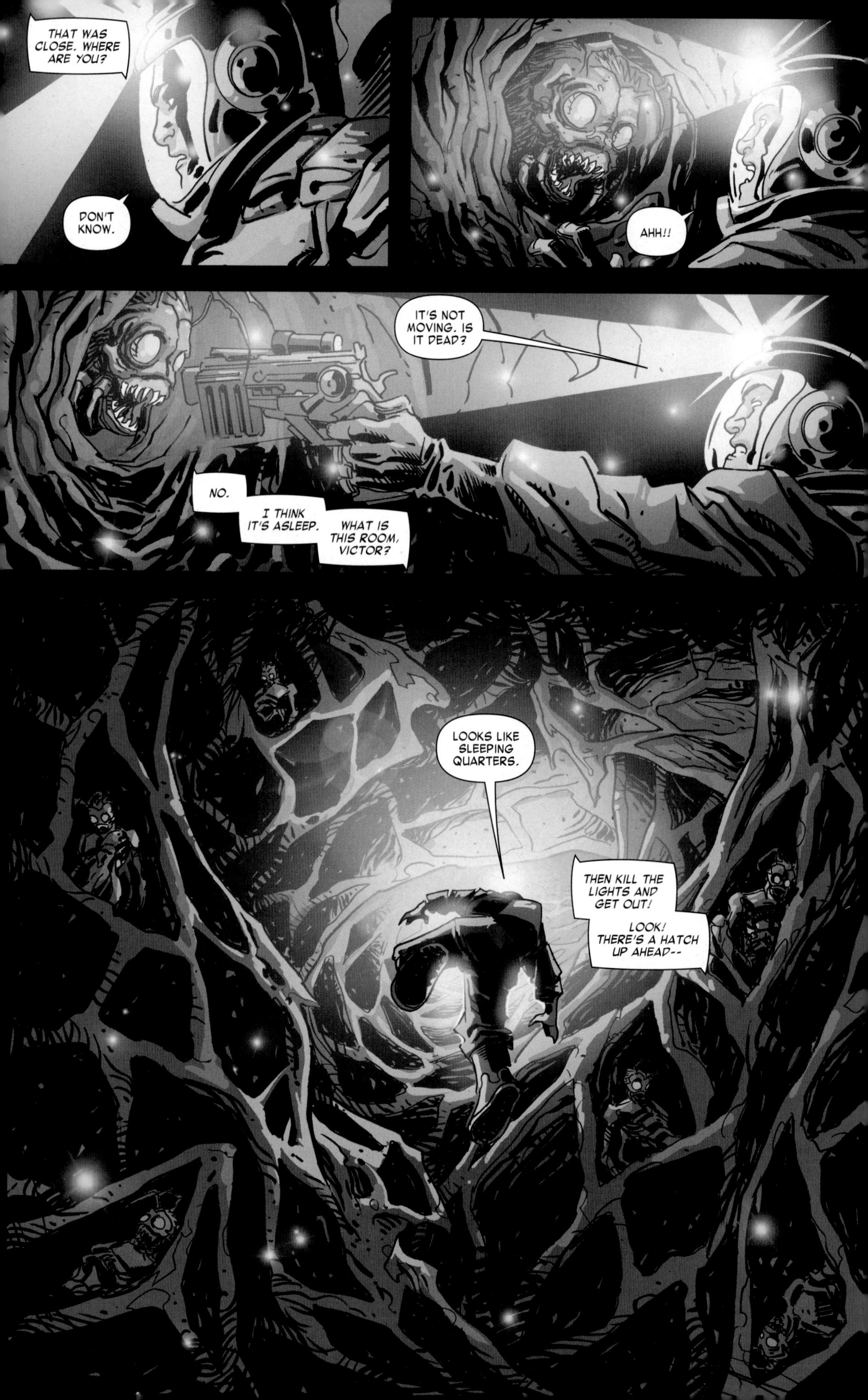
THAT WAS CLOSE. WHERE ARE YOU?
DON'T KNOW.
AHH!!
IT'S NOT MOVING. IS IT DEAD?
NO.
I THINK IT'S ASLEEP.
WHAT IS THIS ROOM, VICTOR?
LOOKS LIKE SLEEPING QUARTERS.
THEN KILL THE LIGHTS AND GET OUT!
LOOK! THERE'S A HATCH UP AHEAD--

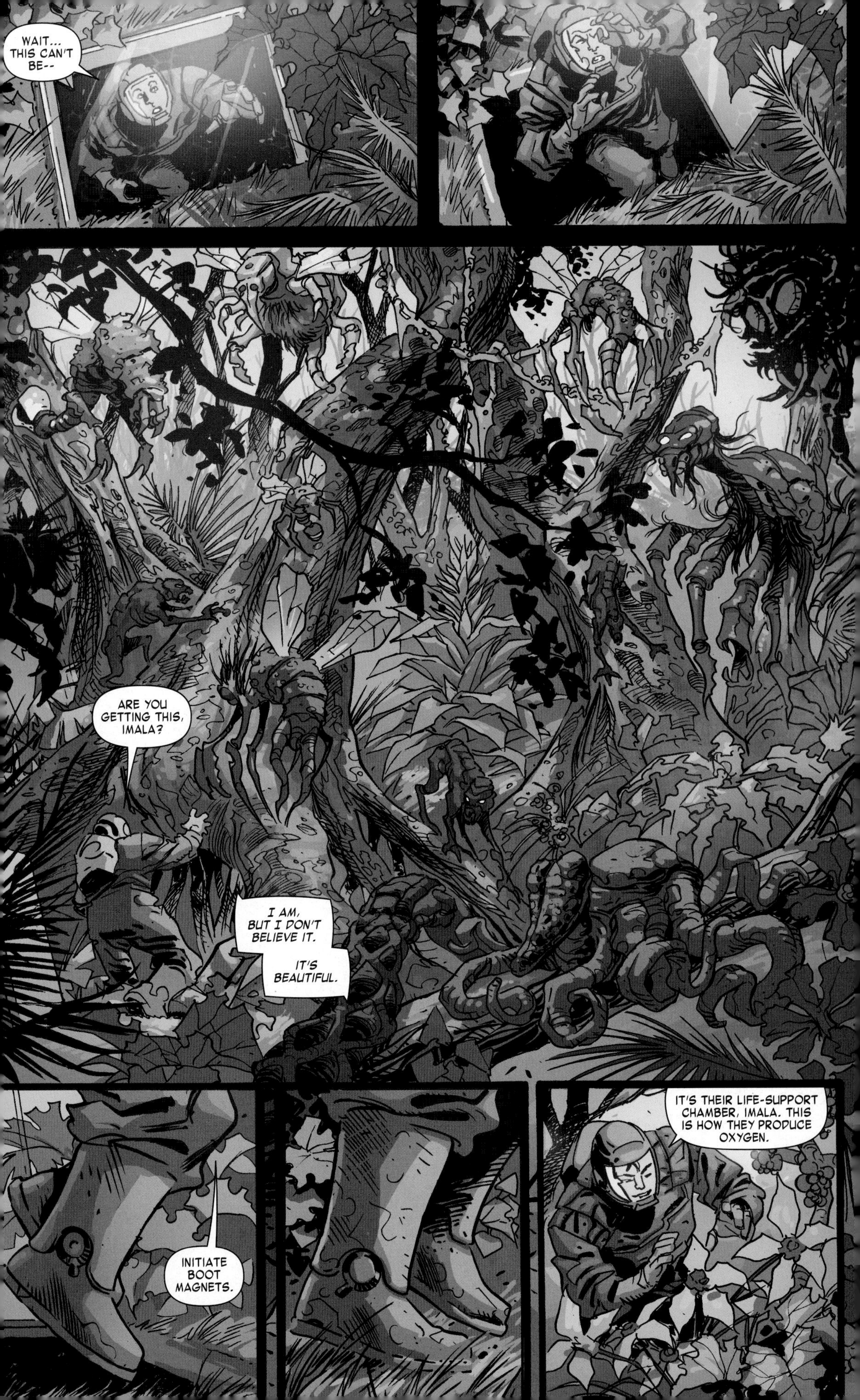
WAIT... THIS CAN'T BE--
ARE YOU GETTING THIS, IMALA?
I AM, BUT I DON'T BELIEVE IT.
IT'S BEAUTIFUL.
INITIATE BOOT MAGNETS.
IT'S THEIR LIFE-SUPPORT CHAMBER, IMALA. THIS IS HOW THEY PRODUCE OXYGEN.

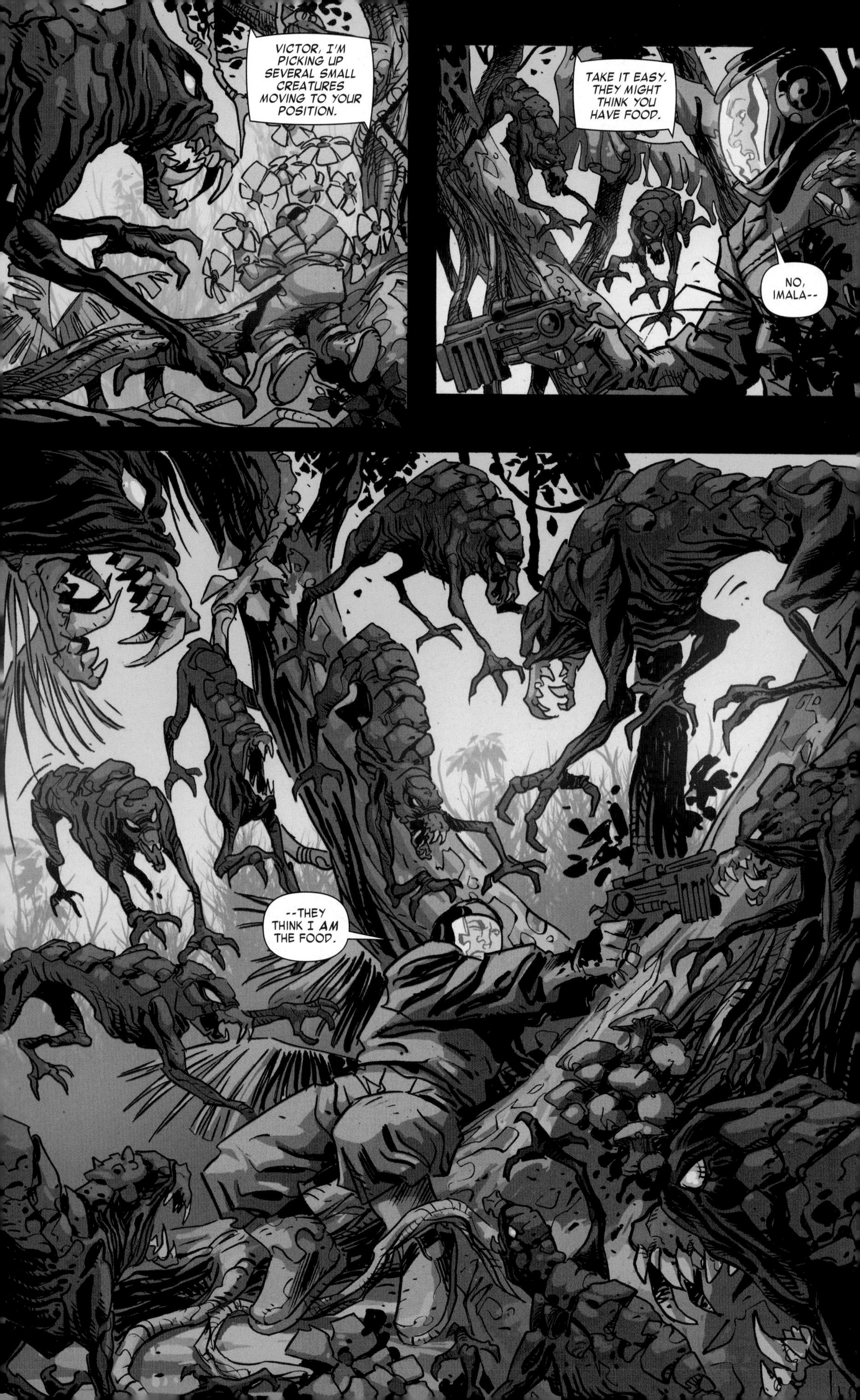
VICTOR, I'M PICKING UP SEVERAL SMALL CREATURES MOVING TO YOUR POSITION.
TAKE IT EASY. THEY MIGHT THINK YOU HAVE FOOD.
NO, IMALA--
--THEY THINK I *AM* THE FOOD.

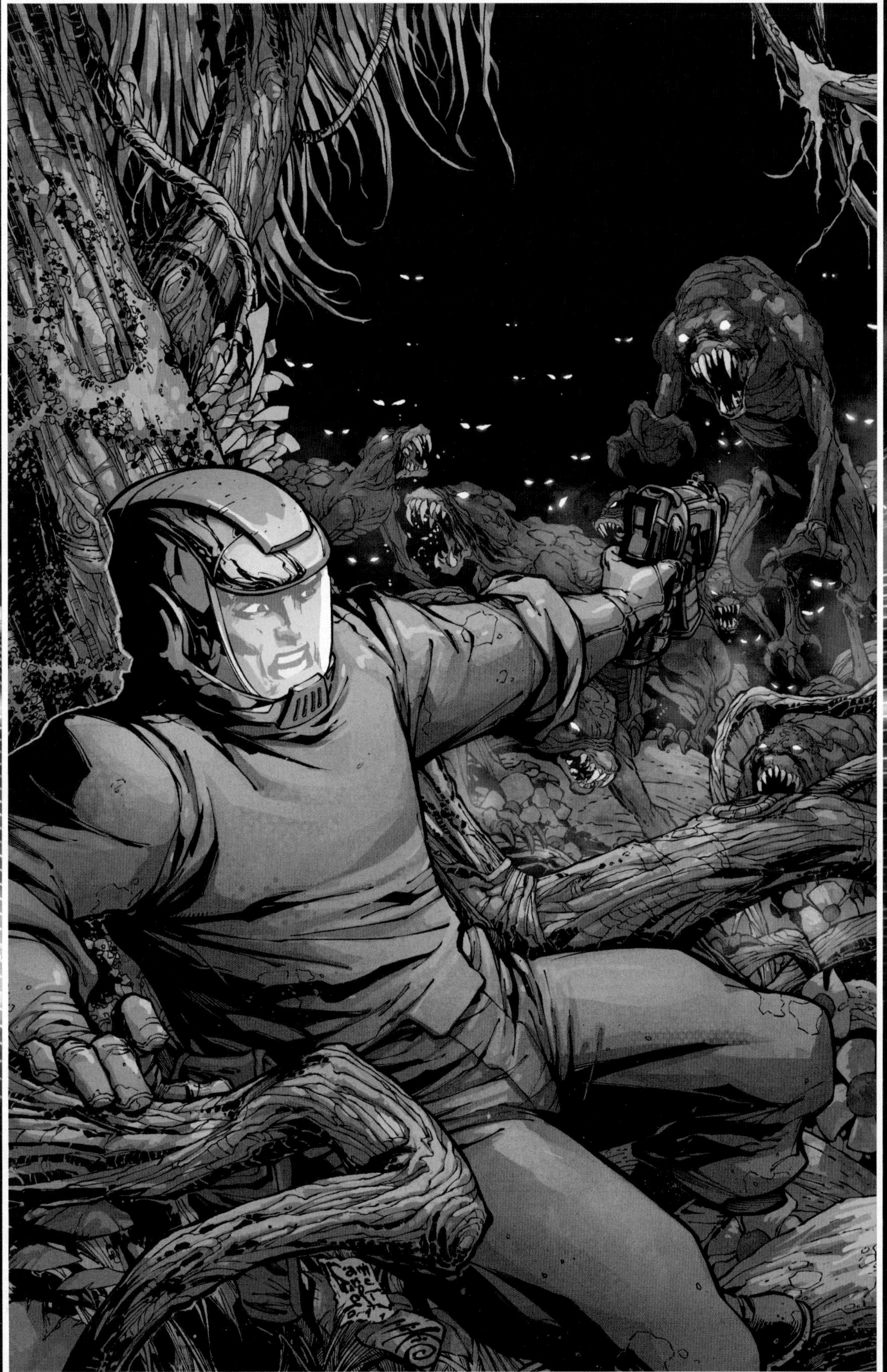

T W O

Partial Transcript. Congressional Hearings: "Failure of the US Army to Adequately Respond to the Formic Invasion." PRESIDING: CONGRESSMAN NICK CAVASETTES (R) Ohio, Chairman, Armed Services Committee.

CAVASETTES: Mazer Rackham, you served with Captain Wit O'Toole of the Mobile Operations Police, or MOPs, during the war, correct?

RACKHAM: Yes, sir.

C: And how would you describe Captain O'Toole?

R: A soldier deserving of the highest regard, sir. Tactically, strategically, personally–

C: Were you aware that Captain O'Toole had disobeyed a direct order by crossing into China?

R: Yes, sir.

C: You're smiling, Lieutenant. Do you endorse Captain O'Toole's flagrant insubordination?

R: I support any decision that saves lives, sir.

C: Even if a superior officer has given you contradictory orders?

R: The military, sir, is like the government. There are a lot of bumbling idiots in positions of authority. A good soldier knows who to ignore and who to follow.

C: You offend the United States of America, son.

R: I didn't specify which military or which government, sir, but if you believe it fits the U.S., I can't argue with your experience and authority.

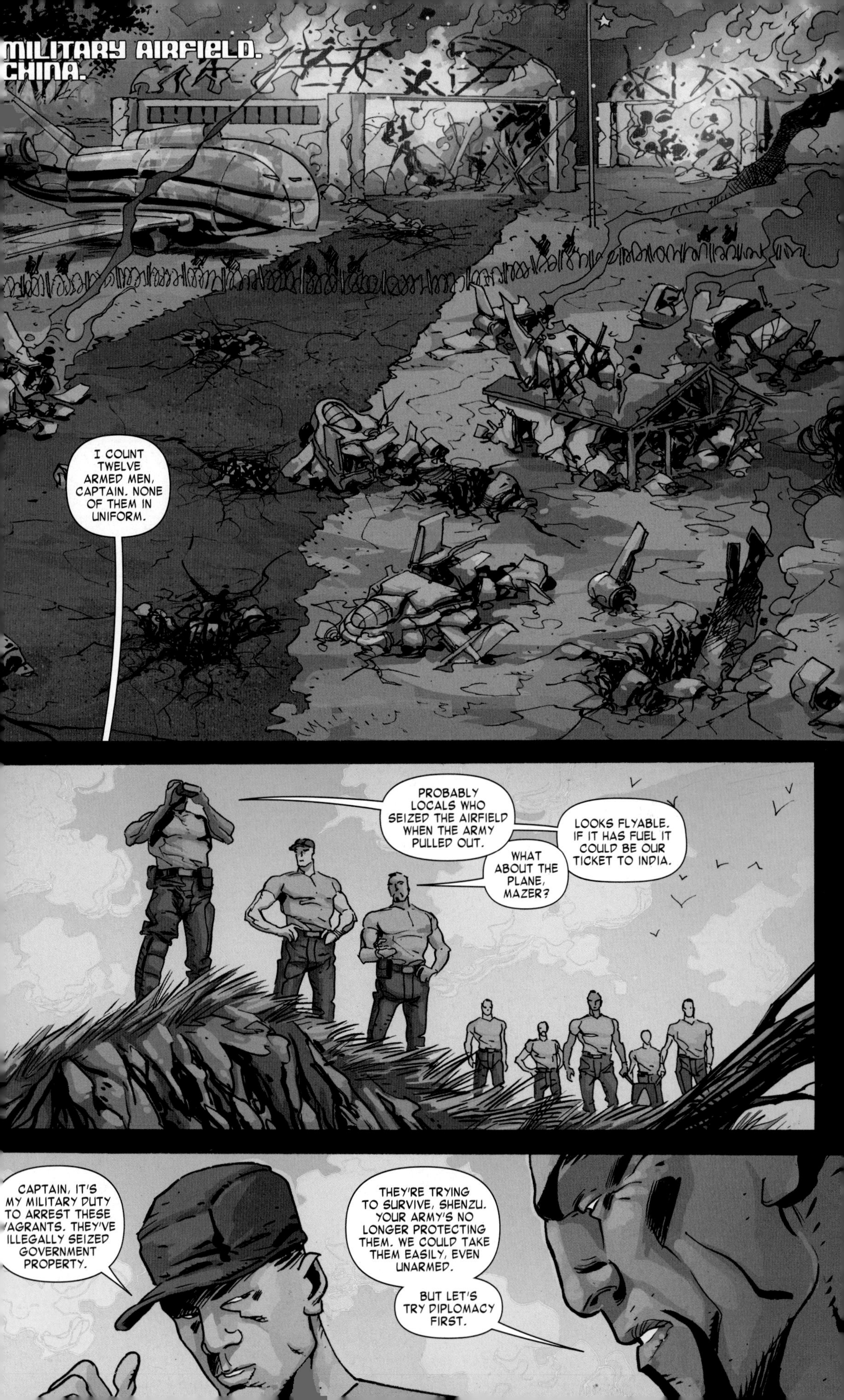
MILITARY AIRFIELD. CHINA.
I COUNT TWELVE ARMED MEN, CAPTAIN. NONE OF THEM IN UNIFORM.
PROBABLY LOCALS WHO SEIZED THE AIRFIELD WHEN THE ARMY PULLED OUT.
WHAT ABOUT THE PLANE, MAZER?
LOOKS FLYABLE. IF IT HAS FUEL IT COULD BE OUR TICKET TO INDIA.
CAPTAIN, IT'S MY MILITARY DUTY TO ARREST THESE VAGRANTS. THEY'VE ILLEGALLY SEIZED GOVERNMENT PROPERTY.
THEY'RE TRYING TO SURVIVE, SHENZU. YOUR ARMY'S NO LONGER PROTECTING THEM. WE COULD TAKE THEM EASILY, EVEN UNARMED.
BUT LET'S TRY DIPLOMACY FIRST.

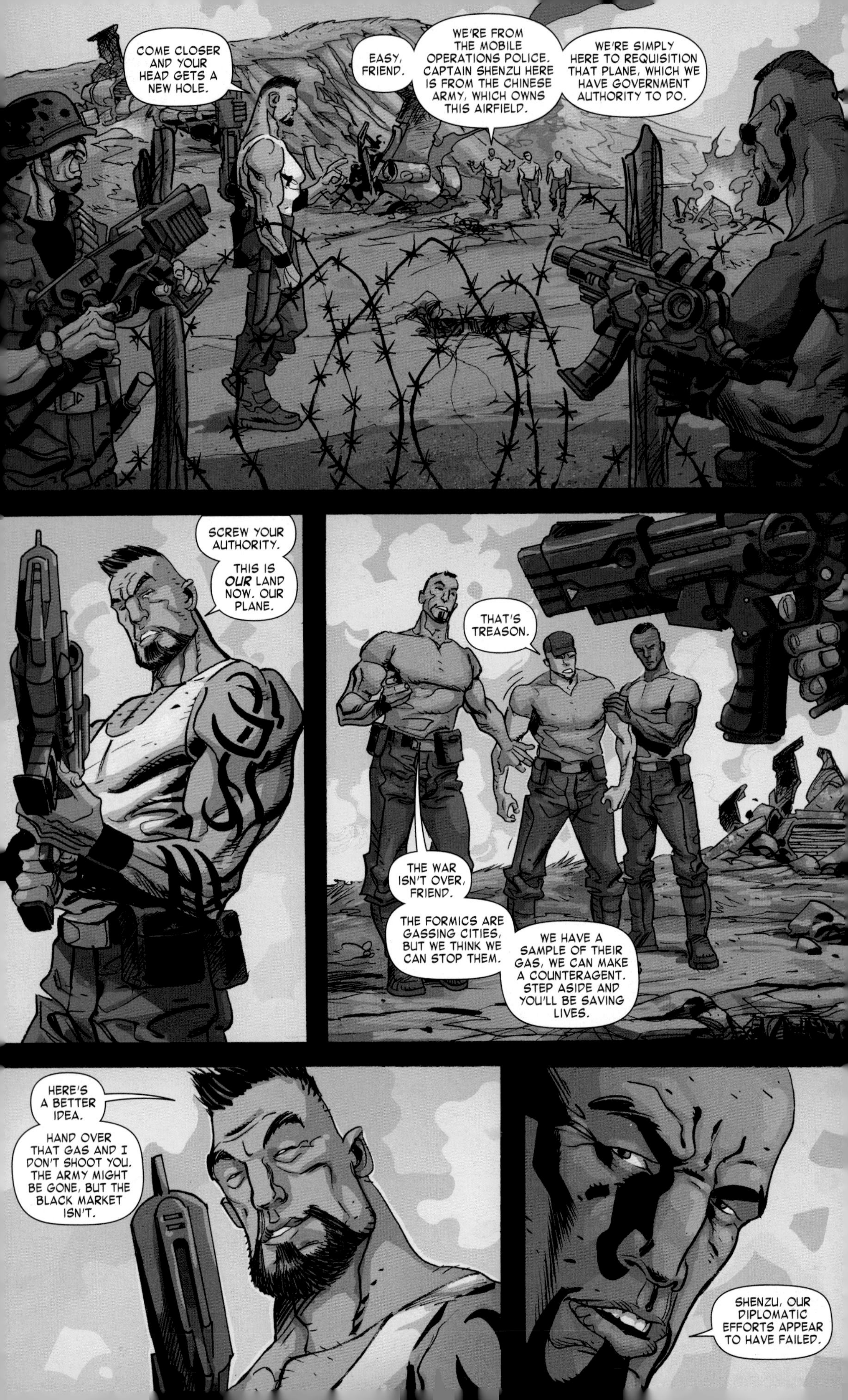
COME CLOSER AND YOUR HEAD GETS A NEW HOLE.
EASY, FRIEND.
WE'RE FROM THE MOBILE OPERATIONS POLICE. CAPTAIN SHENZU HERE IS FROM THE CHINESE ARMY, WHICH OWNS THIS AIRFIELD.
WE'RE SIMPLY HERE TO REQUISITION THAT PLANE, WHICH WE HAVE GOVERNMENT AUTHORITY TO DO.
SCREW YOUR AUTHORITY.
THIS IS *OUR* LAND NOW. OUR PLANE.
THAT'S TREASON.
THE WAR ISN'T OVER, FRIEND.
THE FORMICS ARE GASSING CITIES, BUT WE THINK WE CAN STOP THEM.
WE HAVE A SAMPLE OF THEIR GAS, WE CAN MAKE A COUNTERAGENT. STEP ASIDE AND YOU'LL BE SAVING LIVES.
HERE'S A BETTER IDEA.
HAND OVER THAT GAS AND I DON'T SHOOT YOU. THE ARMY MIGHT BE GONE, BUT THE BLACK MARKET ISN'T.
SHENZU, OUR DIPLOMATIC EFFORTS APPEAR TO HAVE FAILED.

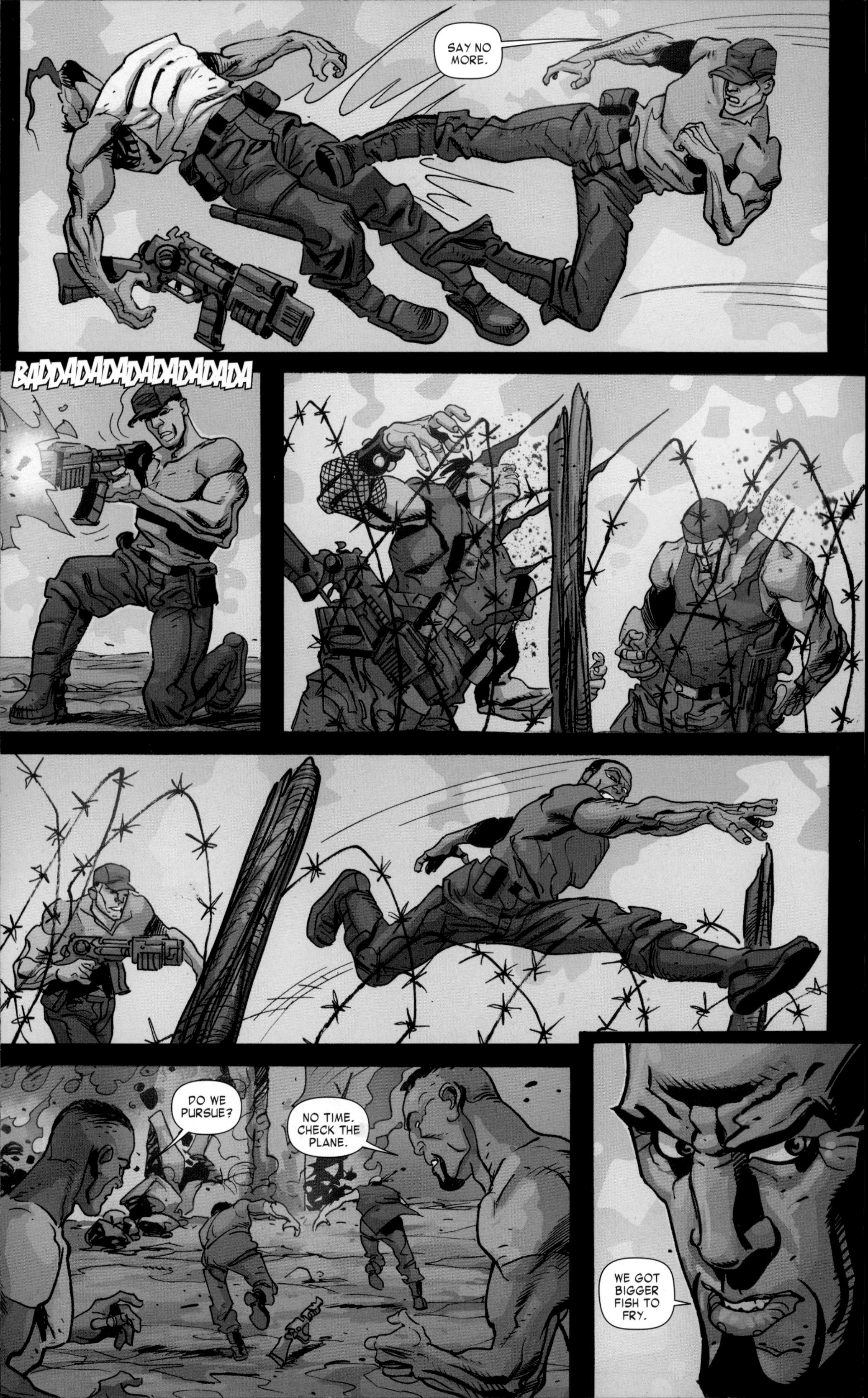
SAY NO MORE.
BADDADADADADADADADADA
DO WE PURSUE?
NO TIME. CHECK THE PLANE.
WE GOT BIGGER FISH TO FRY.

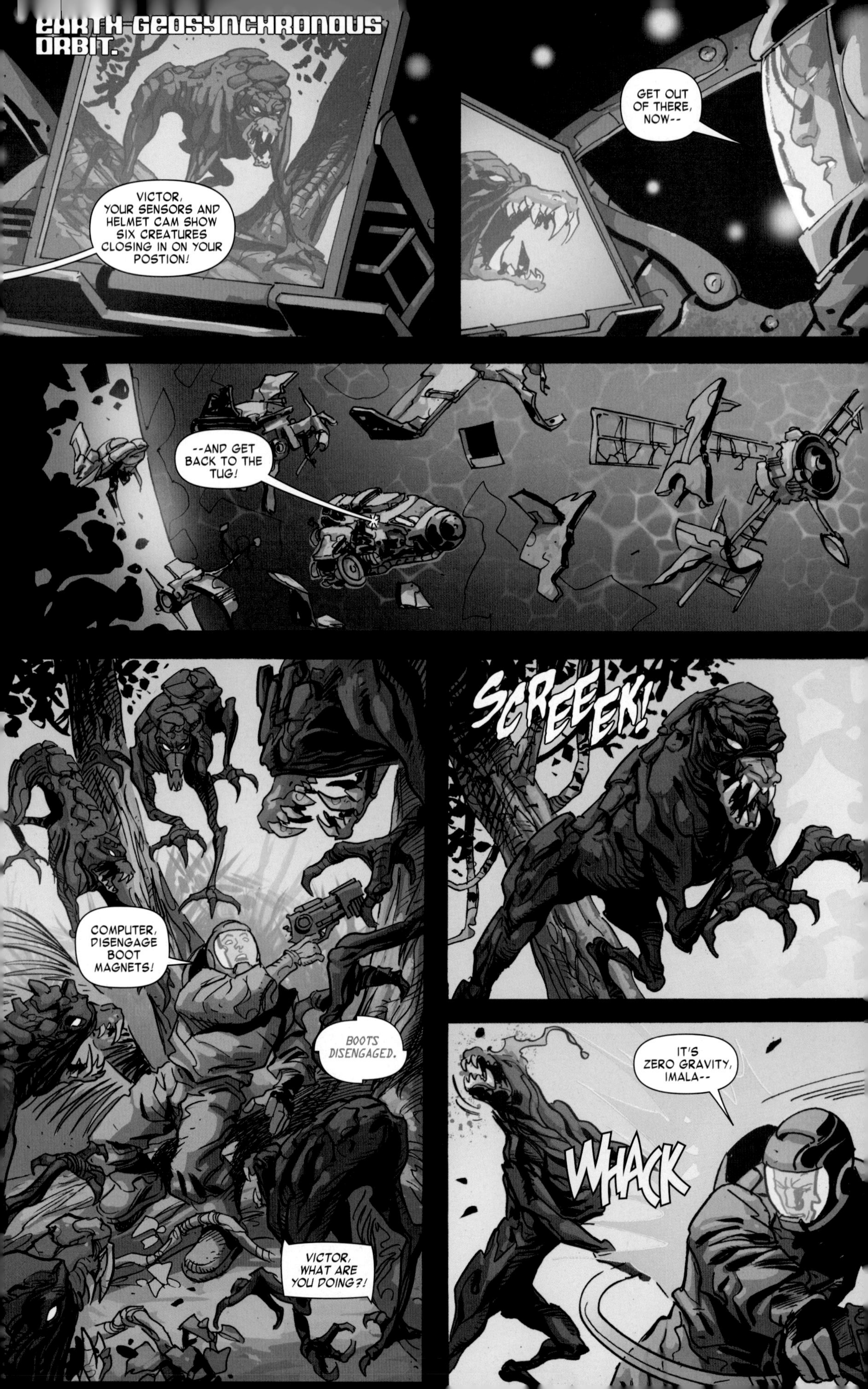
EARTH GEOSYNCHRONOUS ORBIT.
VICTOR, YOUR SENSORS AND HELMET CAM SHOW SIX CREATURES CLOSING IN ON YOUR POSTION!
GET OUT OF THERE, NOW--
--AND GET BACK TO THE TUG!
COMPUTER, DISENGAGE BOOT MAGNETS!
BOOTS DISENGAGED.
VICTOR, WHAT ARE YOU DOING?!
SCREEEEK!
IT'S ZERO GRAVITY, IMALA--
WHACK

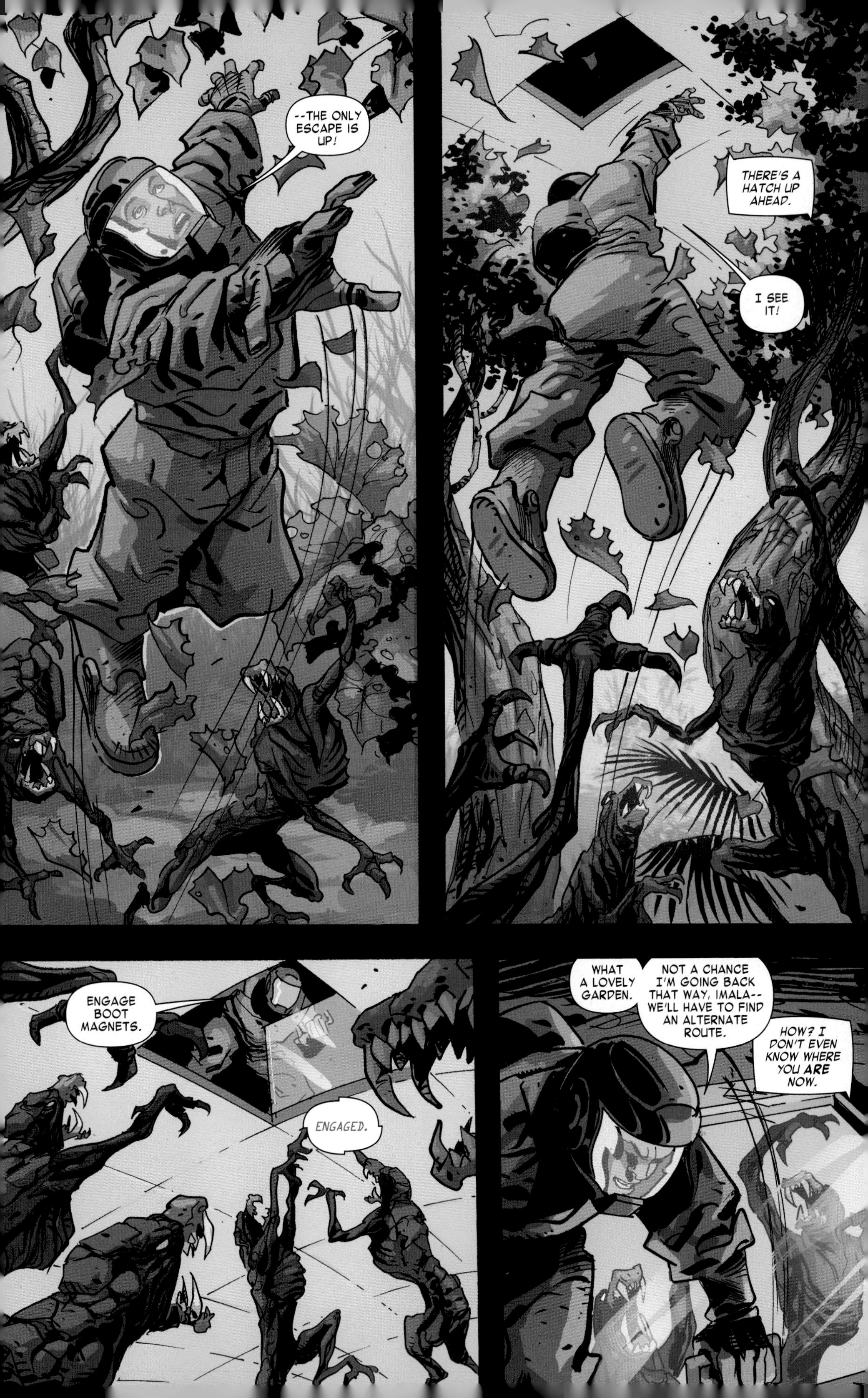
--THE ONLY ESCAPE IS UP!
THERE'S A HATCH UP AHEAD.
I SEE IT!
ENGAGE BOOT MAGNETS.
ENGAGED.
WHAT A LOVELY GARDEN.
NOT A CHANCE I'M GOING BACK THAT WAY, IMALA--WE'LL HAVE TO FIND AN ALTERNATE ROUTE.
HOW? I DON'T EVEN KNOW WHERE YOU ARE NOW.

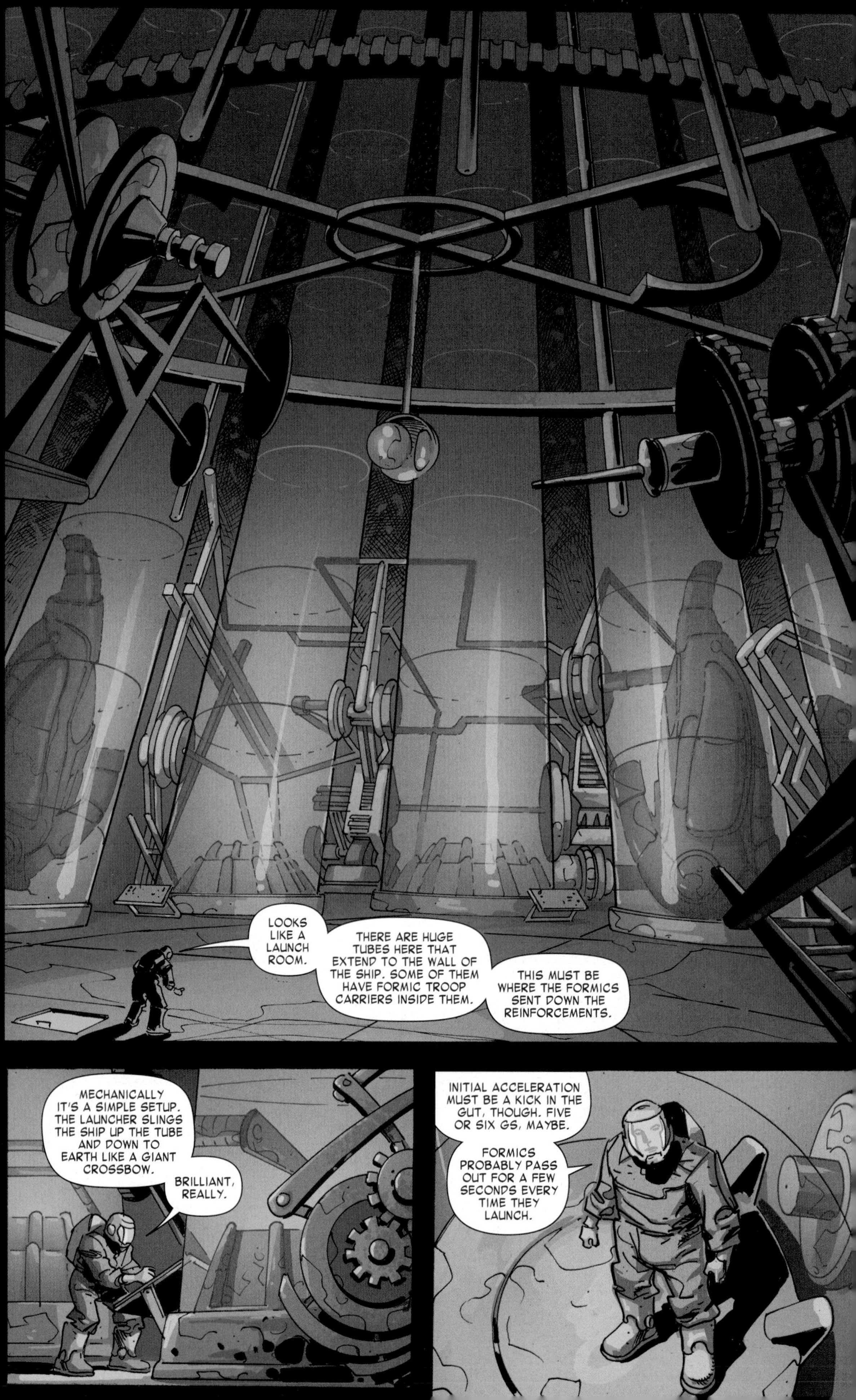
LOOKS LIKE A LAUNCH ROOM.
THERE ARE HUGE TUBES HERE THAT EXTEND TO THE WALL OF THE SHIP. SOME OF THEM HAVE FORMIC TROOP CARRIERS INSIDE THEM.
THIS MUST BE WHERE THE FORMICS SENT DOWN THE REINFORCEMENTS.
MECHANICALLY IT'S A SIMPLE SETUP. THE LAUNCHER SLINGS THE SHIP UP THE TUBE AND DOWN TO EARTH LIKE A GIANT CROSSBOW.
BRILLIANT, REALLY.
INITIAL ACCELERATION MUST BE A KICK IN THE GUT, THOUGH. FIVE OR SIX GS, MAYBE.
FORMICS PROBABLY PASS OUT FOR A FEW SECONDS EVERY TIME THEY LAUNCH.

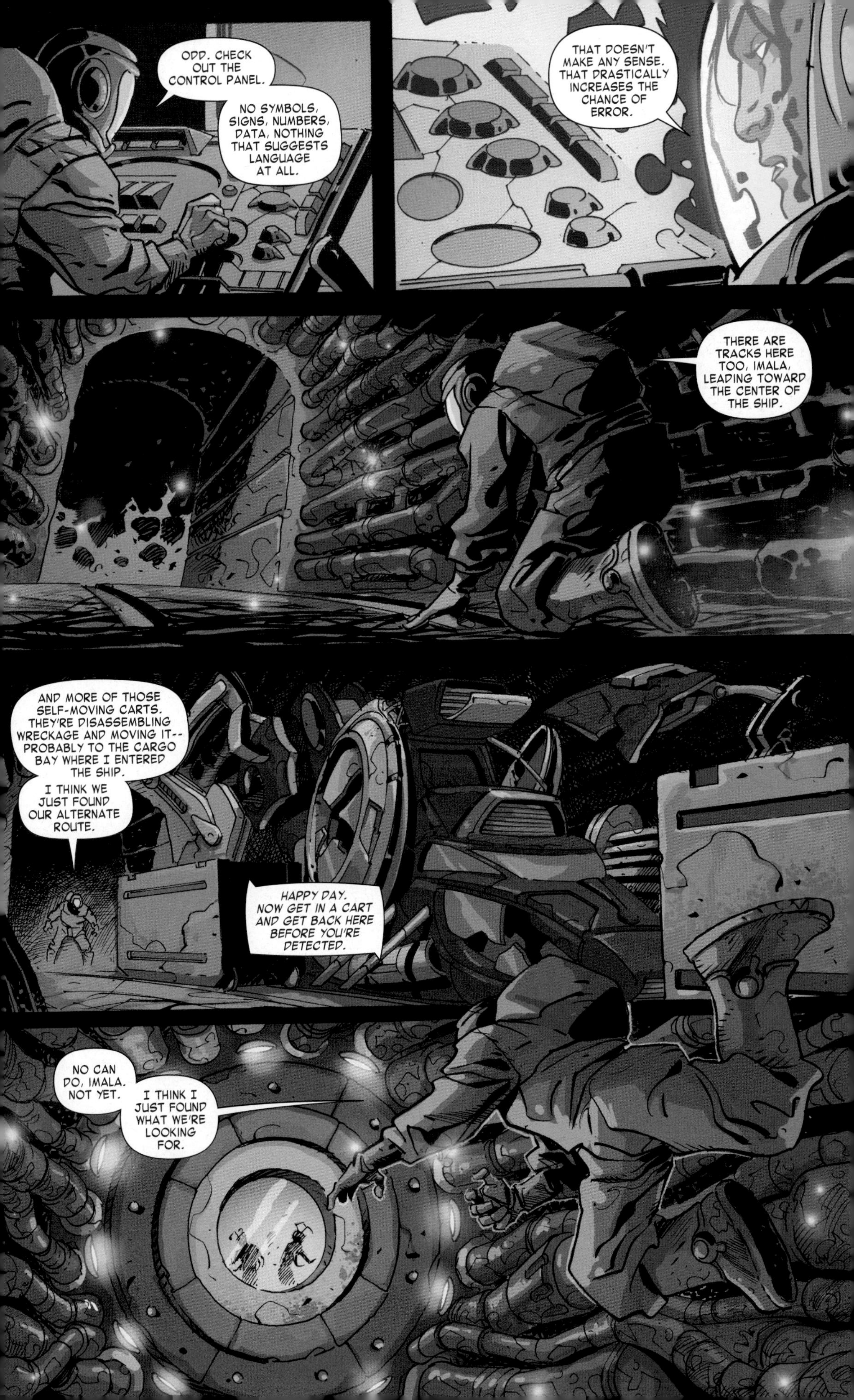

ODD. CHECK OUT THE CONTROL PANEL.
NO SYMBOLS, SIGNS, NUMBERS, DATA, NOTHING THAT SUGGESTS LANGUAGE AT ALL.
THAT DOESN'T MAKE ANY SENSE. THAT DRASTICALLY INCREASES THE CHANCE OF ERROR.
THERE ARE TRACKS HERE TOO, IMALA, LEADING TOWARD THE CENTER OF THE SHIP.
AND MORE OF THOSE SELF-MOVING CARTS. THEY'RE DISASSEMBLING WRECKAGE AND MOVING IT-- PROBABLY TO THE CARGO BAY WHERE I ENTERED THE SHIP.
I THINK WE JUST FOUND OUR ALTERNATE ROUTE.
HAPPY DAY. NOW GET IN A CART AND GET BACK HERE BEFORE YOU'RE DETECTED.
NO CAN DO, IMALA. NOT YET.
I THINK I JUST FOUND WHAT WE'RE LOOKING FOR.

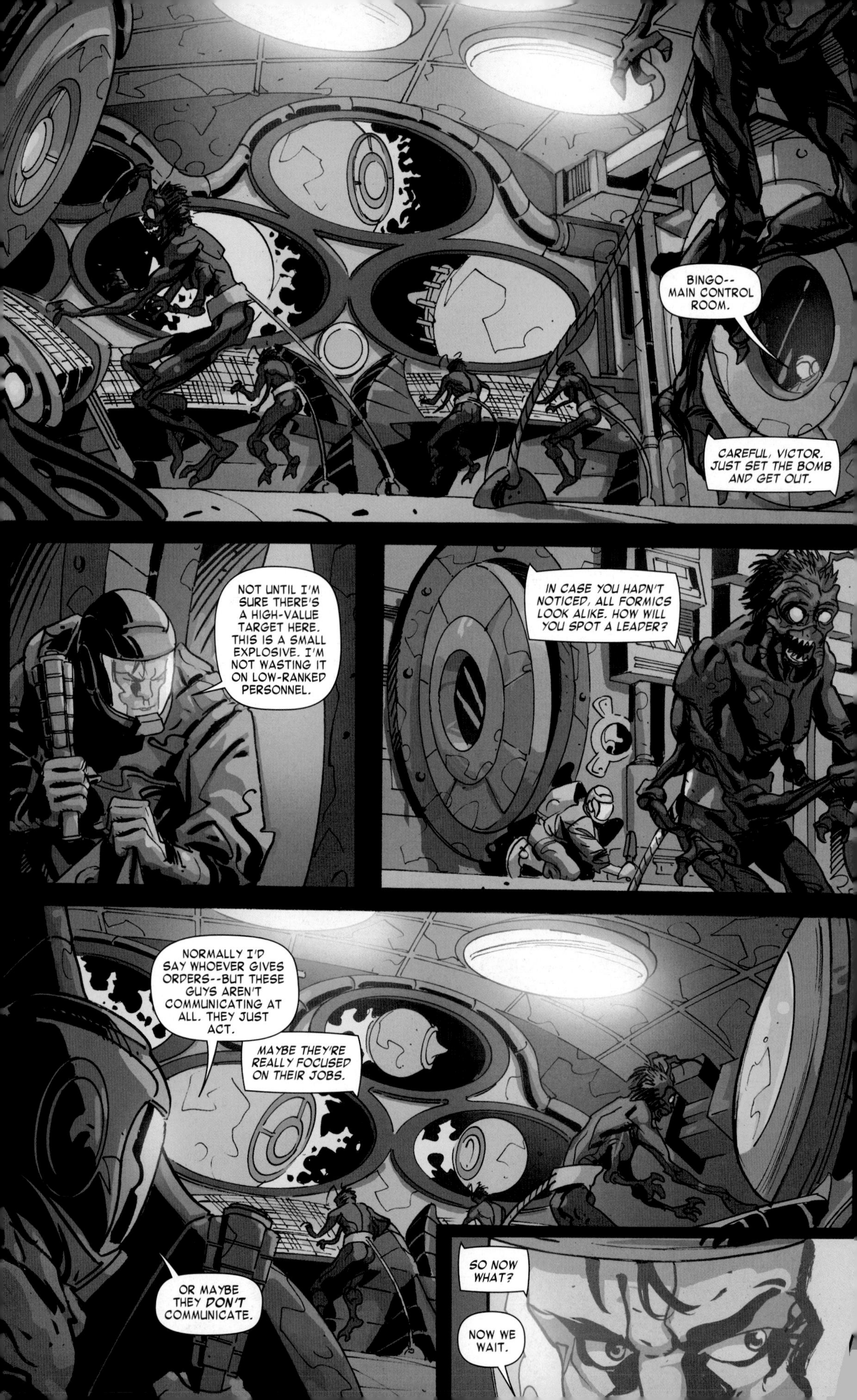
BINGO-- MAIN CONTROL ROOM.
CAREFUL, VICTOR. JUST SET THE BOMB AND GET OUT.
NOT UNTIL I'M SURE THERE'S A HIGH-VALUE TARGET HERE. THIS IS A SMALL EXPLOSIVE. I'M NOT WASTING IT ON LOW-RANKED PERSONNEL.
IN CASE YOU HADN'T NOTICED, ALL FORMICS LOOK ALIKE. HOW WILL YOU SPOT A LEADER?
NORMALLY I'D SAY WHOEVER GIVES ORDERS--BUT THESE GUYS AREN'T COMMUNICATING AT ALL. THEY JUST ACT.
MAYBE THEY'RE REALLY FOCUSED ON THEIR JOBS.
OR MAYBE THEY DON'T COMMUNICATE.
SO NOW WHAT?
NOW WE WAIT.

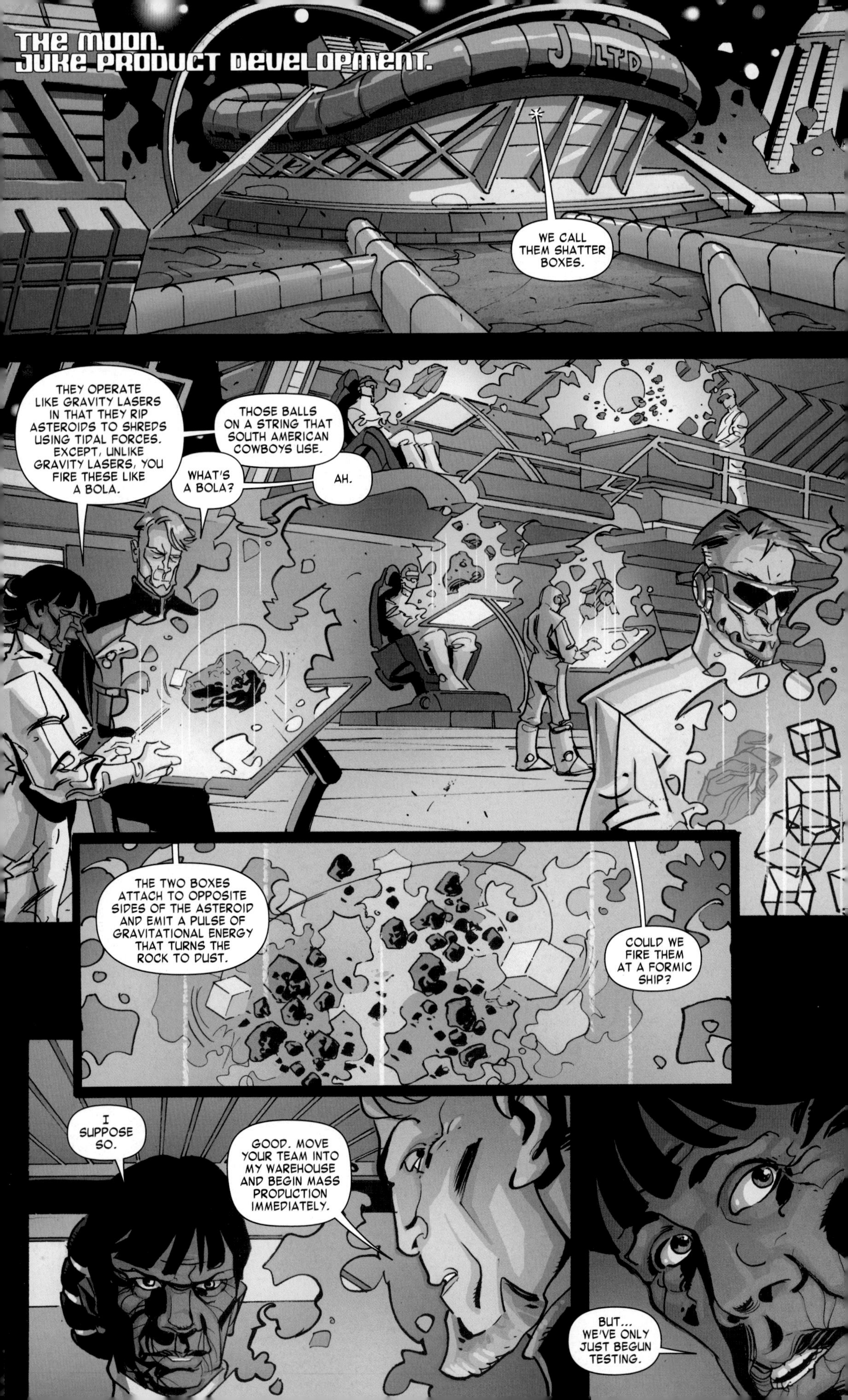
THE MOON.
JUKE PRODUCT DEVELOPMENT.
J LTD
WE CALL THEM SHATTER BOXES.
THEY OPERATE LIKE GRAVITY LASERS IN THAT THEY RIP ASTEROIDS TO SHREDS USING TIDAL FORCES. EXCEPT, UNLIKE GRAVITY LASERS, YOU FIRE THESE LIKE A BOLA.
WHAT'S A BOLA?
THOSE BALLS ON A STRING THAT SOUTH AMERICAN COWBOYS USE.
AH.
THE TWO BOXES ATTACH TO OPPOSITE SIDES OF THE ASTEROID AND EMIT A PULSE OF GRAVITATIONAL ENERGY THAT TURNS THE ROCK TO DUST.
COULD WE FIRE THEM AT A FORMIC SHIP?
I SUPPOSE SO.
GOOD. MOVE YOUR TEAM INTO MY WAREHOUSE AND BEGIN MASS PRODUCTION IMMEDIATELY.
BUT... WE'VE ONLY JUST BEGUN TESTING.

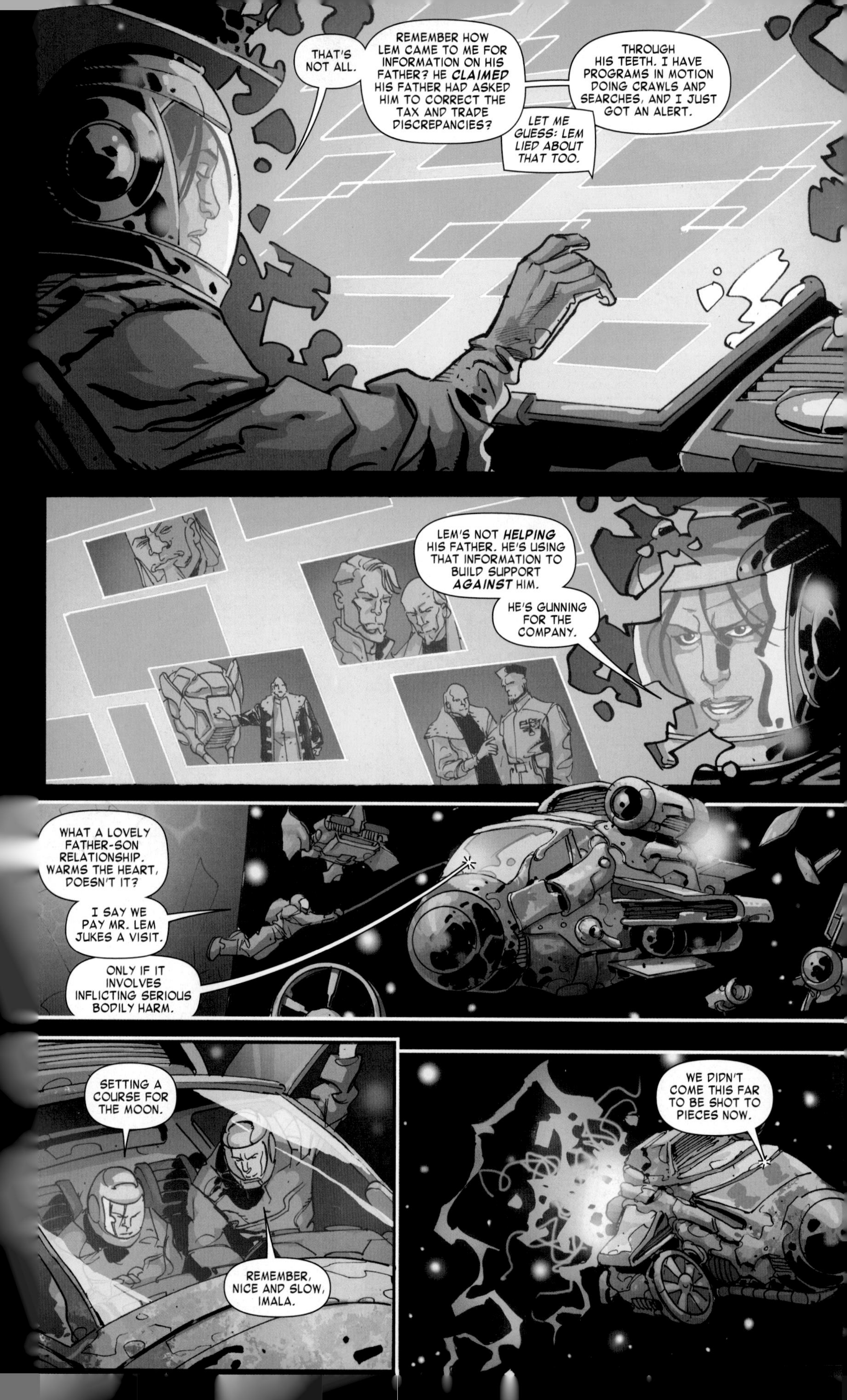
THAT'S NOT ALL.
REMEMBER HOW LEM CAME TO ME FOR INFORMATION ON HIS FATHER? HE CLAIMED HIS FATHER HAD ASKED HIM TO CORRECT THE TAX AND TRADE DISCREPANCIES?
LET ME GUESS: LEM LIED ABOUT THAT TOO.
THROUGH HIS TEETH. I HAVE PROGRAMS IN MOTION DOING CRAWLS AND SEARCHES, AND I JUST GOT AN ALERT.
LEM'S NOT HELPING HIS FATHER. HE'S USING THAT INFORMATION TO BUILD SUPPORT AGAINST HIM.
HE'S GUNNING FOR THE COMPANY.
WHAT A LOVELY FATHER-SON RELATIONSHIP. WARMS THE HEART, DOESN'T IT?
I SAY WE PAY MR. LEM JUKES A VISIT.
ONLY IF IT INVOLVES INFLICTING SERIOUS BODILY HARM.
SETTING A COURSE FOR THE MOON.
REMEMBER, NICE AND SLOW, IMALA.
WE DIDN'T COME THIS FAR TO BE SHOT TO PIECES NOW.

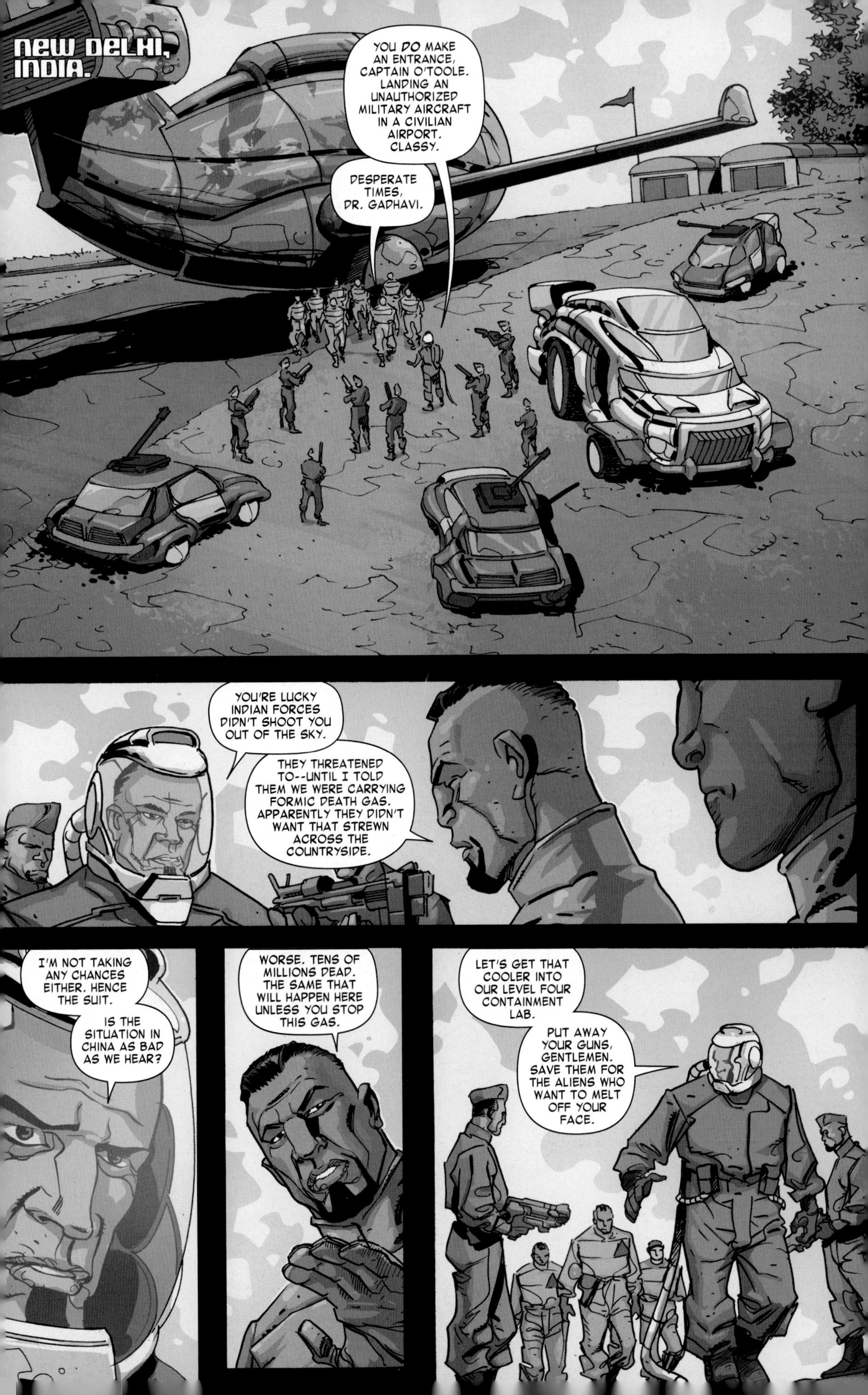
NEW DELHI, INDIA.
YOU DO MAKE AN ENTRANCE, CAPTAIN O'TOOLE. LANDING AN UNAUTHORIZED MILITARY AIRCRAFT IN A CIVILIAN AIRPORT. CLASSY.
DESPERATE TIMES, DR. GADHAVI.
YOU'RE LUCKY INDIAN FORCES DIDN'T SHOOT YOU OUT OF THE SKY.
THEY THREATENED TO--UNTIL I TOLD THEM WE WERE CARRYING FORMIC DEATH GAS. APPARENTLY THEY DIDN'T WANT THAT STREWN ACROSS THE COUNTRYSIDE.
I'M NOT TAKING ANY CHANCES EITHER. HENCE THE SUIT.
IS THE SITUATION IN CHINA AS BAD AS WE HEAR?
WORSE. TENS OF MILLIONS DEAD. THE SAME THAT WILL HAPPEN HERE UNLESS YOU STOP THIS GAS.
LET'S GET THAT COOLER INTO OUR LEVEL FOUR CONTAINMENT LAB.
PUT AWAY YOUR GUNS, GENTLEMEN. SAVE THEM FOR THE ALIENS WHO WANT TO MELT OFF YOUR FACE.

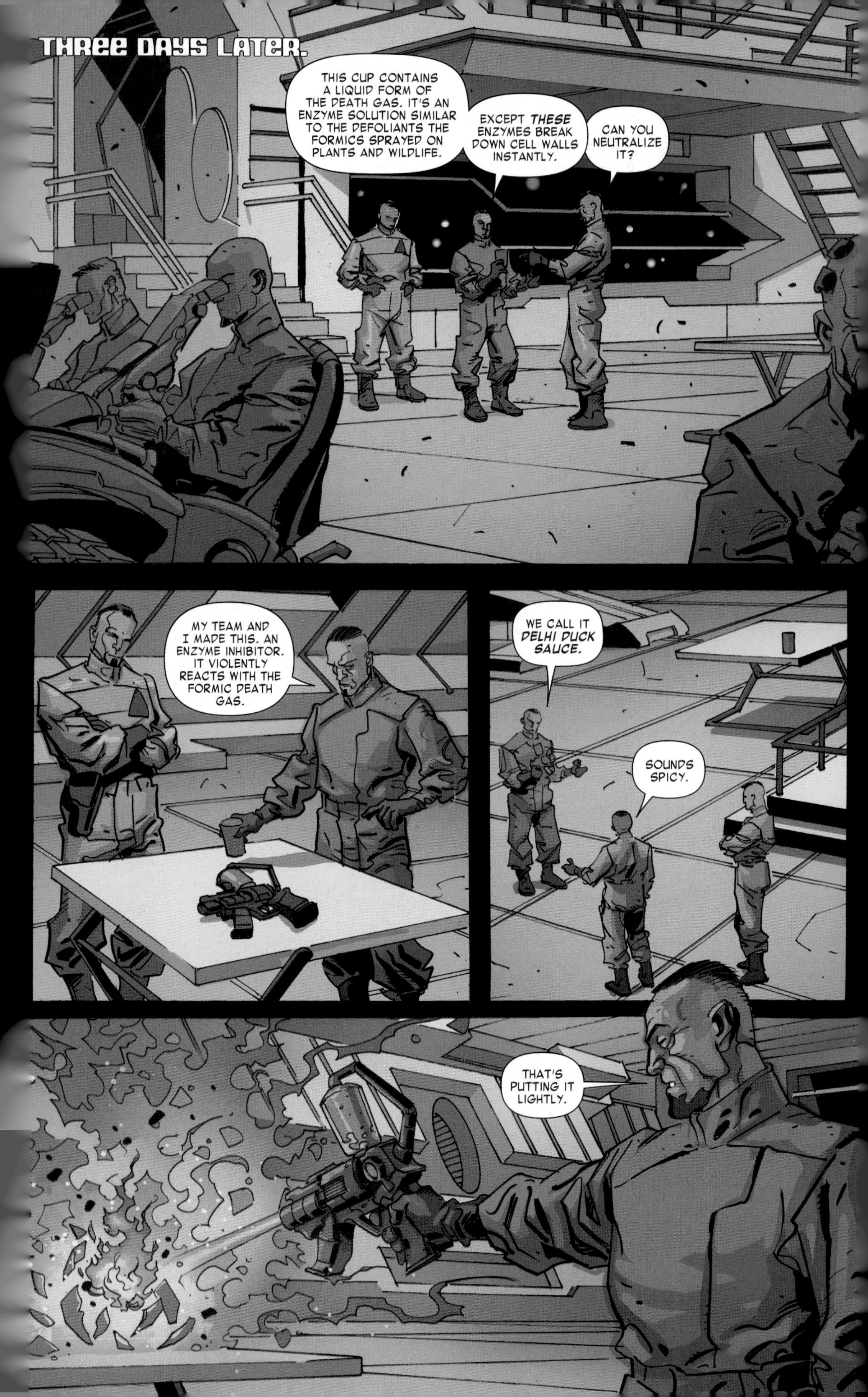
THREE DAYS LATER.
THIS CUP CONTAINS A LIQUID FORM OF THE DEATH GAS. IT'S AN ENZYME SOLUTION SIMILAR TO THE DEFOLIANTS THE FORMICS SPRAYED ON PLANTS AND WILDLIFE.
EXCEPT THESE ENZYMES BREAK DOWN CELL WALLS INSTANTLY.
CAN YOU NEUTRALIZE IT?
MY TEAM AND I MADE THIS. AN ENZYME INHIBITOR. IT VIOLENTLY REACTS WITH THE FORMIC DEATH GAS.
WE CALL IT DELHI DUCK SAUCE.
SOUNDS SPICY.
THAT'S PUTTING IT LIGHTLY.

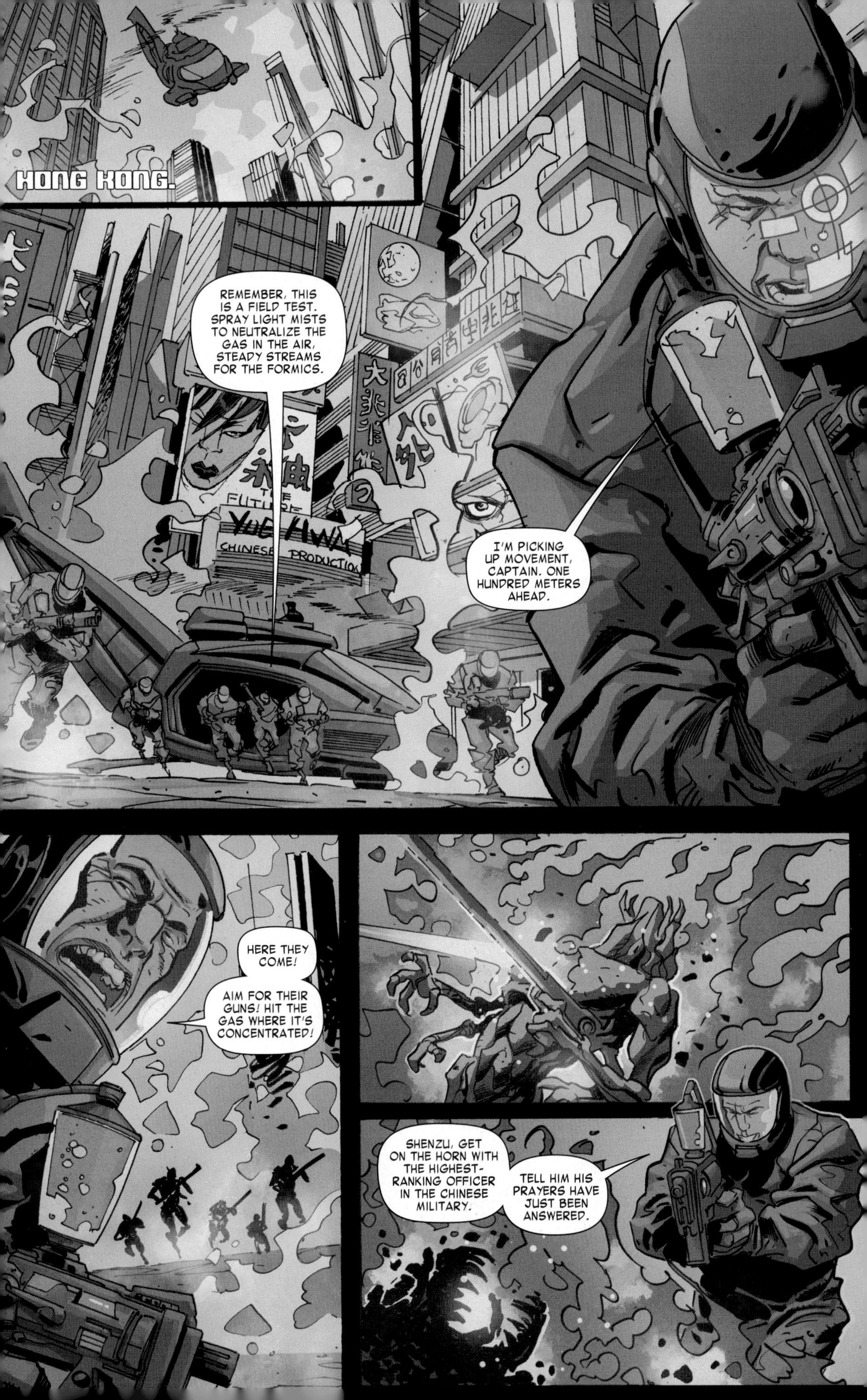
HONG KONG.
REMEMBER, THIS IS A FIELD TEST. SPRAY LIGHT MISTS TO NEUTRALIZE THE GAS IN THE AIR, STEADY STREAMS FOR THE FORMICS.
I'M PICKING UP MOVEMENT, CAPTAIN. ONE HUNDRED METERS AHEAD.
THE FUTURE
YUE HWA
CHINESE PRODUCTION
HERE THEY COME!
AIM FOR THEIR GUNS! HIT THE GAS WHERE IT'S CONCENTRATED!
SHENZU, GET ON THE HORN WITH THE HIGHEST-RANKING OFFICER IN THE CHINESE MILITARY.
TELL HIM HIS PRAYERS HAVE JUST BEEN ANSWERED.

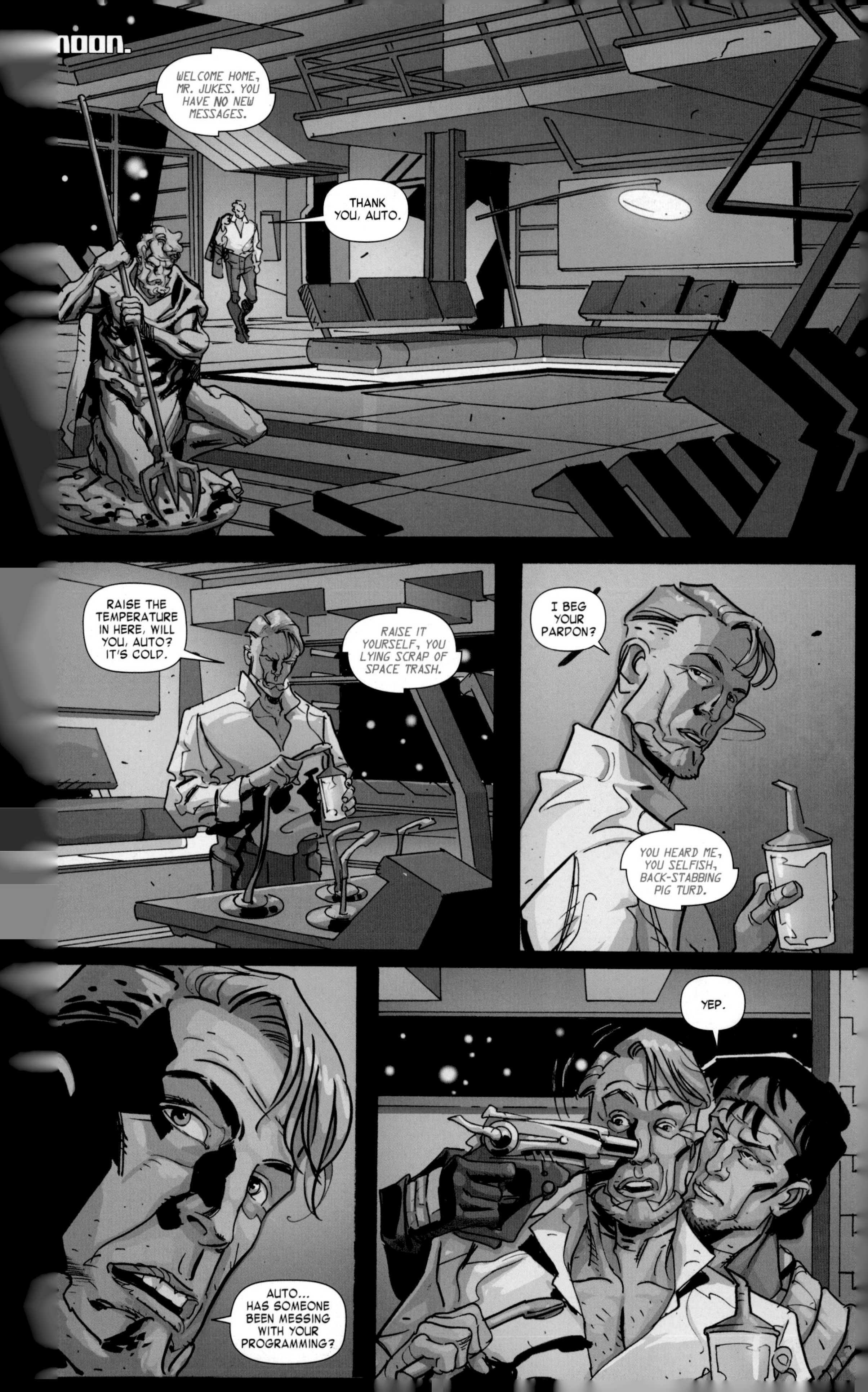

...NOON.
WELCOME HOME, MR. JUKES. YOU HAVE NO NEW MESSAGES.
THANK YOU, AUTO.
RAISE THE TEMPERATURE IN HERE, WILL YOU, AUTO? IT'S COLD.
RAISE IT YOURSELF, YOU LYING SCRAP OF SPACE TRASH.
I BEG YOUR PARDON?
YOU HEARD ME, YOU SELFISH, BACK-STABBING PIG TURD.
AUTO... HAS SOMEONE BEEN MESSING WITH YOUR PROGRAMMING?
YEP.

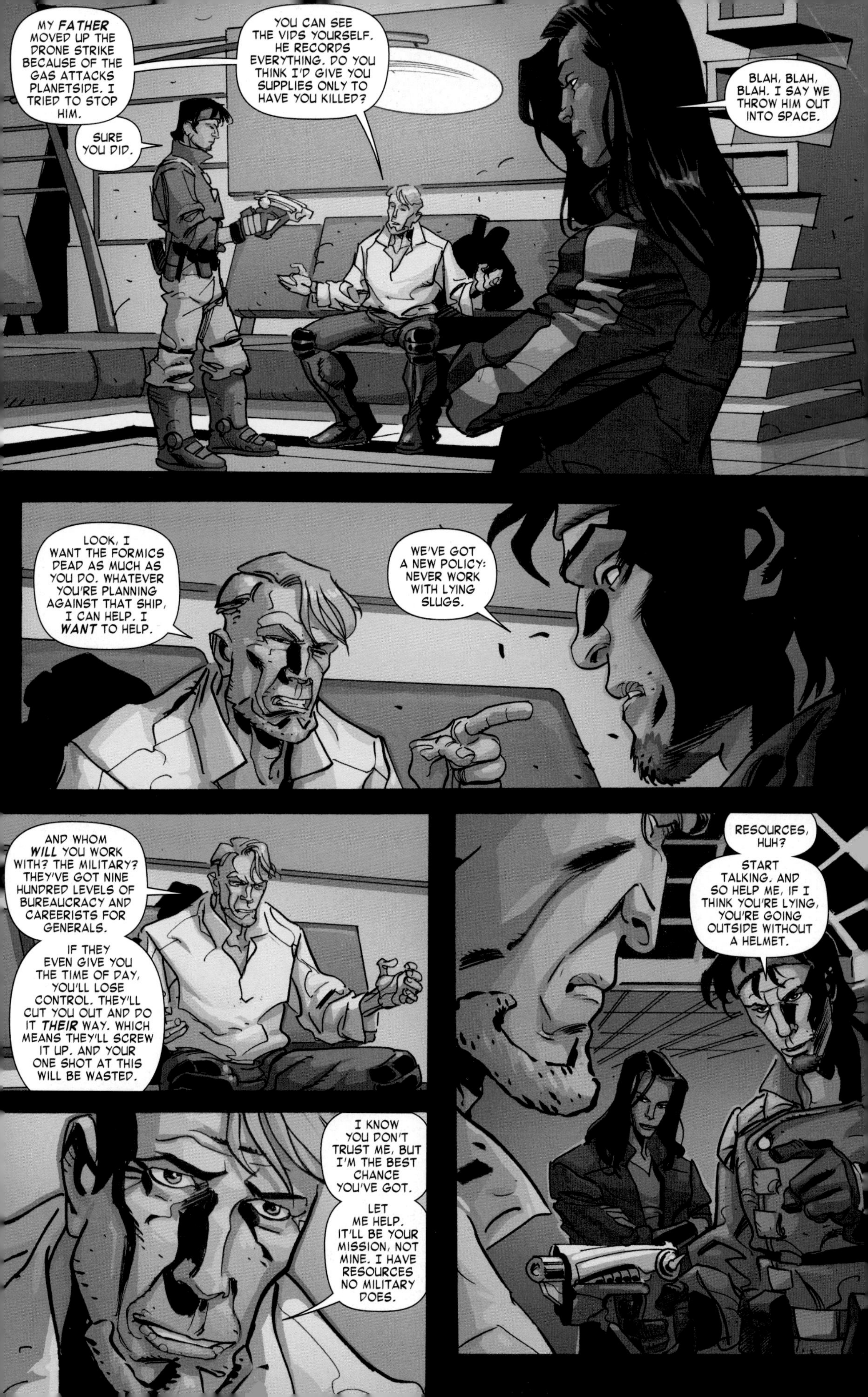
MY FATHER MOVED UP THE DRONE STRIKE BECAUSE OF THE GAS ATTACKS PLANETSIDE. I TRIED TO STOP HIM.
YOU CAN SEE THE VIDS YOURSELF. HE RECORDS EVERYTHING. DO YOU THINK I'D GIVE YOU SUPPLIES ONLY TO HAVE YOU KILLED?
SURE YOU DID.
BLAH, BLAH, BLAH. I SAY WE THROW HIM OUT INTO SPACE.
LOOK, I WANT THE FORMICS DEAD AS MUCH AS YOU DO. WHATEVER YOU'RE PLANNING AGAINST THAT SHIP, I CAN HELP. I WANT TO HELP.
WE'VE GOT A NEW POLICY: NEVER WORK WITH LYING SLUGS.
AND WHOM WILL YOU WORK WITH? THE MILITARY? THEY'VE GOT NINE HUNDRED LEVELS OF BUREAUCRACY AND CAREERISTS FOR GENERALS.
IF THEY EVEN GIVE YOU THE TIME OF DAY, YOU'LL LOSE CONTROL. THEY'LL CUT YOU OUT AND DO IT THEIR WAY. WHICH MEANS THEY'LL SCREW IT UP. AND YOUR ONE SHOT AT THIS WILL BE WASTED.
I KNOW YOU DON'T TRUST ME, BUT I'M THE BEST CHANCE YOU'VE GOT.
LET ME HELP. IT'LL BE YOUR MISSION, NOT MINE. I HAVE RESOURCES NO MILITARY DOES.
RESOURCES, HUH?
START TALKING. AND SO HELP ME, IF I THINK YOU'RE LYING, YOU'RE GOING OUTSIDE WITHOUT A HELMET.

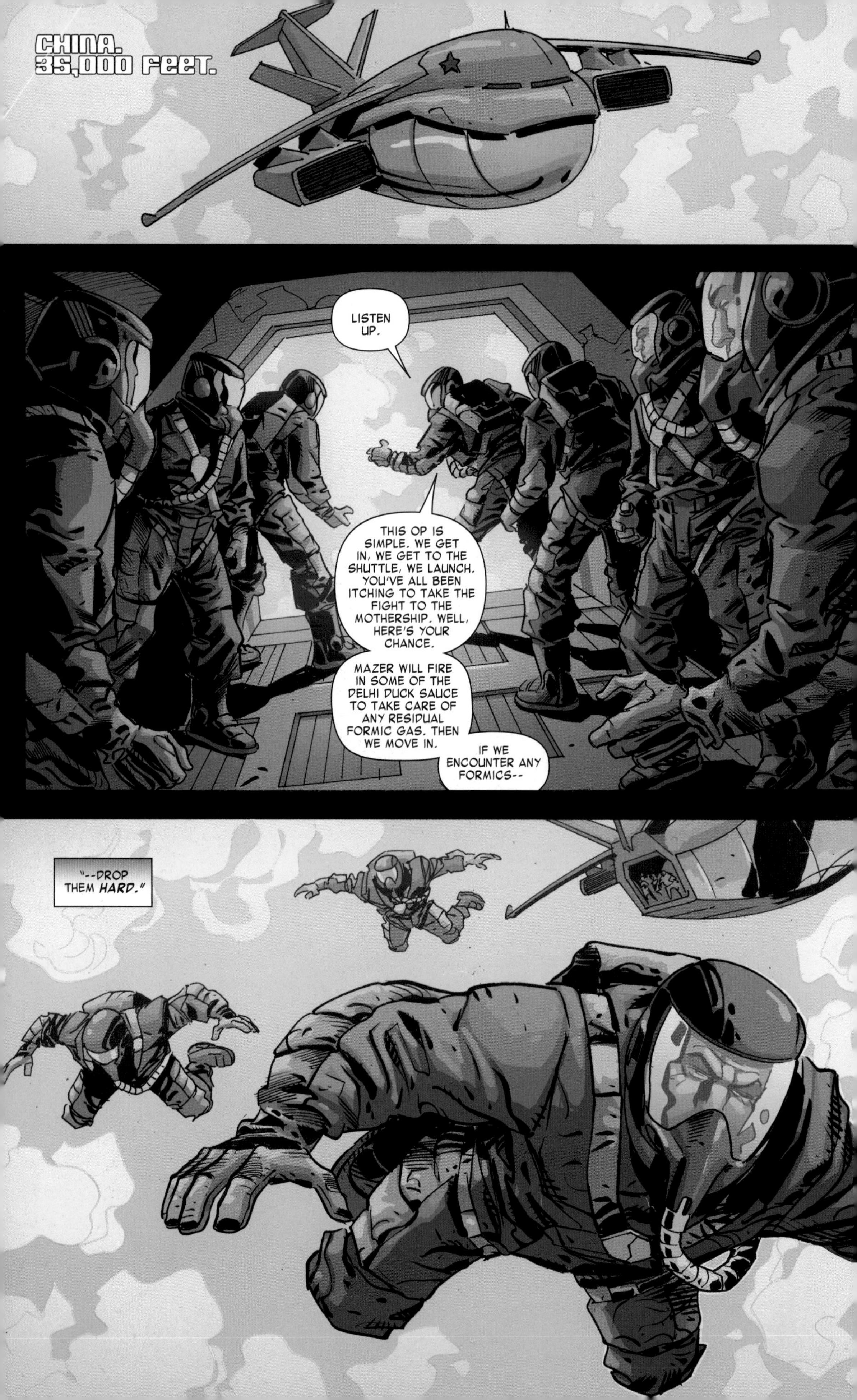
CHINA. 35,000 FEET.
LISTEN UP.
THIS OP IS SIMPLE. WE GET IN, WE GET TO THE SHUTTLE, WE LAUNCH. YOU'VE ALL BEEN ITCHING TO TAKE THE FIGHT TO THE MOTHERSHIP. WELL, HERE'S YOUR CHANCE.
MAZER WILL FIRE IN SOME OF THE DELHI DUCK SAUCE TO TAKE CARE OF ANY RESIDUAL FORMIC GAS. THEN WE MOVE IN.
IF WE ENCOUNTER ANY FORMICS--
"--DROP THEM HARD."

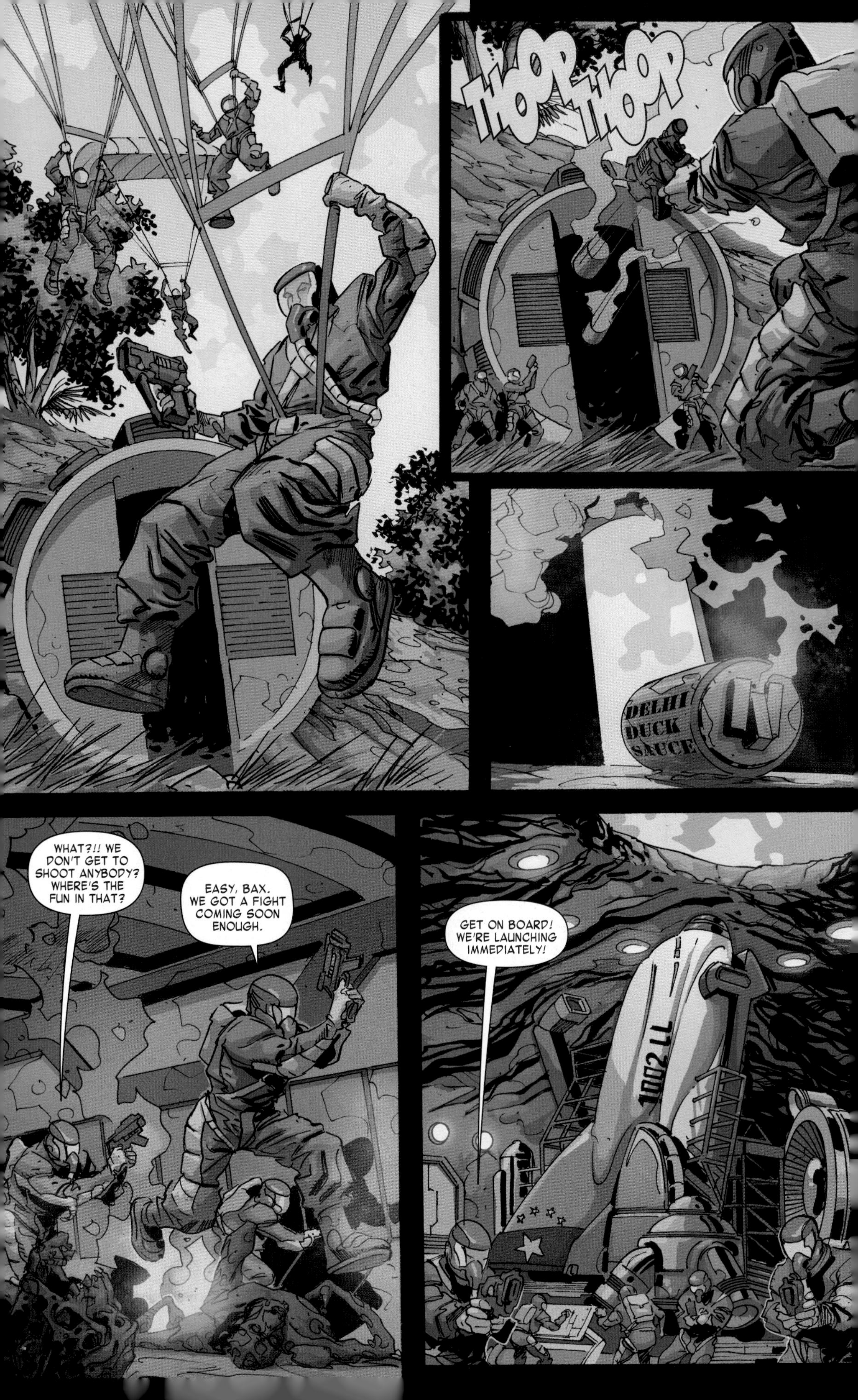
THOOP THOOP
DELHI DUCK SAUCE
WHAT?!! WE DON'T GET TO SHOOT ANYBODY? WHERE'S THE FUN IN THAT?
EASY, BAX. WE GOT A FIGHT COMING SOON ENOUGH.
GET ON BOARD! WE'RE LAUNCHING IMMEDIATELY!

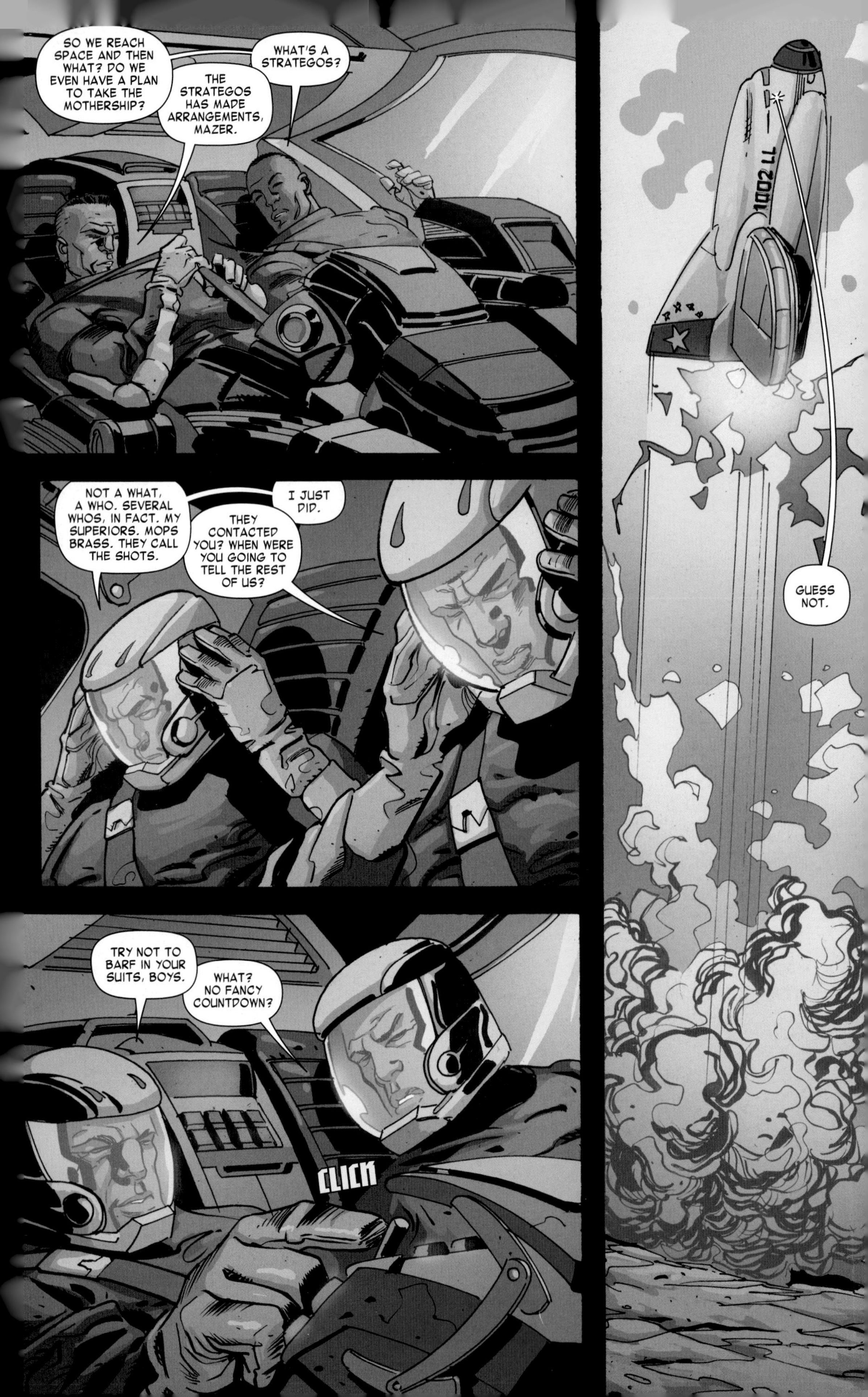

SO WE REACH SPACE AND THEN WHAT? DO WE EVEN HAVE A PLAN TO TAKE THE MOTHERSHIP?
THE STRATEGOS HAS MADE ARRANGEMENTS, MAZER.
WHAT'S A STRATEGOS?
NOT A WHAT, A WHO. SEVERAL WHOS, IN FACT. MY SUPERIORS. MOPS BRASS. THEY CALL THE SHOTS.
THEY CONTACTED YOU? WHEN WERE YOU GOING TO TELL THE REST OF US?
I JUST DID.
TRY NOT TO BARF IN YOUR SUITS, BOYS.
WHAT? NO FANCY COUNTDOWN?
CLICK
1002 LL
GUESS NOT.

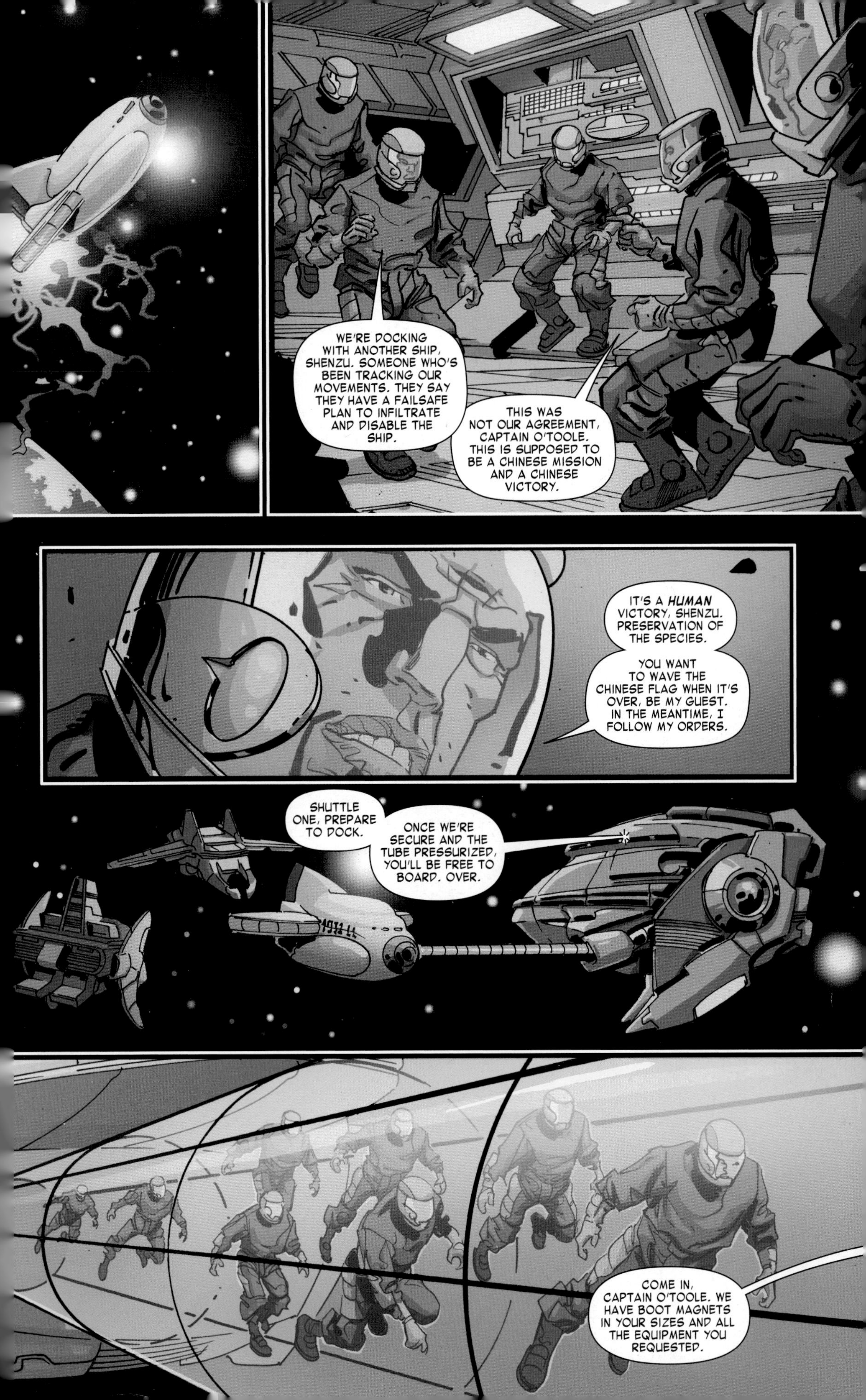
WE'RE DOCKING WITH ANOTHER SHIP, SHENZU. SOMEONE WHO'S BEEN TRACKING OUR MOVEMENTS. THEY SAY THEY HAVE A FAILSAFE PLAN TO INFILTRATE AND DISABLE THE SHIP.
THIS WAS NOT OUR AGREEMENT, CAPTAIN O'TOOLE. THIS IS SUPPOSED TO BE A CHINESE MISSION AND A CHINESE VICTORY.
IT'S A *HUMAN* VICTORY, SHENZU. PRESERVATION OF THE SPECIES.
YOU WANT TO WAVE THE CHINESE FLAG WHEN IT'S OVER, BE MY GUEST. IN THE MEANTIME, I FOLLOW MY ORDERS.
SHUTTLE ONE, PREPARE TO DOCK.
ONCE WE'RE SECURE AND THE TUBE PRESSURIZED, YOU'LL BE FREE TO BOARD. OVER.
COME IN, CAPTAIN O'TOOLE. WE HAVE BOOT MAGNETS IN YOUR SIZES AND ALL THE EQUIPMENT YOU REQUESTED.

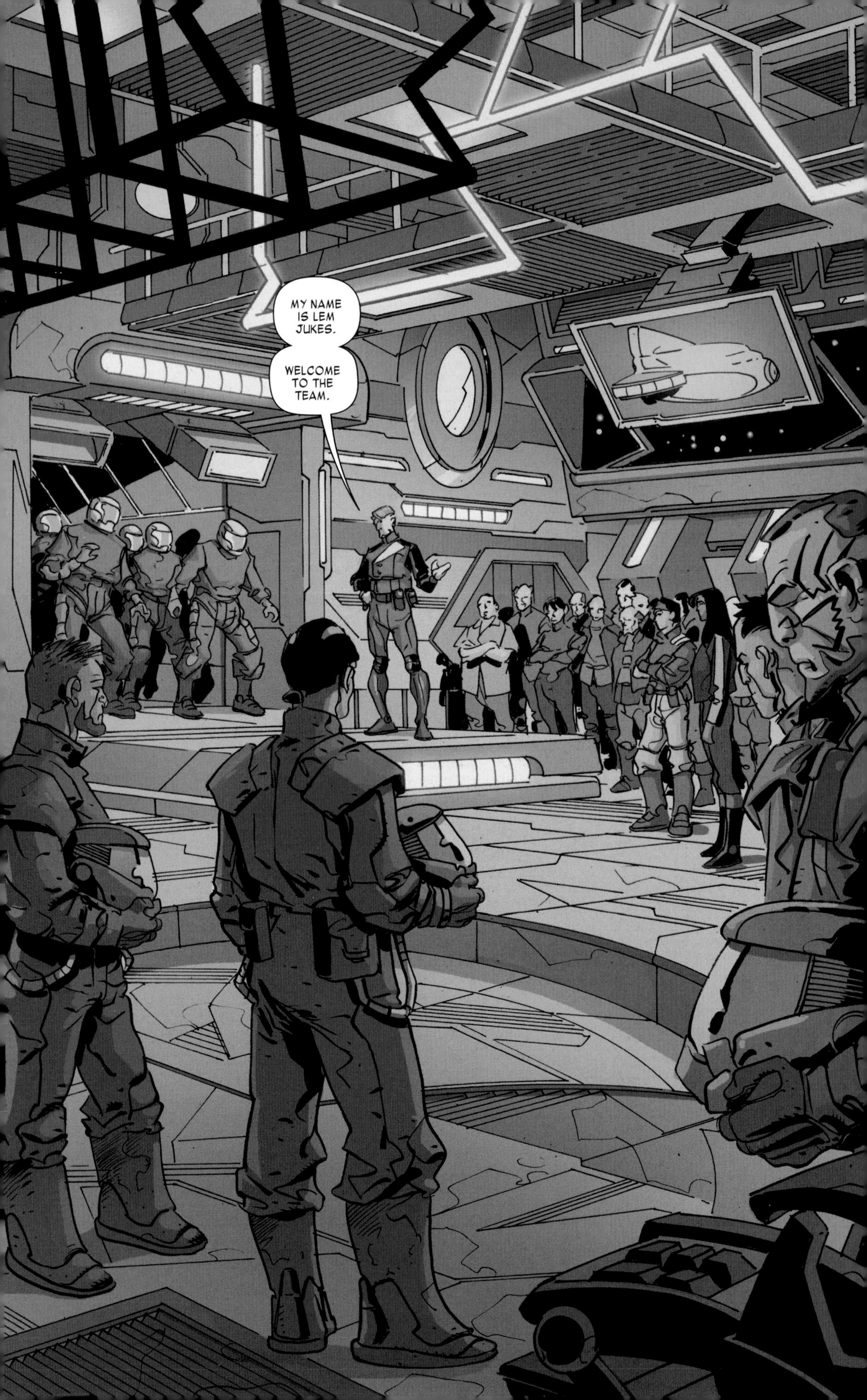
MY NAME IS LEM JUKES.
WELCOME TO THE TEAM.

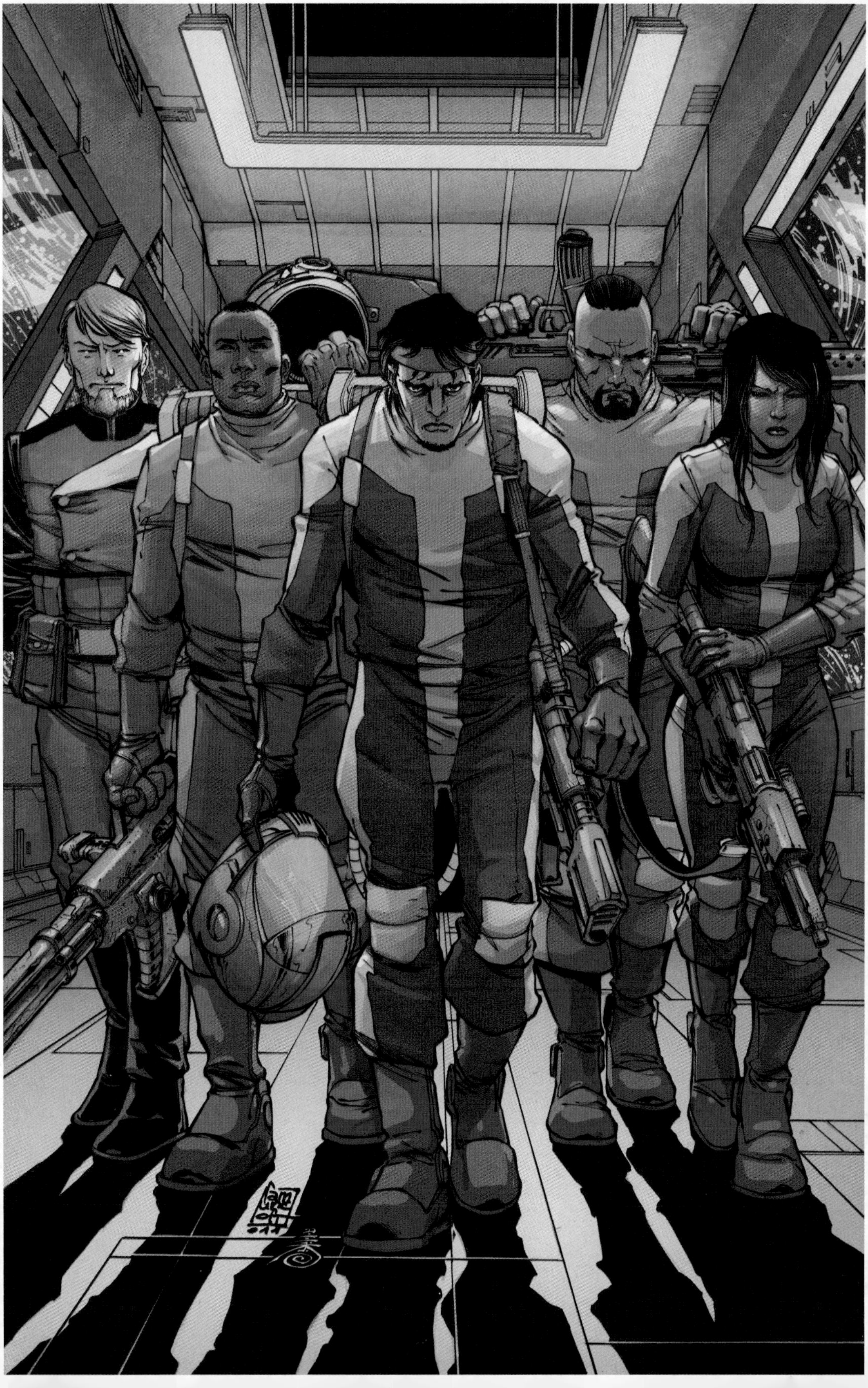

TO: hannini.granger@jukeslimited.com
FROM: lem.jukes@jukeslimited.com
SUBJECT: the future of our organization

Mr. Hannini,

If you're reading this, then the holocam on your screen has performed a discreet yet thorough retinal scan and confirmed that you are indeed the chairman of the board and not some nosy sneak, poking around in your netmail. In short, rest easy. This is a secure message.

You are no doubt aware of my father's recent failure with the Vanguard drones and gravity lasers. While his attack on the Formic ship was well intentioned, it has unfortunately brought this company to the brink of financial ruin. We have nose-dived from being the most fiscally sound corporation in the universe to "the stock that sank like lead" as one journalist recently wrote.

While I love my father, his rash behavior unsettles me. Your recent remarks on the matter suggest you feel the same. I propose a meeting to discuss our options.

When your eyes reach the end of this message, it will delete.

All best,
Lem Jukes

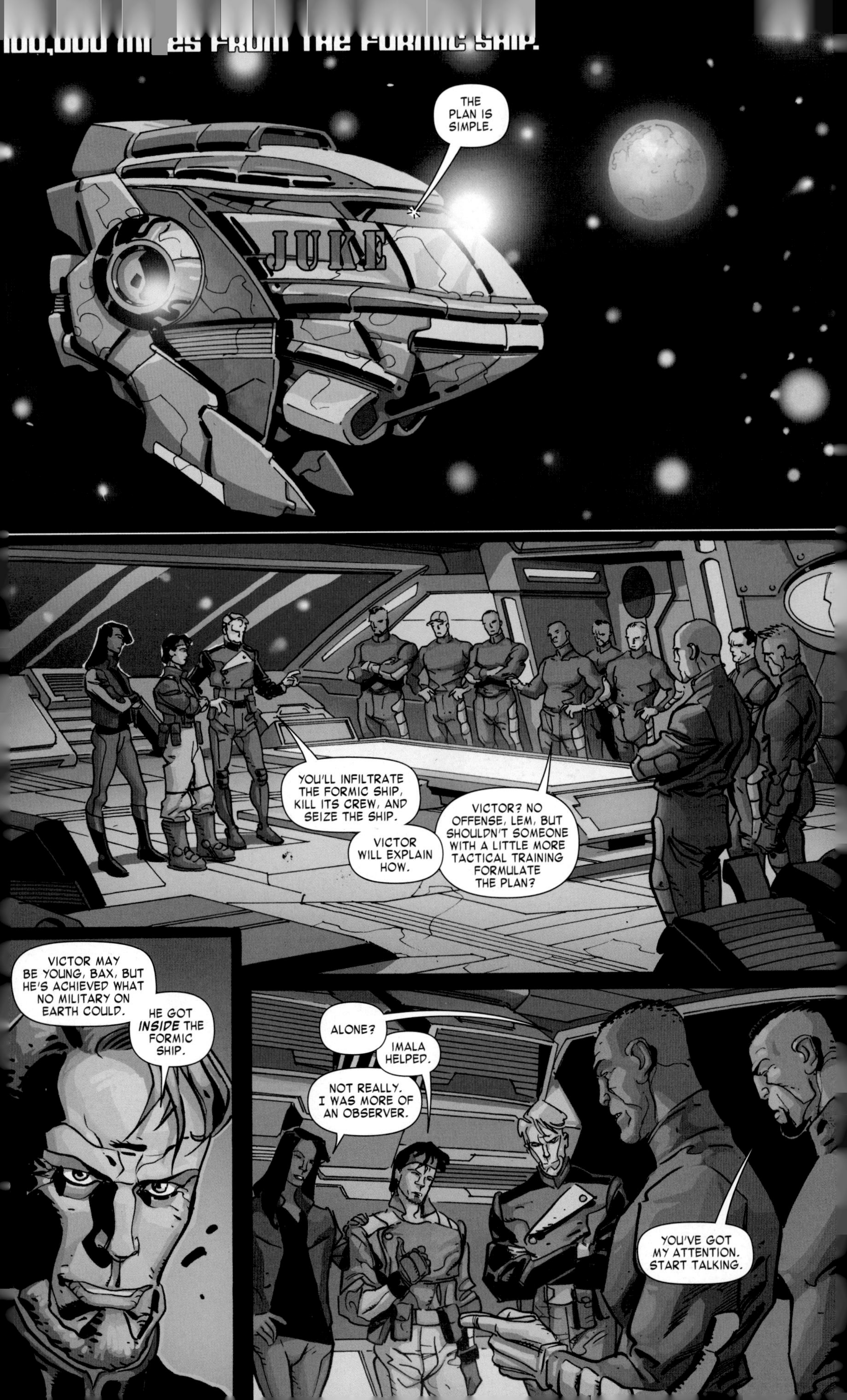
ES FROM THE FORMIC SHIP.
THE PLAN IS SIMPLE.
JUKE
YOU'LL INFILTRATE THE FORMIC SHIP, KILL ITS CREW, AND SEIZE THE SHIP.
VICTOR WILL EXPLAIN HOW.
VICTOR? NO OFFENSE, LEM, BUT SHOULDN'T SOMEONE WITH A LITTLE MORE TACTICAL TRAINING FORMULATE THE PLAN?
VICTOR MAY BE YOUNG, BAX, BUT HE'S ACHIEVED WHAT NO MILITARY ON EARTH COULD.
HE GOT INSIDE THE FORMIC SHIP.
ALONE?
IMALA HELPED.
NOT REALLY. I WAS MORE OF AN OBSERVER.
YOU'VE GOT MY ATTENTION. START TALKING.

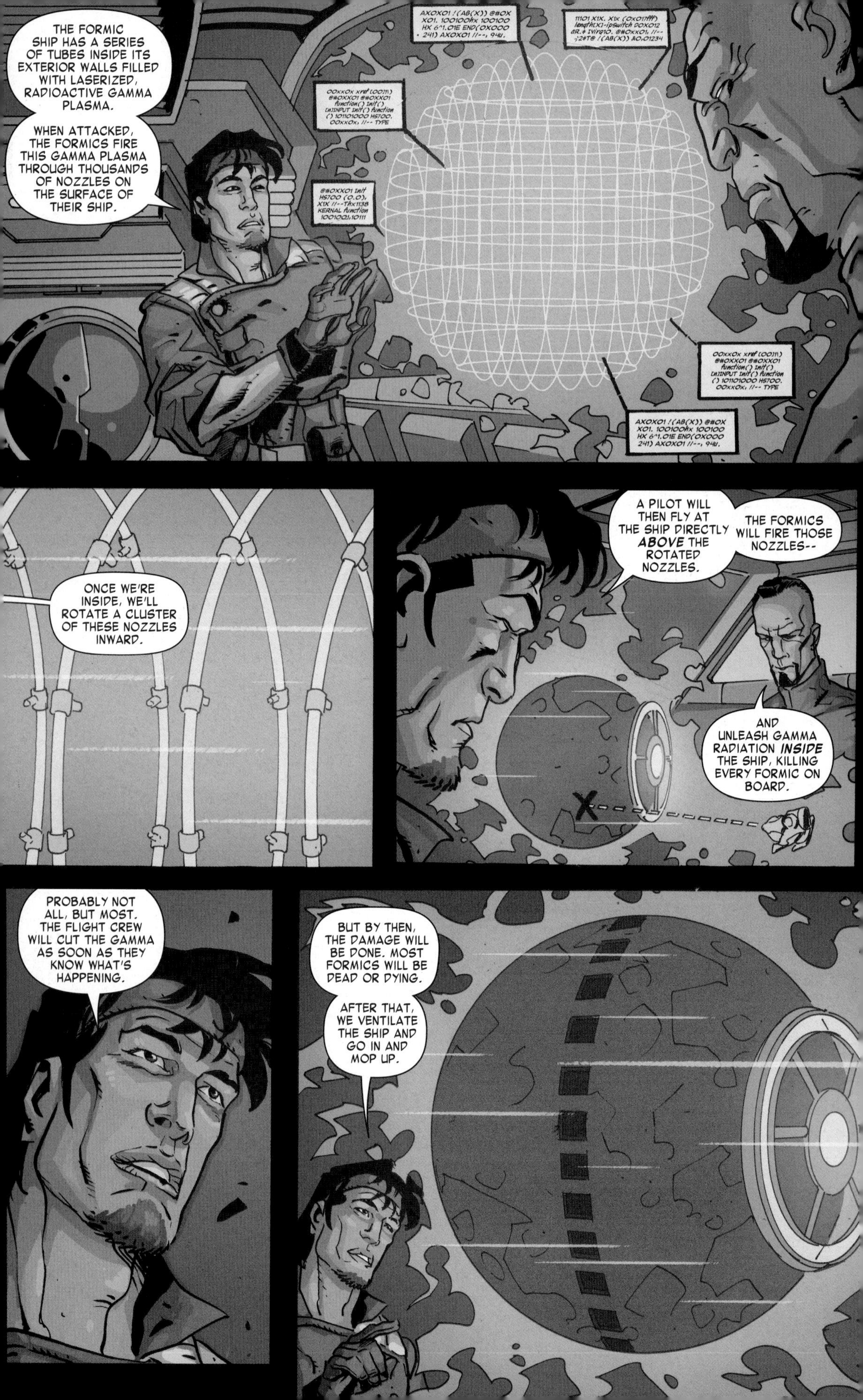

THE FORMIC SHIP HAS A SERIES OF TUBES INSIDE ITS EXTERIOR WALLS FILLED WITH LASERIZED, RADIOACTIVE GAMMA PLASMA.
WHEN ATTACKED, THE FORMICS FIRE THIS GAMMA PLASMA THROUGH THOUSANDS OF NOZZLES ON THE SURFACE OF THEIR SHIP.
ONCE WE'RE INSIDE, WE'LL ROTATE A CLUSTER OF THESE NOZZLES INWARD.
A PILOT WILL THEN FLY AT THE SHIP DIRECTLY ABOVE THE ROTATED NOZZLES.
THE FORMICS WILL FIRE THOSE NOZZLES--
AND UNLEASH GAMMA RADIATION INSIDE THE SHIP, KILLING EVERY FORMIC ON BOARD.
PROBABLY NOT ALL, BUT MOST. THE FLIGHT CREW WILL CUT THE GAMMA AS SOON AS THEY KNOW WHAT'S HAPPENING.
BUT BY THEN, THE DAMAGE WILL BE DONE. MOST FORMICS WILL BE DEAD OR DYING.
AFTER THAT, WE VENTILATE THE SHIP AND GO IN AND MOP UP.

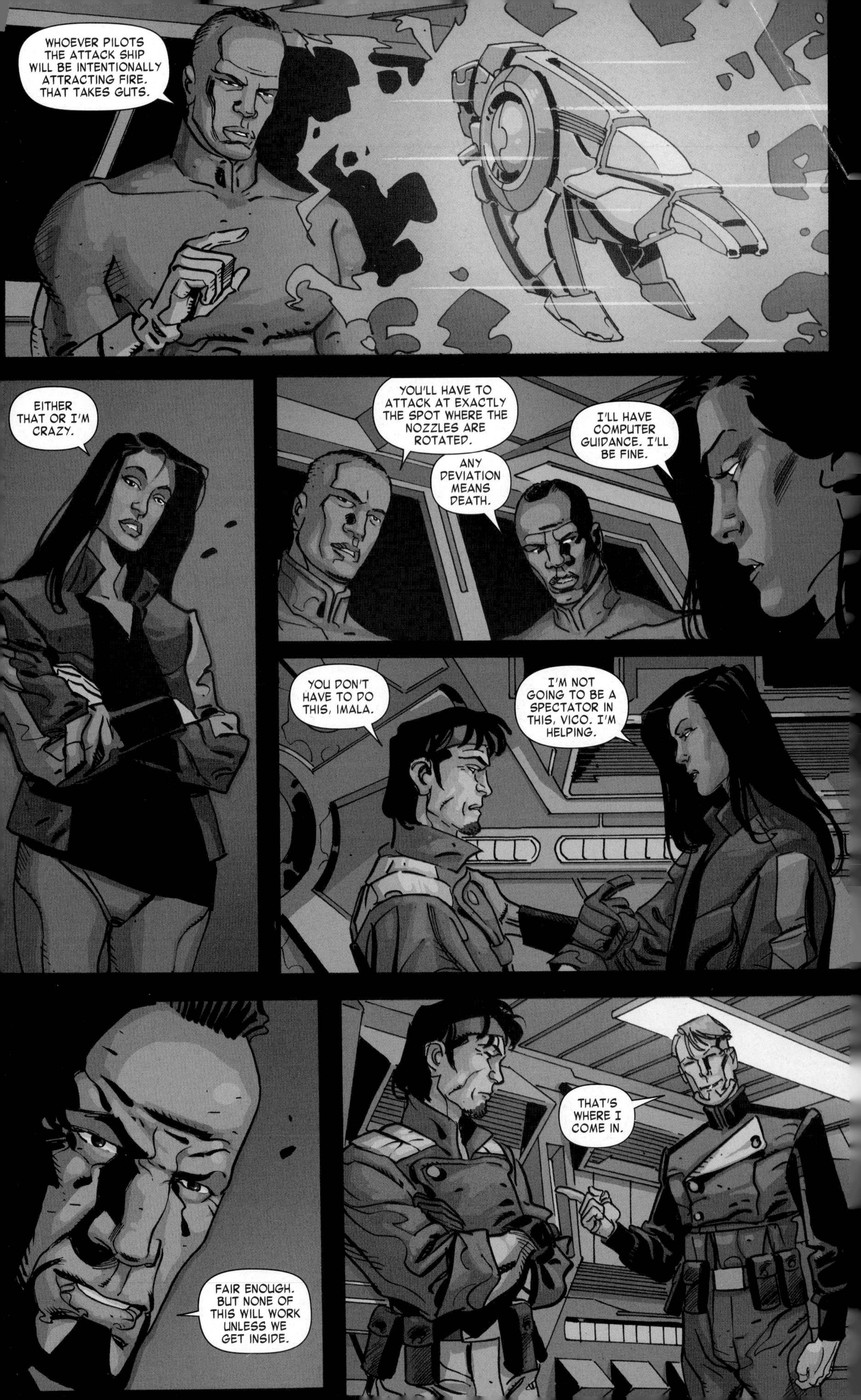
WHOEVER PILOTS THE ATTACK SHIP WILL BE INTENTIONALLY ATTRACTING FIRE. THAT TAKES GUTS.
EITHER THAT OR I'M CRAZY.
YOU'LL HAVE TO ATTACK AT EXACTLY THE SPOT WHERE THE NOZZLES ARE ROTATED.
ANY DEVIATION MEANS DEATH.
I'LL HAVE COMPUTER GUIDANCE. I'LL BE FINE.
YOU DON'T HAVE TO DO THIS, IMALA.
I'M NOT GOING TO BE A SPECTATOR IN THIS, VICO. I'M HELPING.
FAIR ENOUGH. BUT NONE OF THIS WILL WORK UNLESS WE GET INSIDE.
THAT'S WHERE I COME IN.

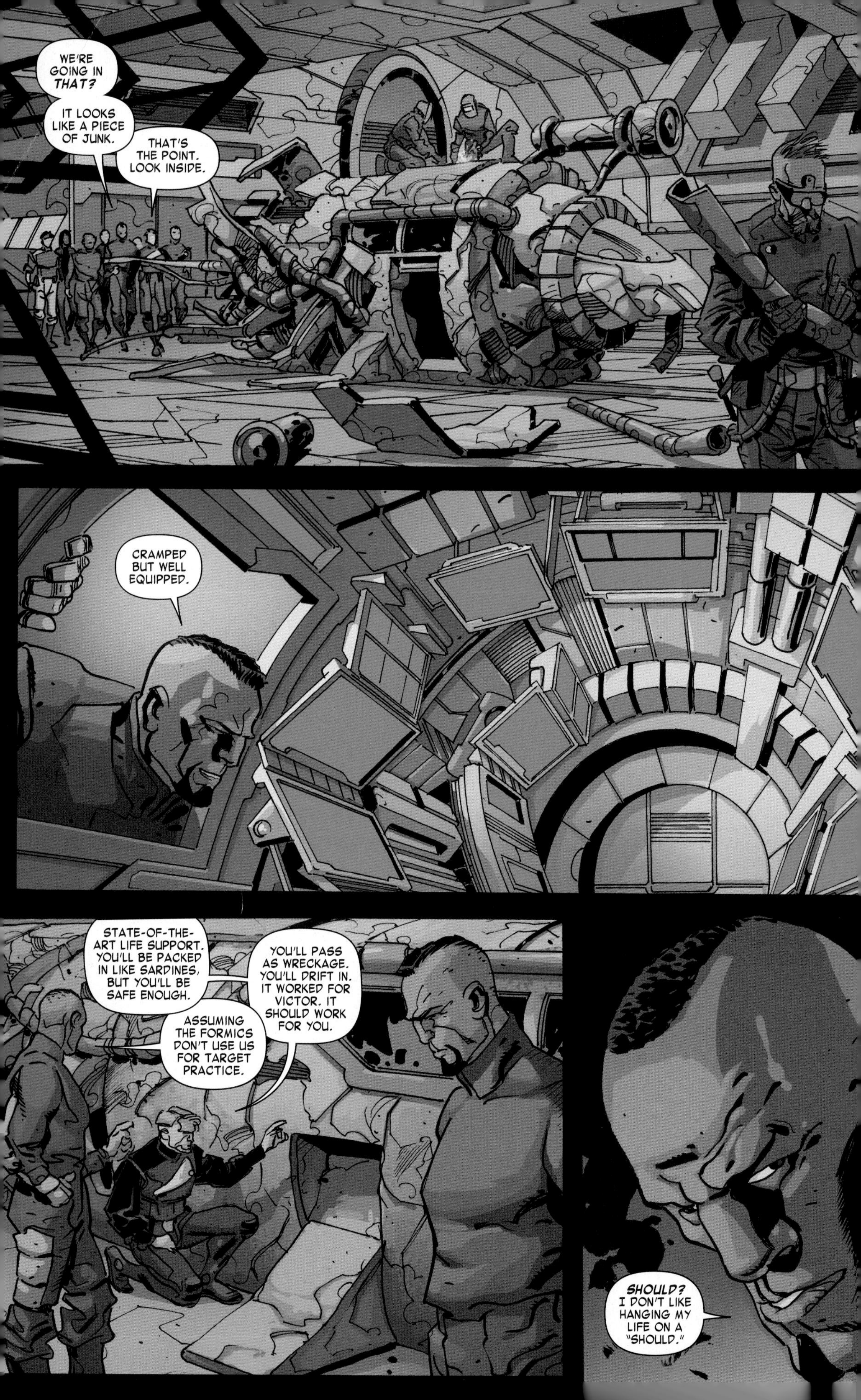
WE'RE GOING IN *THAT?*
IT LOOKS LIKE A PIECE OF JUNK.
THAT'S THE POINT. LOOK INSIDE.
CRAMPED BUT WELL EQUIPPED.
STATE-OF-THE-ART LIFE SUPPORT. YOU'LL BE PACKED IN LIKE SARDINES, BUT YOU'LL BE SAFE ENOUGH.
YOU'LL PASS AS WRECKAGE. YOU'LL DRIFT IN. IT WORKED FOR VICTOR. IT SHOULD WORK FOR YOU.
ASSUMING THE FORMICS DON'T USE US FOR TARGET PRACTICE.
SHOULD? I DON'T LIKE HANGING MY LIFE ON A "SHOULD."

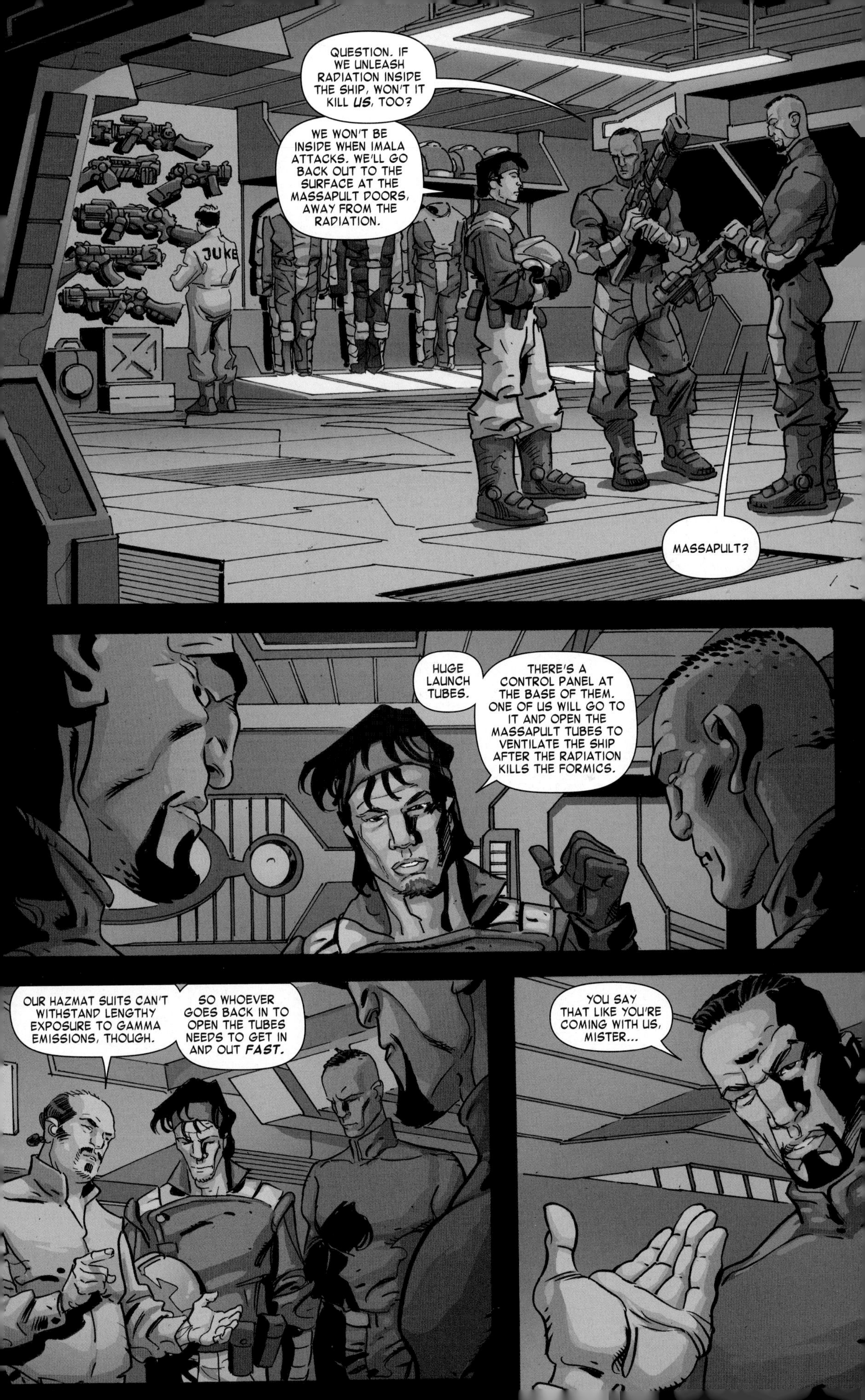
QUESTION. IF WE UNLEASH RADIATION INSIDE THE SHIP, WON'T IT KILL US, TOO?
WE WON'T BE INSIDE WHEN IMALA ATTACKS. WE'LL GO BACK OUT TO THE SURFACE AT THE MASSAPULT DOORS, AWAY FROM THE RADIATION.
JUKE
MASSAPULT?
HUGE LAUNCH TUBES.
THERE'S A CONTROL PANEL AT THE BASE OF THEM. ONE OF US WILL GO TO IT AND OPEN THE MASSAPULT TUBES TO VENTILATE THE SHIP AFTER THE RADIATION KILLS THE FORMICS.
OUR HAZMAT SUITS CAN'T WITHSTAND LENGTHY EXPOSURE TO GAMMA EMISSIONS, THOUGH.
SO WHOEVER GOES BACK IN TO OPEN THE TUBES NEEDS TO GET IN AND OUT FAST.
YOU SAY THAT LIKE YOU'RE COMING WITH US, MISTER...

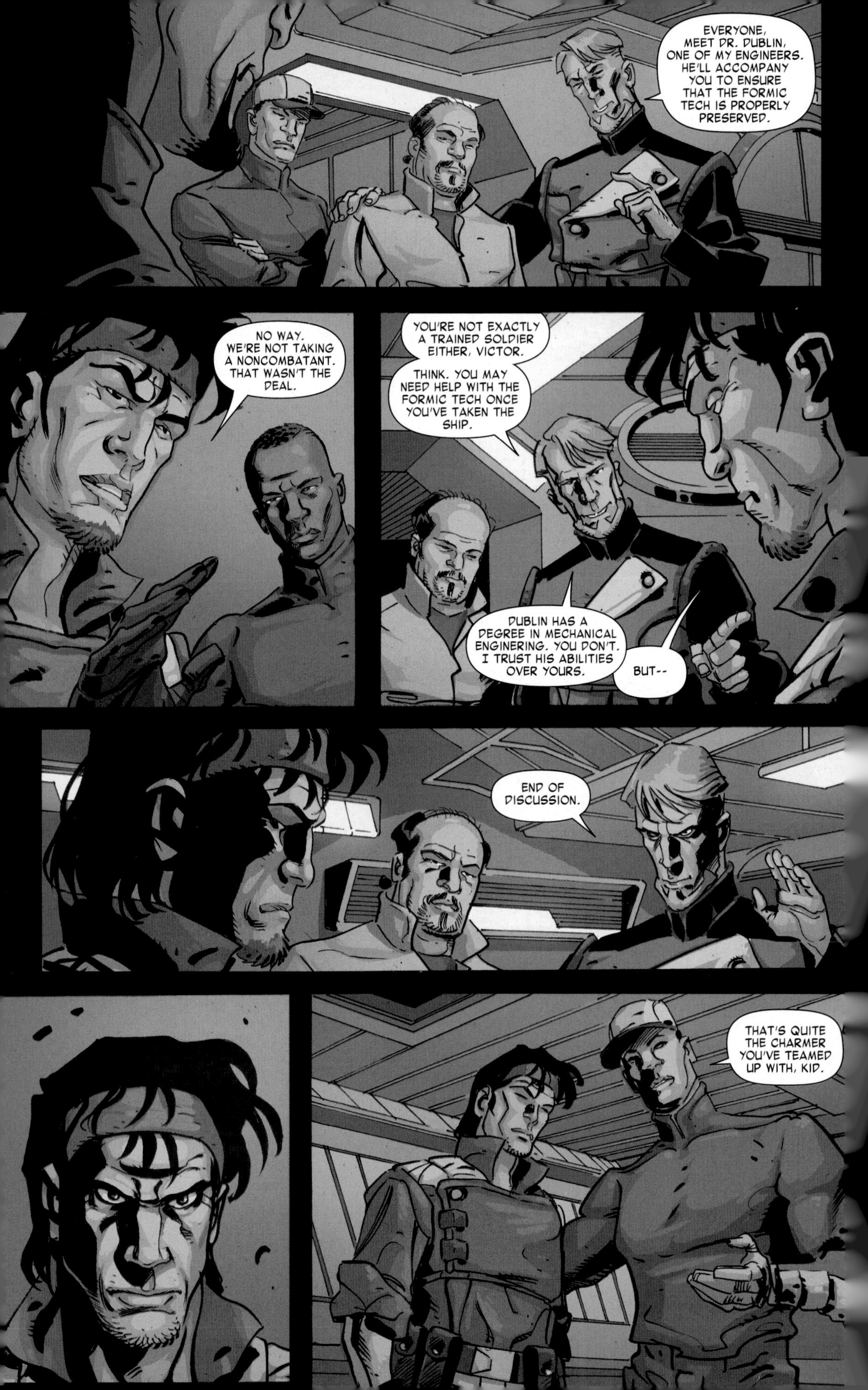
EVERYONE, MEET DR. DUBLIN, ONE OF MY ENGINEERS. HE'LL ACCOMPANY YOU TO ENSURE THAT THE FORMIC TECH IS PROPERLY PRESERVED.
NO WAY. WE'RE NOT TAKING A NONCOMBATANT. THAT WASN'T THE DEAL.
YOU'RE NOT EXACTLY A TRAINED SOLDIER EITHER, VICTOR.
THINK. YOU MAY NEED HELP WITH THE FORMIC TECH ONCE YOU'VE TAKEN THE SHIP.
DUBLIN HAS A DEGREE IN MECHANICAL ENGINERING. YOU DON'T. I TRUST HIS ABILITIES OVER YOURS.
BUT--
END OF DISCUSSION.
THAT'S QUITE THE CHARMER YOU'VE TEAMED UP WITH, KID.

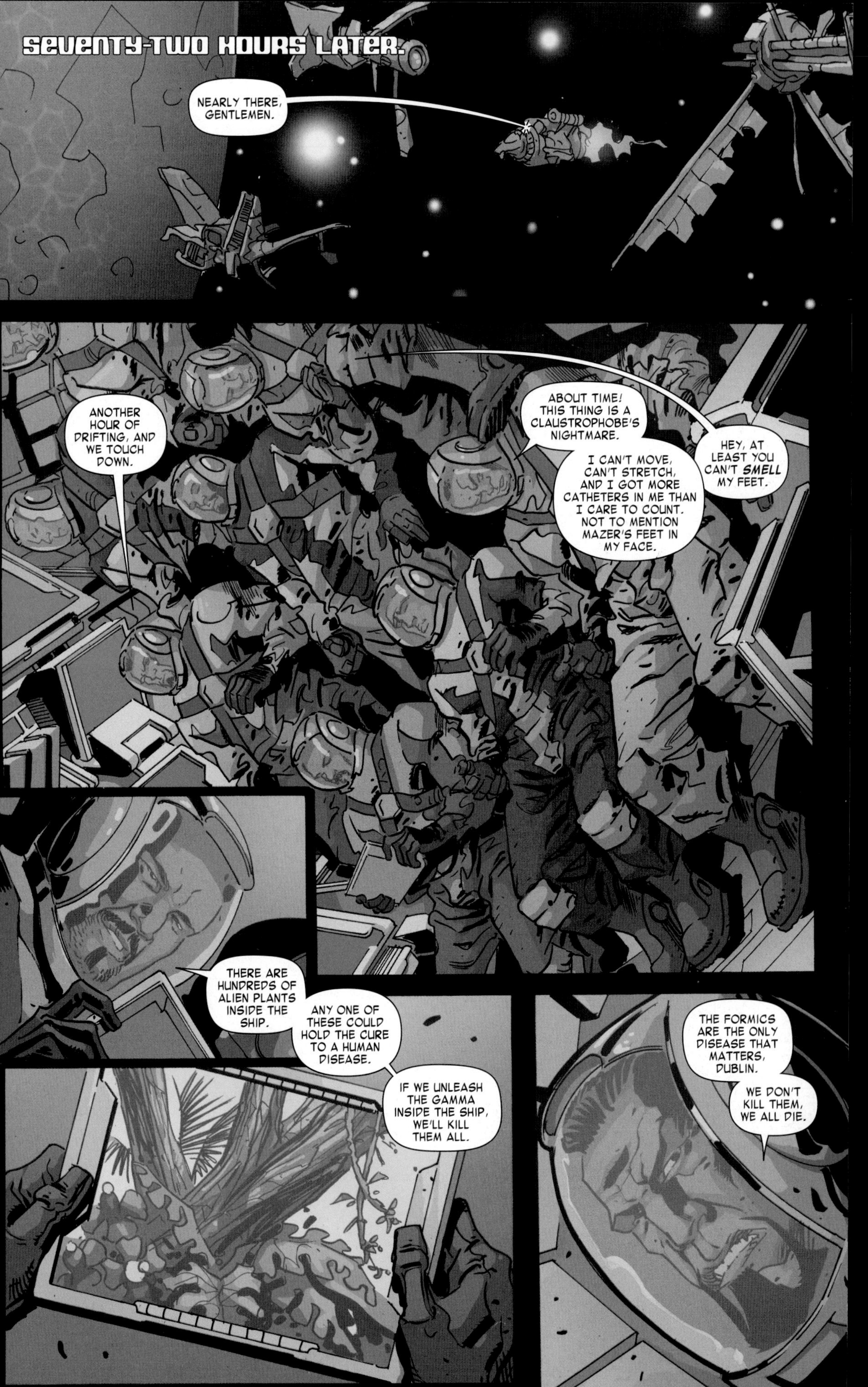
SEVENTY-TWO HOURS LATER.
NEARLY THERE, GENTLEMEN.
ANOTHER HOUR OF DRIFTING, AND WE TOUCH DOWN.
ABOUT TIME! THIS THING IS A CLAUSTROPHOBE'S NIGHTMARE.
I CAN'T MOVE, CAN'T STRETCH, AND I GOT MORE CATHETERS IN ME THAN I CARE TO COUNT. NOT TO MENTION MAZER'S FEET IN MY FACE.
HEY, AT LEAST YOU CAN'T SMELL MY FEET.
THERE ARE HUNDREDS OF ALIEN PLANTS INSIDE THE SHIP.
ANY ONE OF THESE COULD HOLD THE CURE TO A HUMAN DISEASE.
IF WE UNLEASH THE GAMMA INSIDE THE SHIP, WE'LL KILL THEM ALL.
THE FORMICS ARE THE ONLY DISEASE THAT MATTERS, DUBLIN.
WE DON'T KILL THEM, WE ALL DIE.

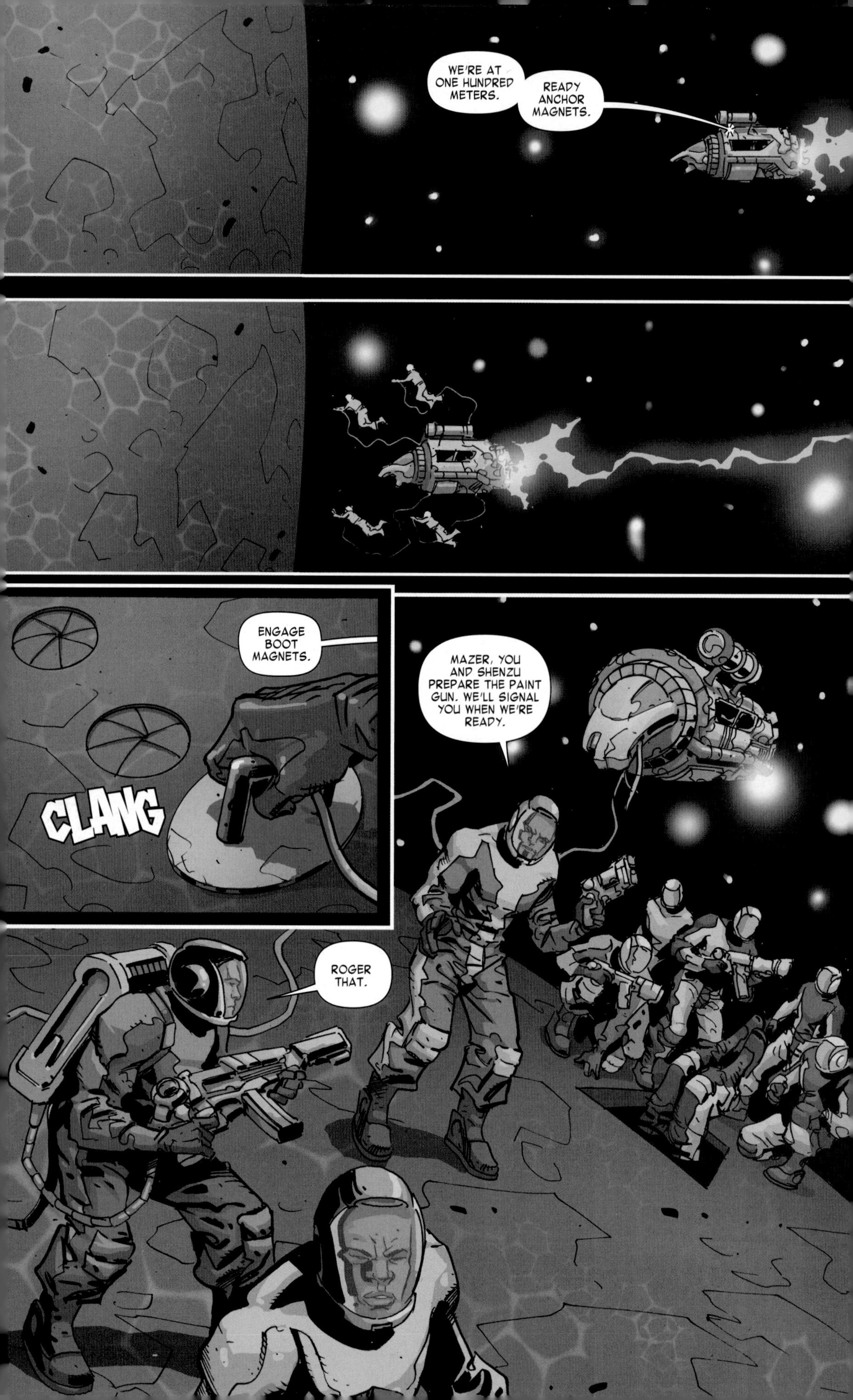
WE'RE AT ONE HUNDRED METERS.
READY ANCHOR MAGNETS.
ENGAGE BOOT MAGNETS.
CLANG
MAZER, YOU AND SHENZU PREPARE THE PAINT GUN. WE'LL SIGNAL YOU WHEN WE'RE READY.
ROGER THAT.

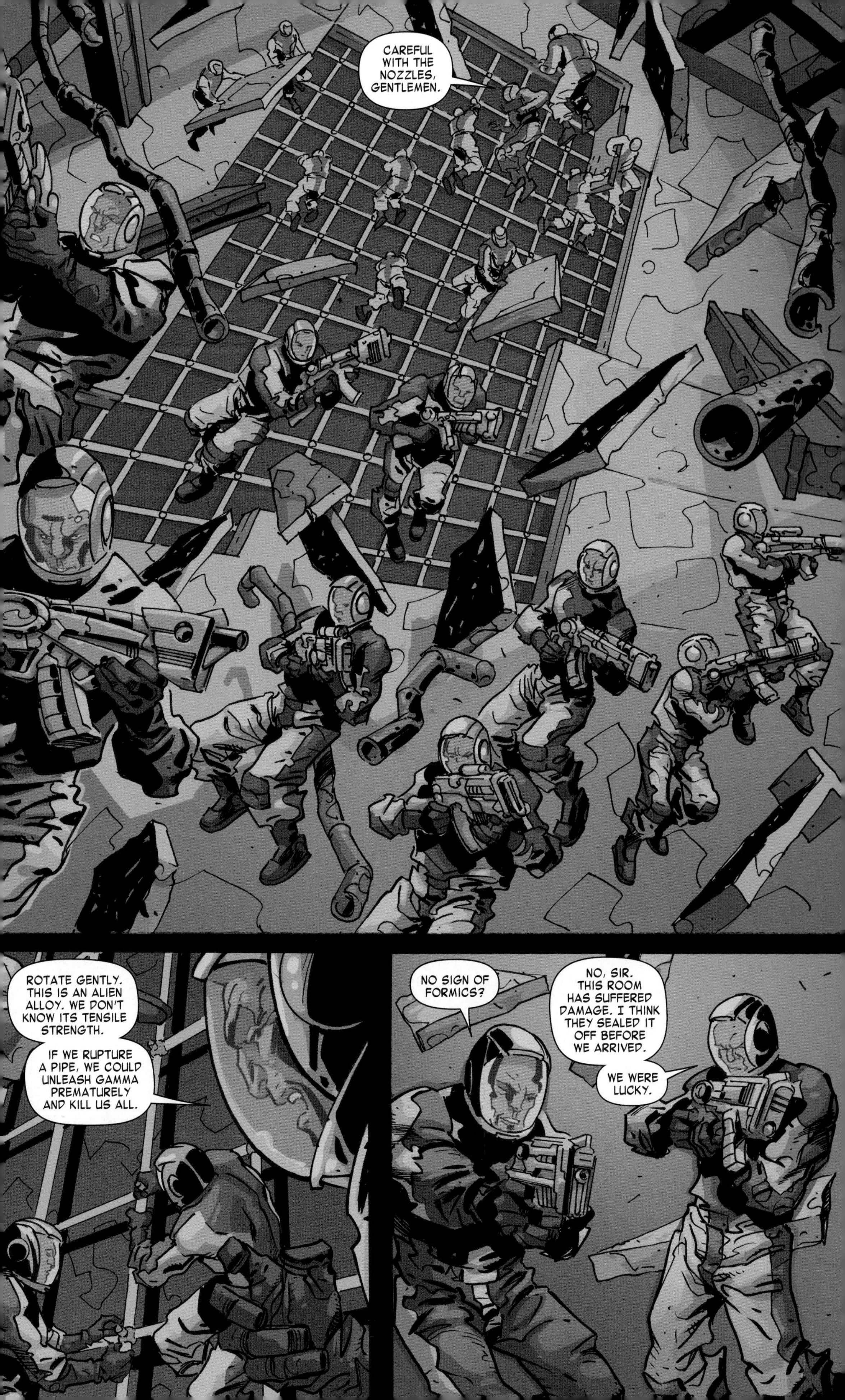
CAREFUL WITH THE NOZZLES, GENTLEMEN.
ROTATE GENTLY. THIS IS AN ALIEN ALLOY. WE DON'T KNOW ITS TENSILE STRENGTH.
IF WE RUPTURE A PIPE, WE COULD UNLEASH GAMMA PREMATURELY AND KILL US ALL.
NO SIGN OF FORMICS?
NO, SIR. THIS ROOM HAS SUFFERED DAMAGE. I THINK THEY SEALED IT OFF BEFORE WE ARRIVED.
WE WERE LUCKY.

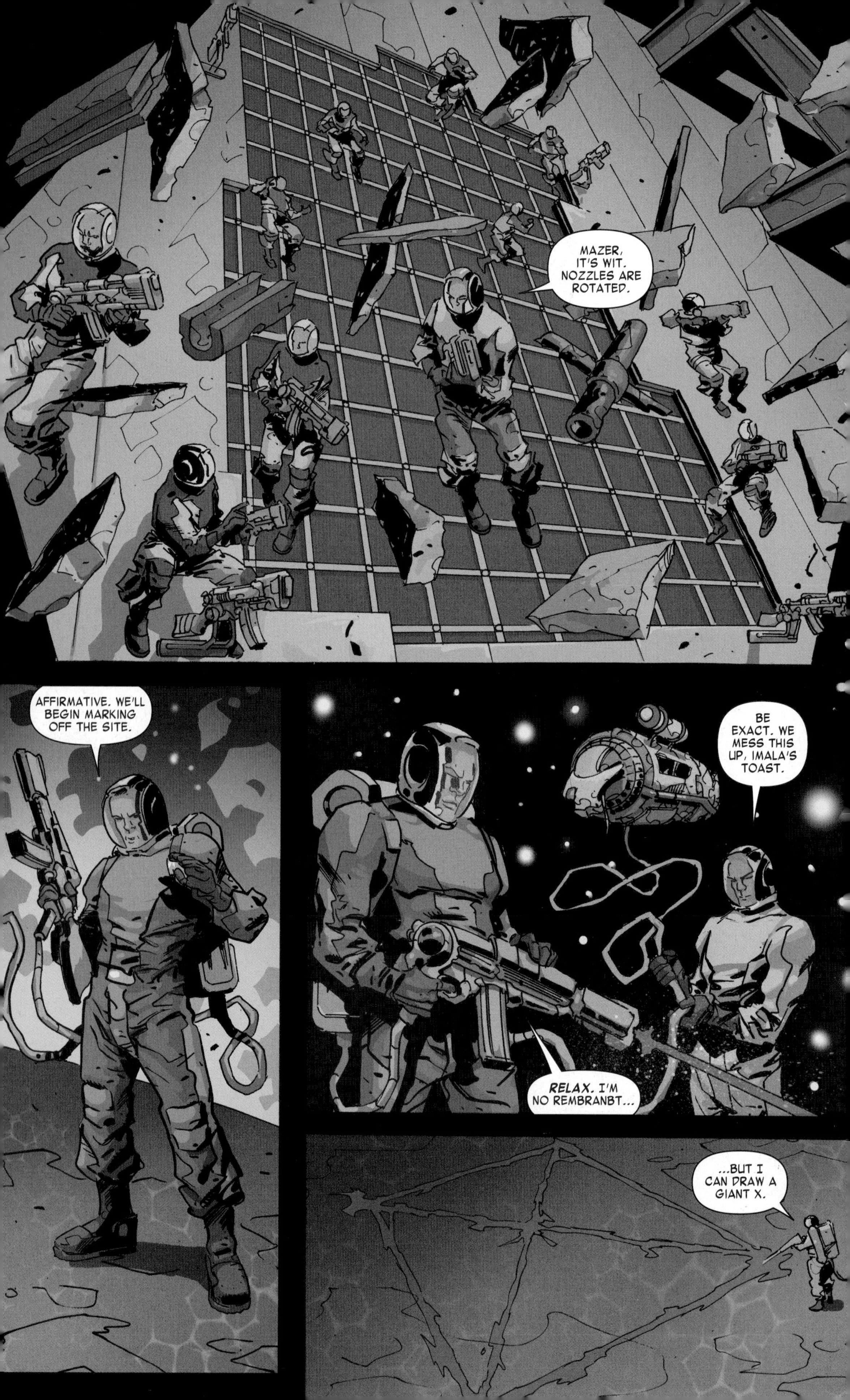
MAZER, IT'S WIT. NOZZLES ARE ROTATED.
AFFIRMATIVE. WE'LL BEGIN MARKING OFF THE SITE.
BE EXACT. WE MESS THIS UP, IMALA'S TOAST.
RELAX. I'M NO REMBRANBT...
...BUT I CAN DRAW A GIANT X.

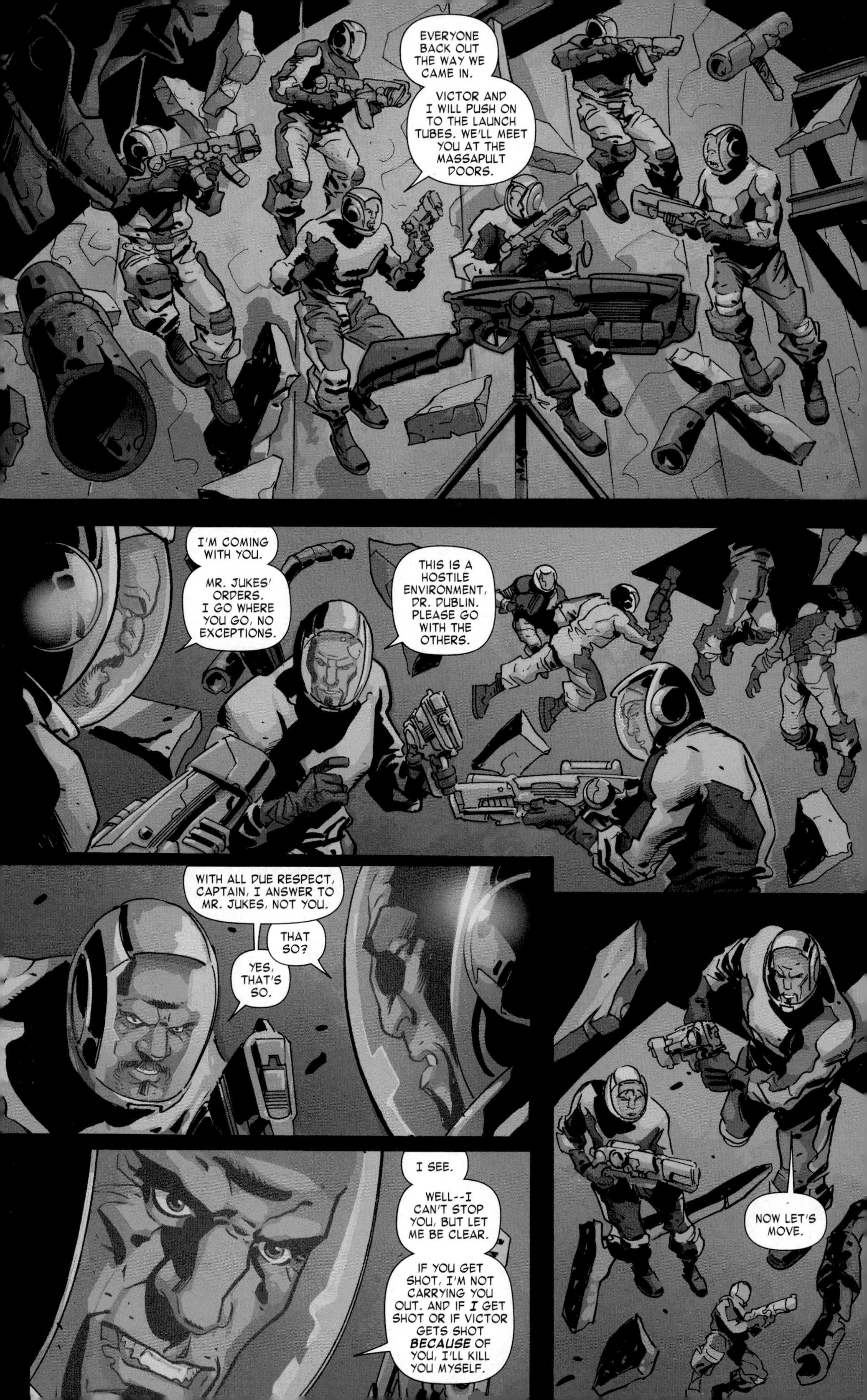
EVERYONE BACK OUT THE WAY WE CAME IN.
VICTOR AND I WILL PUSH ON TO THE LAUNCH TUBES. WE'LL MEET YOU AT THE MASSAPULT DOORS.
I'M COMING WITH YOU.
MR. JUKES' ORDERS. I GO WHERE YOU GO, NO EXCEPTIONS.
THIS IS A HOSTILE ENVIRONMENT, DR. DUBLIN. PLEASE GO WITH THE OTHERS.
WITH ALL DUE RESPECT, CAPTAIN, I ANSWER TO MR. JUKES, NOT YOU.
THAT SO?
YES, THAT'S SO.
I SEE.
WELL--I CAN'T STOP YOU, BUT LET ME BE CLEAR.
IF YOU GET SHOT, I'M NOT CARRYING YOU OUT. AND IF *I* GET SHOT OR IF VICTOR GETS SHOT ***BECAUSE*** OF YOU, I'LL KILL YOU MYSELF.
NOW LET'S MOVE.

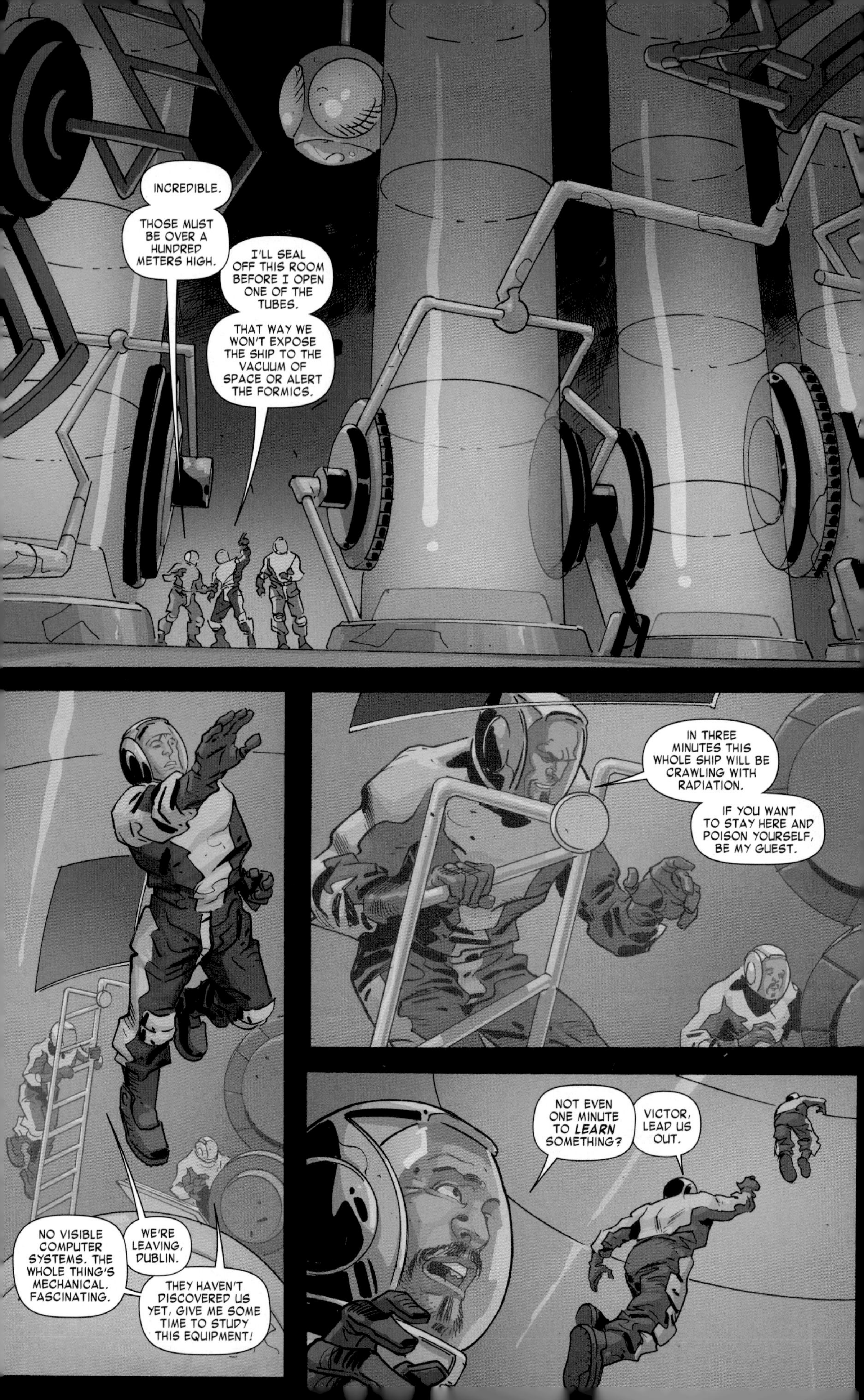
INCREDIBLE.
THOSE MUST BE OVER A HUNDRED METERS HIGH.
I'LL SEAL OFF THIS ROOM BEFORE I OPEN ONE OF THE TUBES.
THAT WAY WE WON'T EXPOSE THE SHIP TO THE VACUUM OF SPACE OR ALERT THE FORMICS.
NO VISIBLE COMPUTER SYSTEMS. THE WHOLE THING'S MECHANICAL. FASCINATING.
WE'RE LEAVING, DUBLIN.
THEY HAVEN'T DISCOVERED US YET, GIVE ME SOME TIME TO STUDY THIS EQUIPMENT!
IN THREE MINUTES THIS WHOLE SHIP WILL BE CRAWLING WITH RADIATION.
IF YOU WANT TO STAY HERE AND POISON YOURSELF, BE MY GUEST.
NOT EVEN ONE MINUTE TO *LEARN* SOMETHING?
VICTOR, LEAD US OUT.

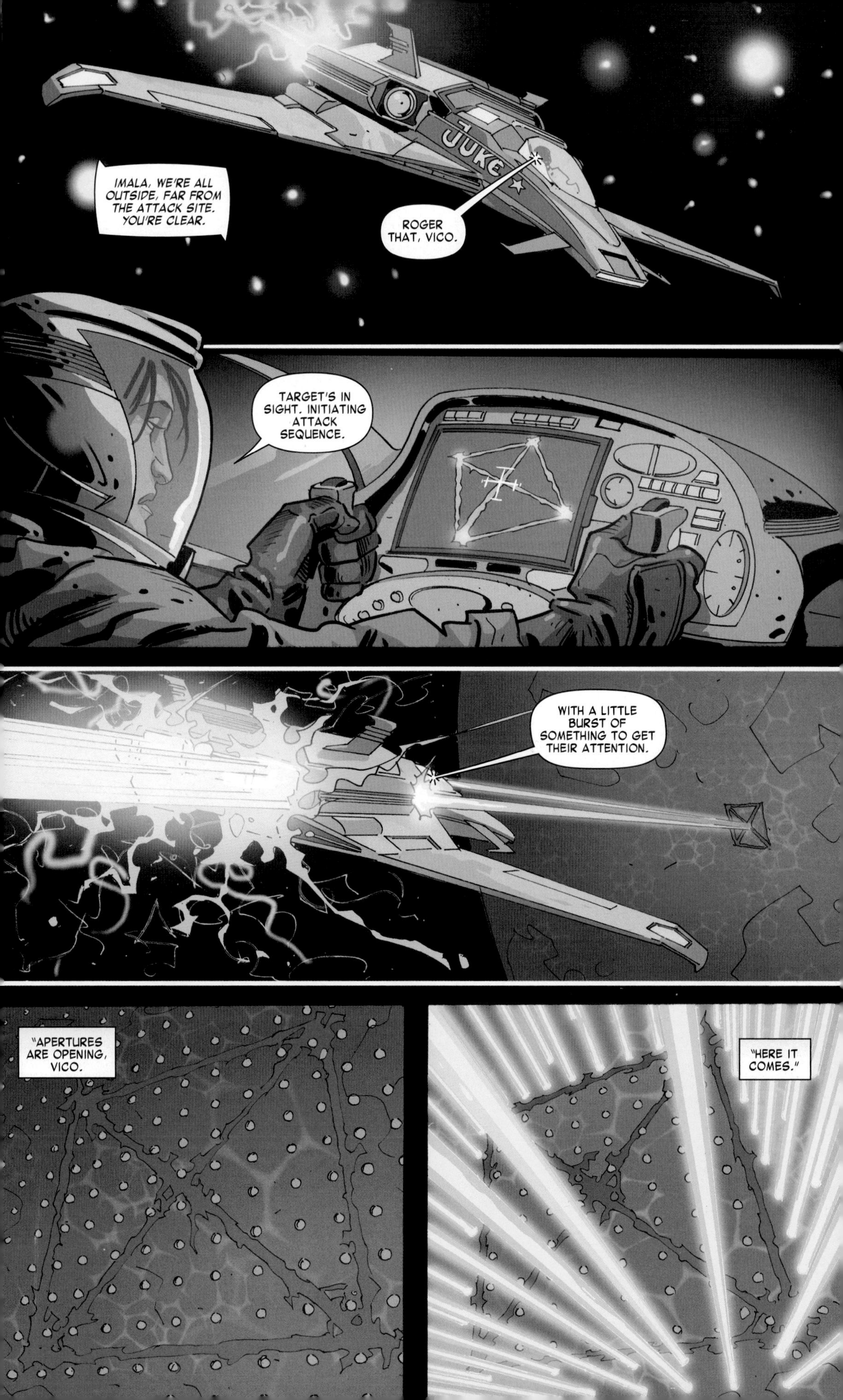

JUKE
IMALA, WE'RE ALL OUTSIDE, FAR FROM THE ATTACK SITE. YOU'RE CLEAR.
ROGER THAT, VICO.
TARGET'S IN SIGHT. INITIATING ATTACK SEQUENCE.
WITH A LITTLE BURST OF SOMETHING TO GET THEIR ATTENTION.
"APERTURES ARE OPENING, VICO.
"HERE IT COMES."

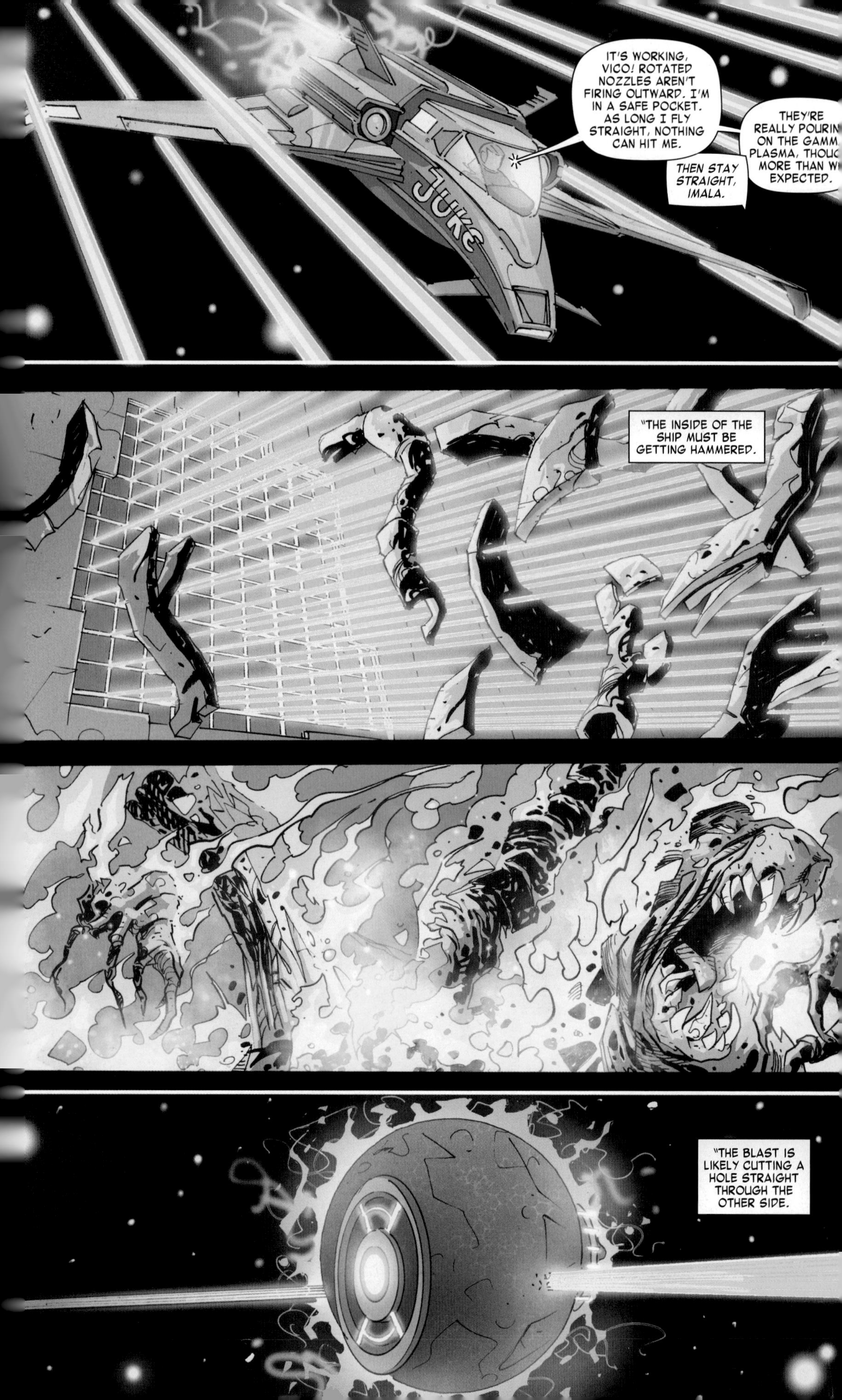

IT'S WORKING, VICO! ROTATED NOZZLES AREN'T FIRING OUTWARD. I'M IN A SAFE POCKET. AS LONG I FLY STRAIGHT, NOTHING CAN HIT ME.
JUKE
THEN STAY STRAIGHT, IMALA.
THEY'RE REALLY POURIN ON THE GAMM PLASMA, THOUG MORE THAN W EXPECTED.
"THE INSIDE OF THE SHIP MUST BE GETTING HAMMERED.
"THE BLAST IS LIKELY CUTTING A HOLE STRAIGHT THROUGH THE OTHER SIDE.

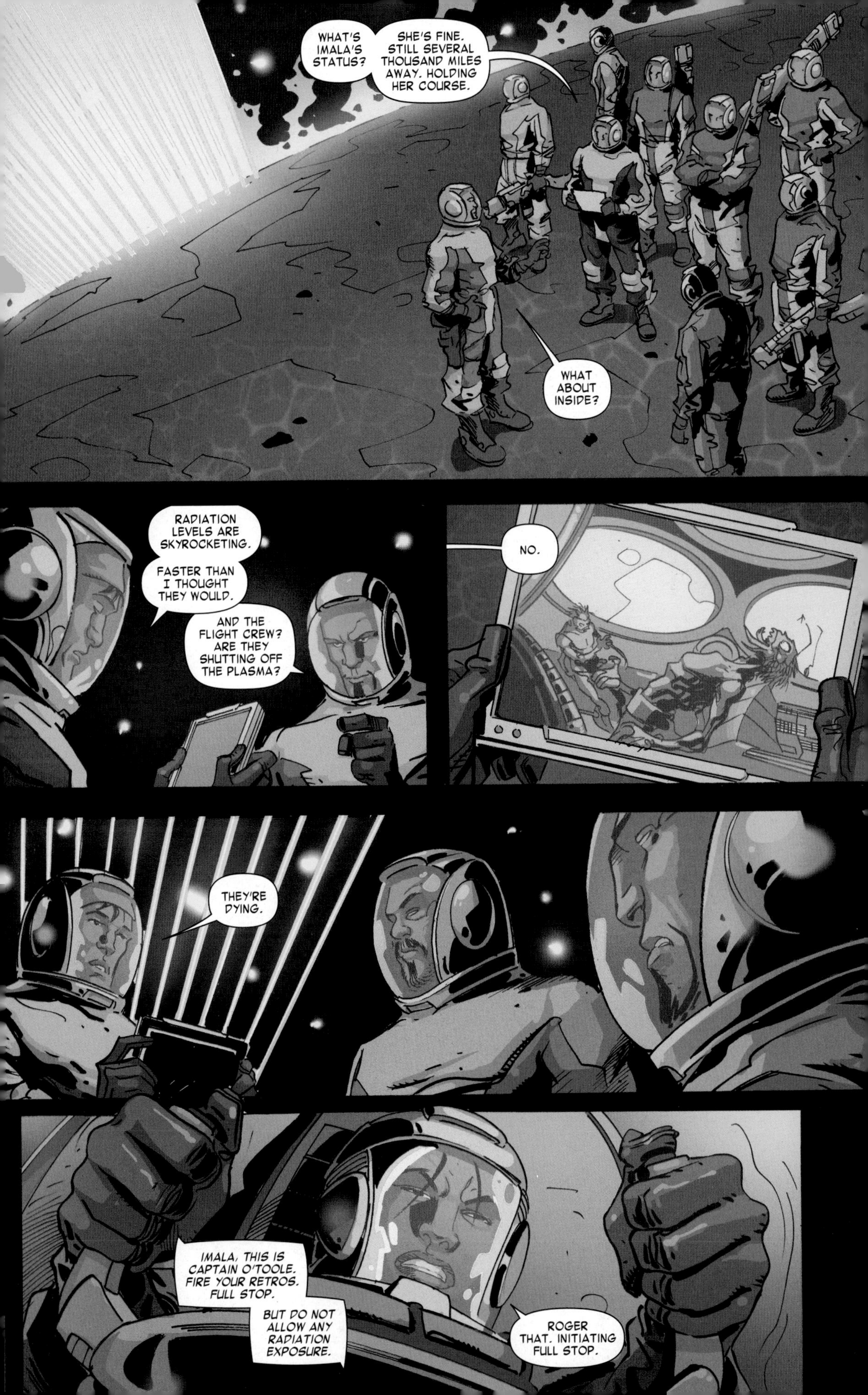
WHAT'S IMALA'S STATUS?
SHE'S FINE. STILL SEVERAL THOUSAND MILES AWAY. HOLDING HER COURSE.
WHAT ABOUT INSIDE?
RADIATION LEVELS ARE SKYROCKETING.
FASTER THAN I THOUGHT THEY WOULD.
AND THE FLIGHT CREW? ARE THEY SHUTTING OFF THE PLASMA?
NO.
THEY'RE DYING.
IMALA, THIS IS CAPTAIN O'TOOLE. FIRE YOUR RETROS. FULL STOP.
BUT DO NOT ALLOW ANY RADIATION EXPOSURE.
ROGER THAT. INITIATING FULL STOP.

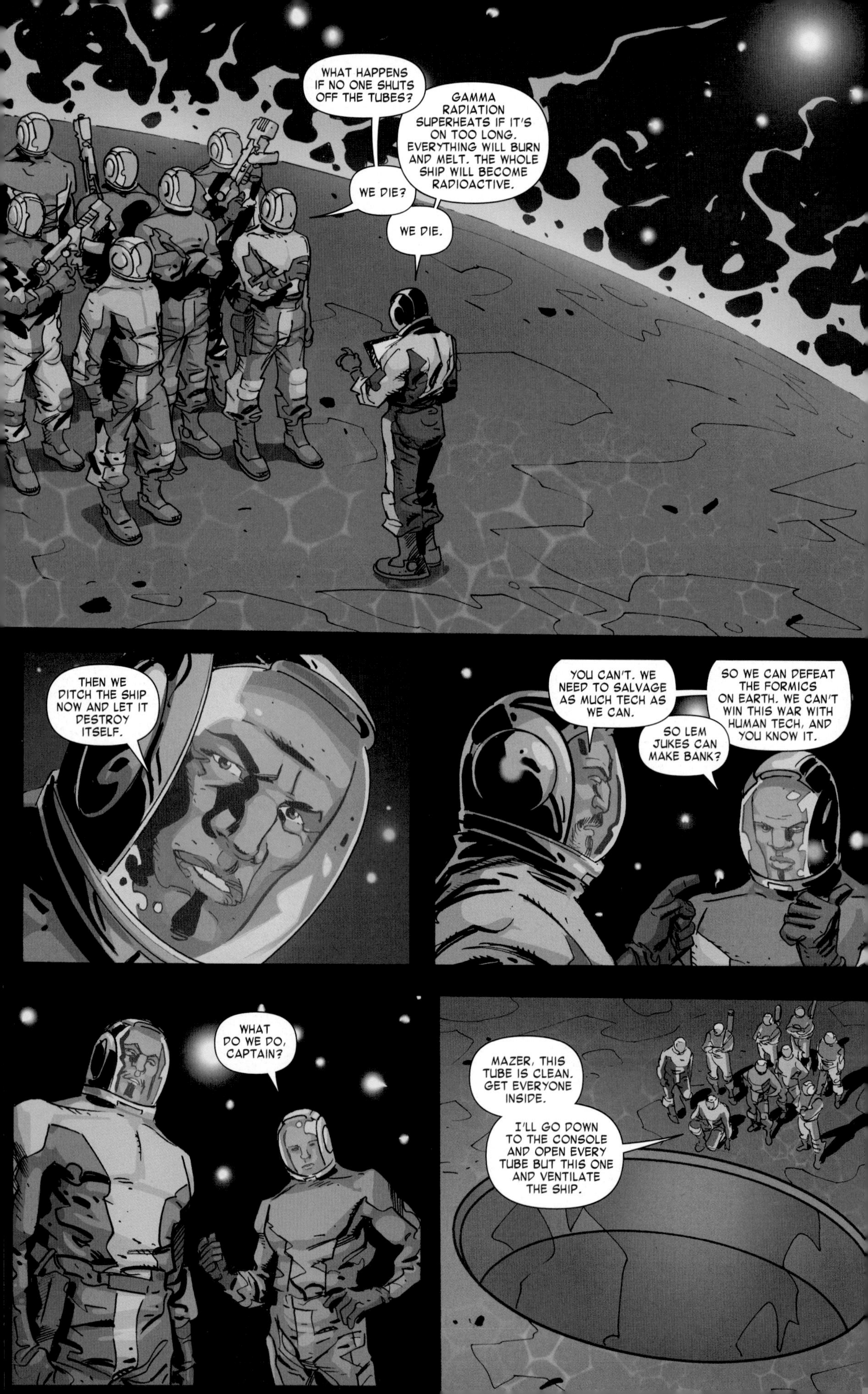
WHAT HAPPENS IF NO ONE SHUTS OFF THE TUBES?
GAMMA RADIATION SUPERHEATS IF IT'S ON TOO LONG. EVERYTHING WILL BURN AND MELT. THE WHOLE SHIP WILL BECOME RADIOACTIVE.
WE DIE?
WE DIE.
THEN WE DITCH THE SHIP NOW AND LET IT DESTROY ITSELF.
YOU CAN'T. WE NEED TO SALVAGE AS MUCH TECH AS WE CAN.
SO WE CAN DEFEAT THE FORMICS ON EARTH. WE CAN'T WIN THIS WAR WITH HUMAN TECH, AND YOU KNOW IT.
SO LEM JUKES CAN MAKE BANK?
WHAT DO WE DO, CAPTAIN?
MAZER, THIS TUBE IS CLEAN. GET EVERYONE INSIDE.
I'LL GO DOWN TO THE CONSOLE AND OPEN EVERY TUBE BUT THIS ONE AND VENTILATE THE SHIP.

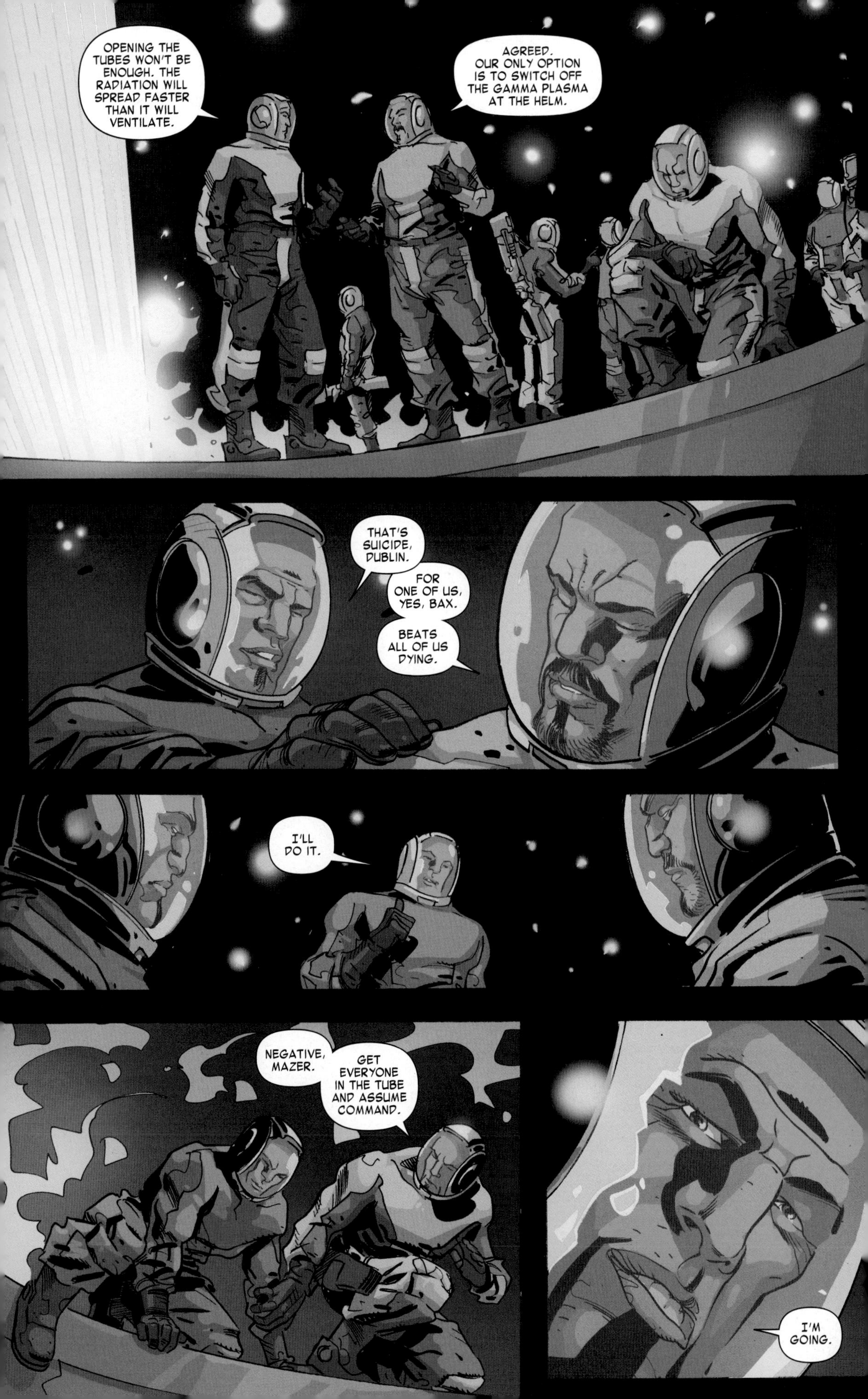
OPENING THE TUBES WON'T BE ENOUGH. THE RADIATION WILL SPREAD FASTER THAN IT WILL VENTILATE.
AGREED. OUR ONLY OPTION IS TO SWITCH OFF THE GAMMA PLASMA AT THE HELM.
THAT'S SUICIDE, DUBLIN.
FOR ONE OF US, YES, BAX.
BEATS ALL OF US DYING.
I'LL DO IT.
NEGATIVE, MAZER.
GET EVERYONE IN THE TUBE AND ASSUME COMMAND.
I'M GOING.

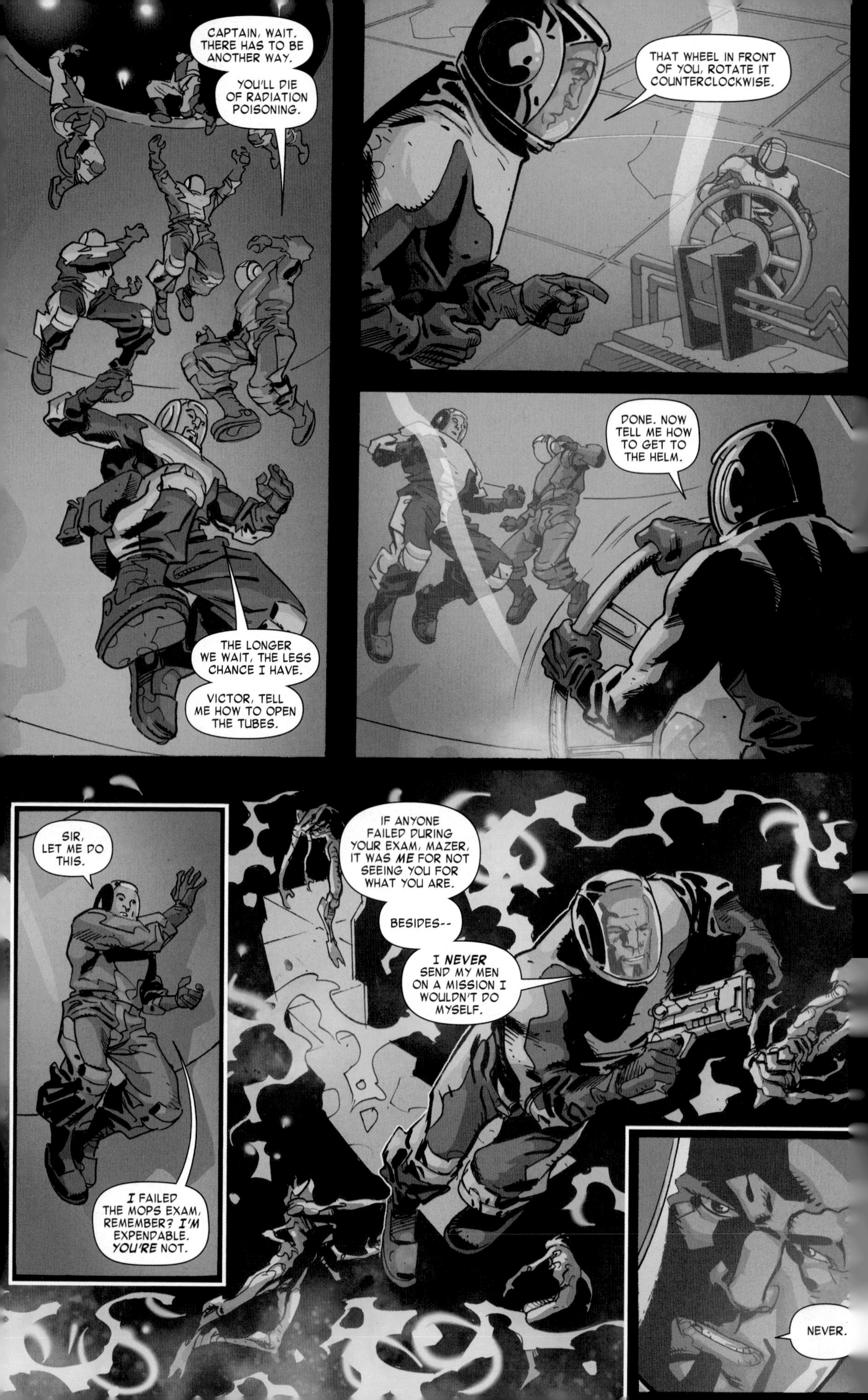
CAPTAIN, WAIT. THERE HAS TO BE ANOTHER WAY.
YOU'LL DIE OF RADIATION POISONING.
THE LONGER WE WAIT, THE LESS CHANCE I HAVE.
VICTOR, TELL ME HOW TO OPEN THE TUBES.
THAT WHEEL IN FRONT OF YOU, ROTATE IT COUNTERCLOCKWISE.
DONE. NOW TELL ME HOW TO GET TO THE HELM.
SIR, LET ME DO THIS.
I FAILED THE MOPS EXAM, REMEMBER? *I'M* EXPENDABLE. *YOU'RE* NOT.
IF ANYONE FAILED DURING YOUR EXAM, MAZER, IT WAS *ME* FOR NOT SEEING YOU FOR WHAT YOU ARE.
BESIDES--
I *NEVER* SEND MY MEN ON A MISSION I WOULDN'T DO MYSELF.
NEVER.

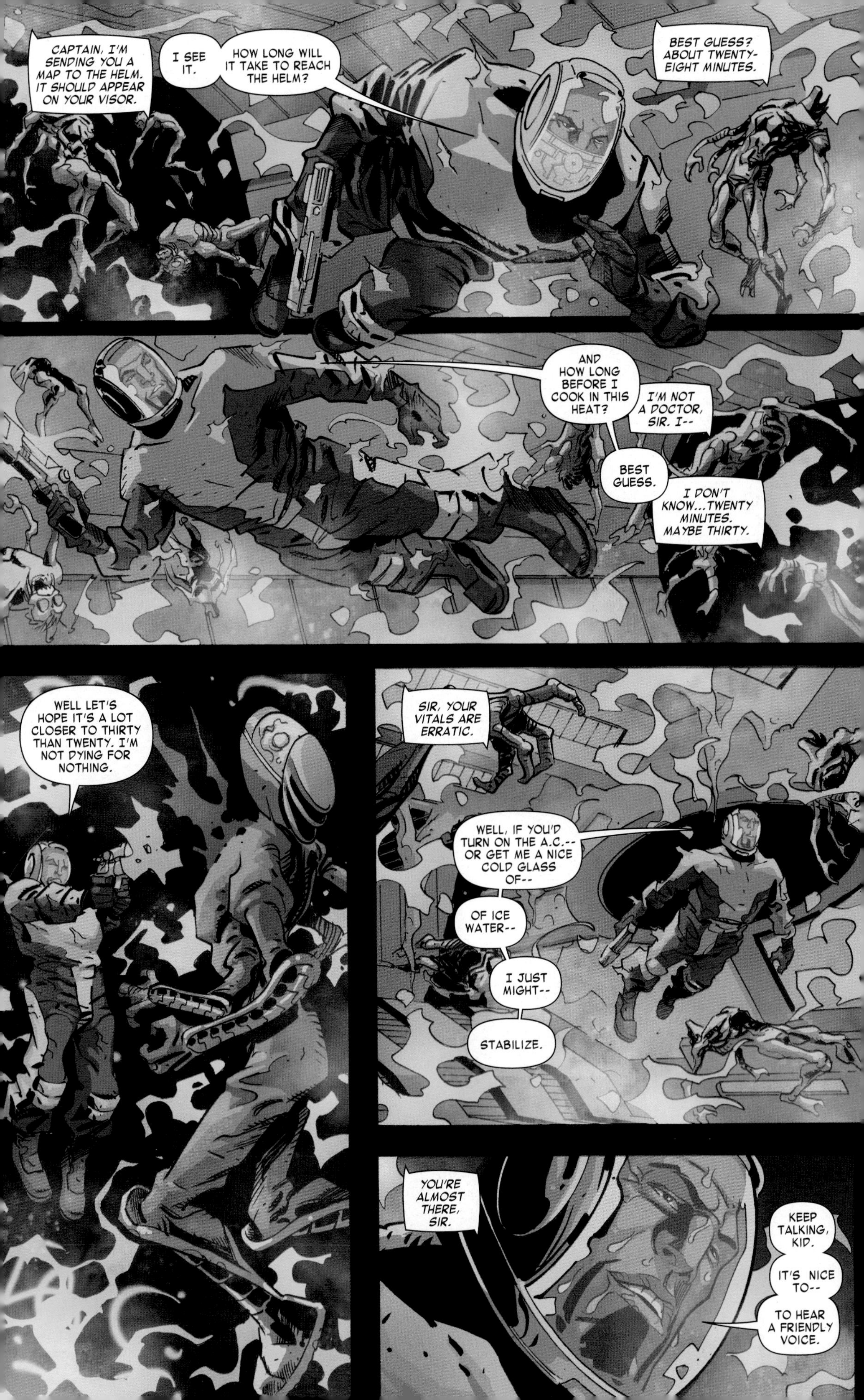
CAPTAIN, I'M SENDING YOU A MAP TO THE HELM. IT SHOULD APPEAR ON YOUR VISOR.
I SEE IT.
HOW LONG WILL IT TAKE TO REACH THE HELM?
BEST GUESS? ABOUT TWENTY-EIGHT MINUTES.
AND HOW LONG BEFORE I COOK IN THIS HEAT?
I'M NOT A DOCTOR, SIR. I--
BEST GUESS.
I DON'T KNOW...TWENTY MINUTES. MAYBE THIRTY.
WELL LET'S HOPE IT'S A LOT CLOSER TO THIRTY THAN TWENTY. I'M NOT DYING FOR NOTHING.
SIR, YOUR VITALS ARE ERRATIC.
WELL, IF YOU'D TURN ON THE A.C.-- OR GET ME A NICE COLD GLASS OF--
OF ICE WATER--
I JUST MIGHT--
STABILIZE.
YOU'RE ALMOST THERE, SIR.
KEEP TALKING, KID.
IT'S NICE TO--
TO HEAR A FRIENDLY VOICE.

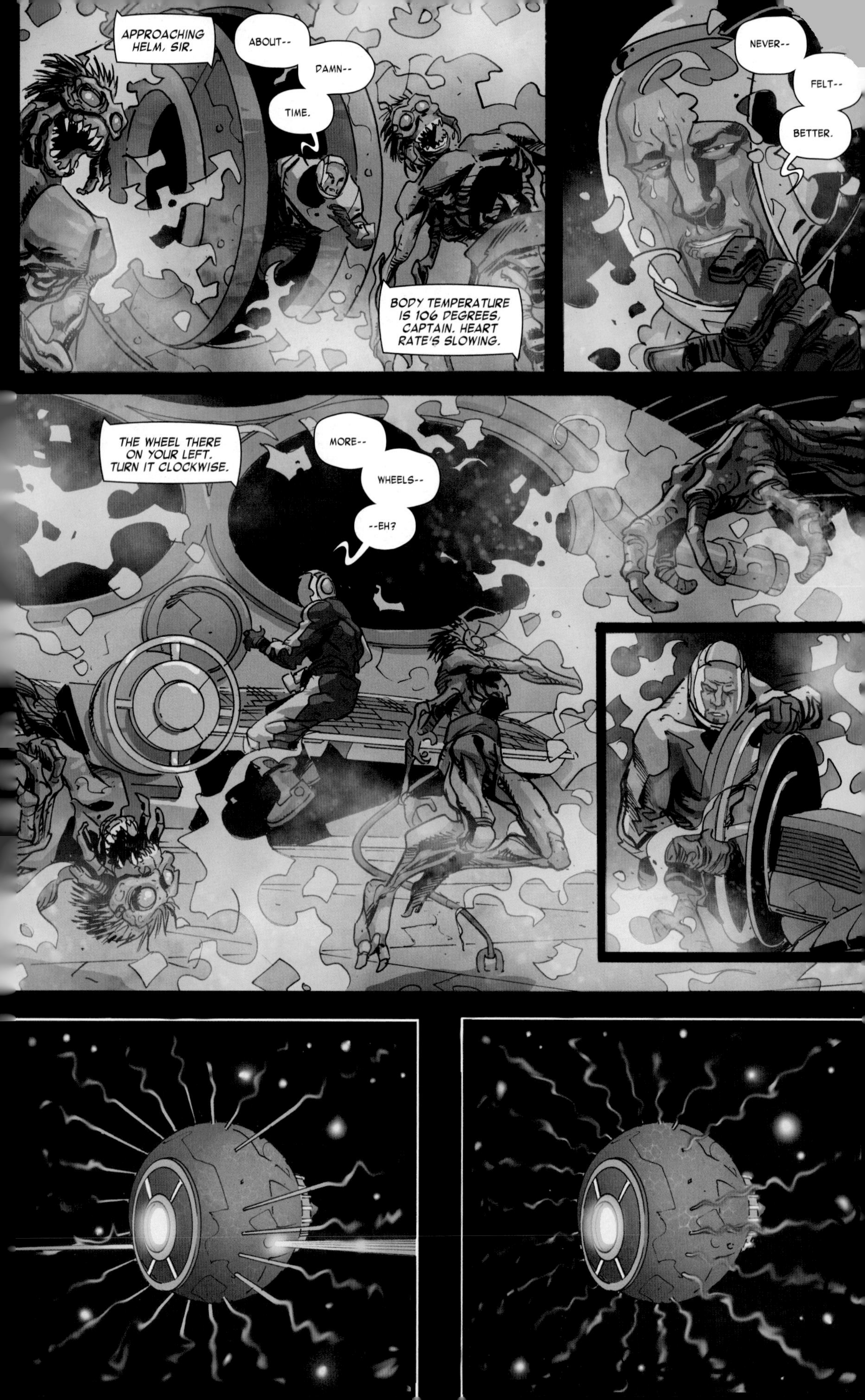
APPROACHING HELM, SIR.
ABOUT--
DAMN--
TIME.
BODY TEMPERATURE IS 106 DEGREES, CAPTAIN. HEART RATE'S SLOWING.
NEVER--
FELT--
BETTER.
THE WHEEL THERE ON YOUR LEFT. TURN IT CLOCKWISE.
MORE--
WHEELS--
--EH?

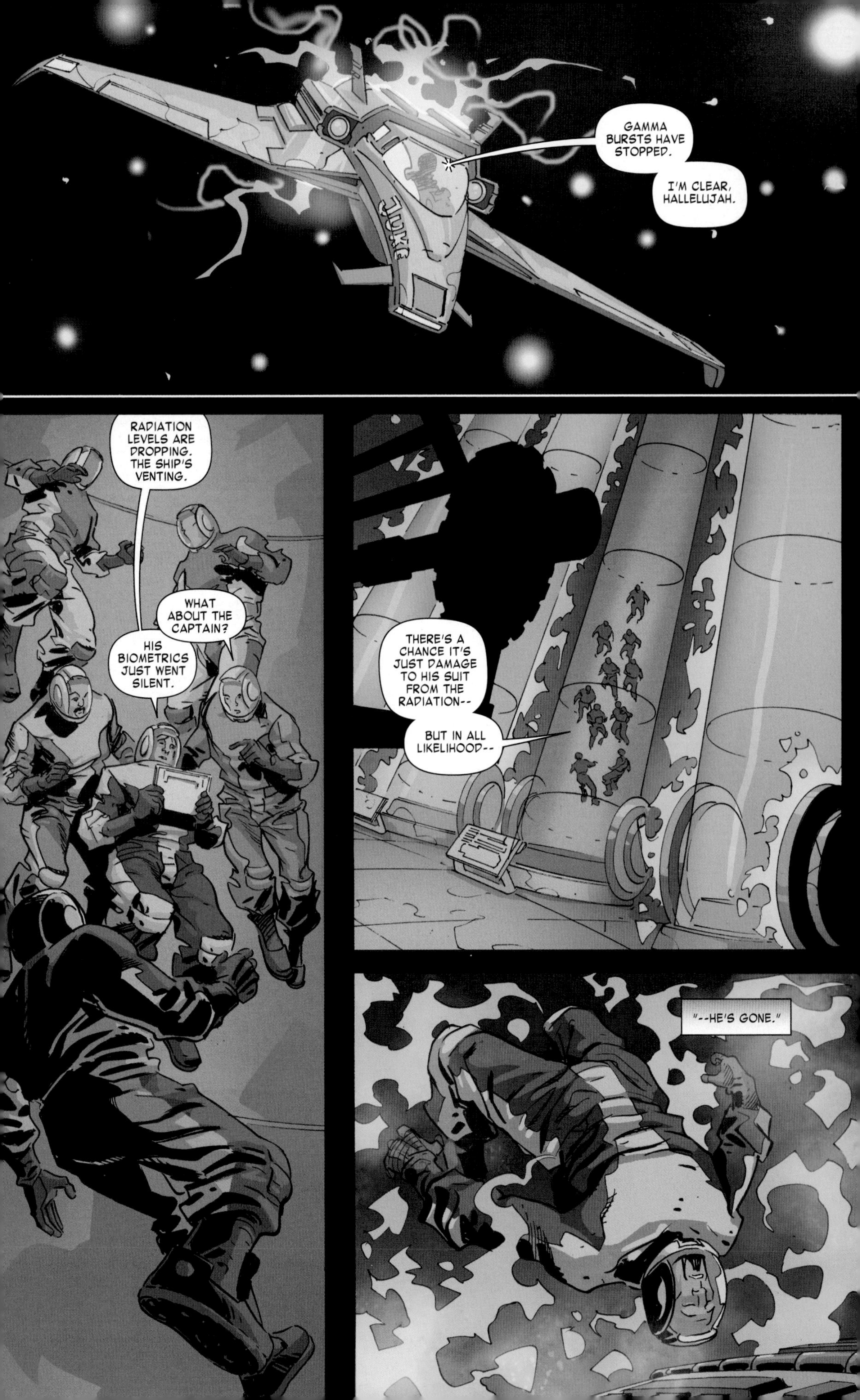
GAMMA BURSTS HAVE STOPPED.
I'M CLEAR, HALLELUJAH.
RADIATION LEVELS ARE DROPPING. THE SHIP'S VENTING.
WHAT ABOUT THE CAPTAIN?
HIS BIOMETRICS JUST WENT SILENT.
THERE'S A CHANCE IT'S JUST DAMAGE TO HIS SUIT FROM THE RADIATION--
BUT IN ALL LIKELIHOOD--
"--HE'S GONE."

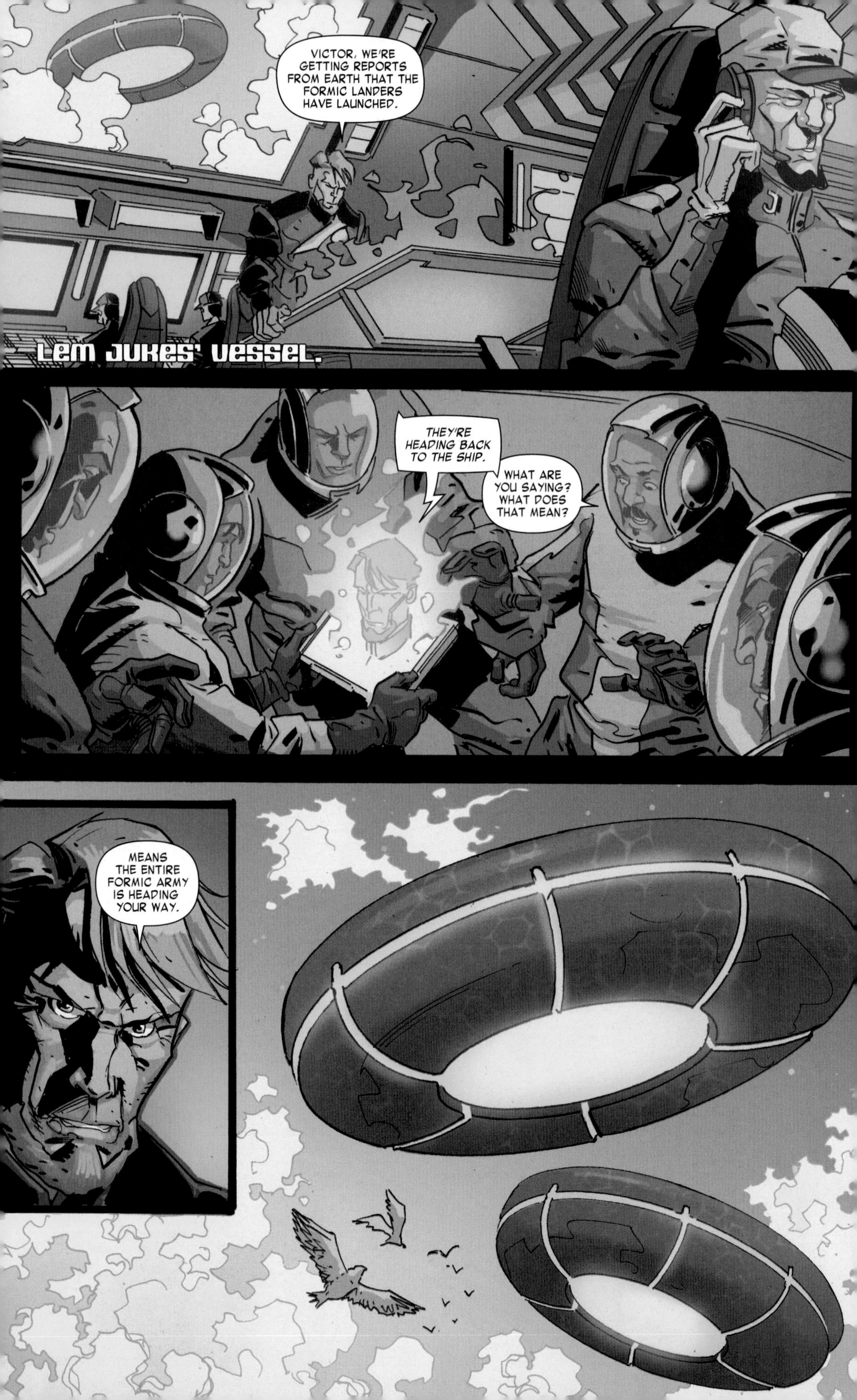
VICTOR, WE'RE GETTING REPORTS FROM EARTH THAT THE FORMIC LANDERS HAVE LAUNCHED.
LEM JUKES' VESSEL.
THEY'RE HEADING BACK TO THE SHIP.
WHAT ARE YOU SAYING? WHAT DOES THAT MEAN?
MEANS THE ENTIRE FORMIC ARMY IS HEADING YOUR WAY.

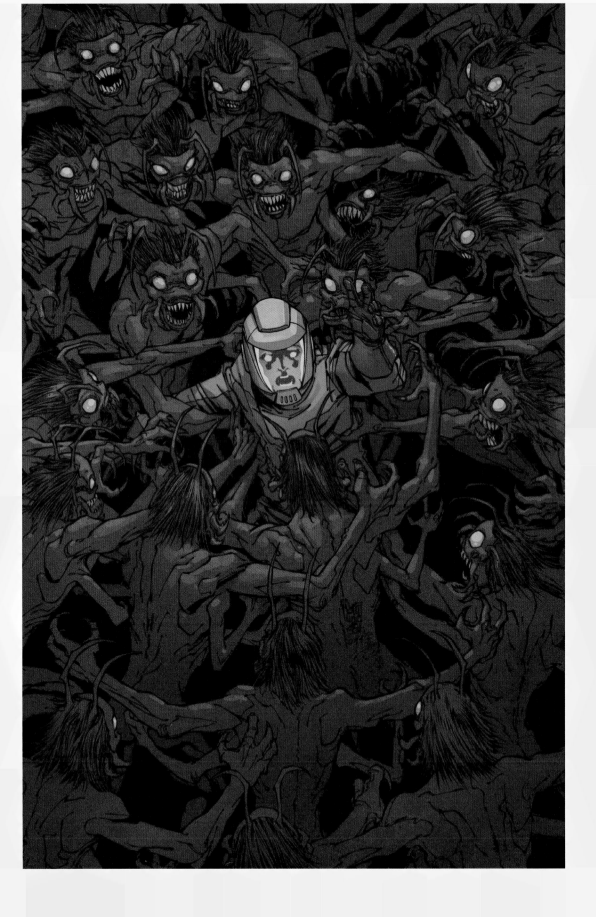

INSTANT MESSAGE INTERCHANGE btwn:
Ukko Jukes, Pres. and CEO, and Rebecca Kline, SVP,
Chief Analytics Officer
Juke Limited File: 39874-UJ1024
Clearance: Restricted

UKKO: Status?
KLINE: All 3 landers have launched. They've cleared
    the atmosphere. Likely heading to mother ship.
UKKO: And Lem?
KLINE: Our people are briefing him. He'll attack.
UKKO: You can't guarantee that.
KLINE: He fits the profile. We've run the behavior
    module three times. It's 87% accurate, plus or
    minus a few points.
UKKO: I know his profile. He's my son.
KLINE: Of course.
UKKO: And the fighters?
KLINE: 78% of ships are flight-ready. 40 pilots
    standing by. 237 employees currently at the
    facility.
UKKO: Will they fight?
KLINE: Pilots, yes. Miners, hard to say. Modules
    predict at least 67% will fight. Personally, I
    think that's high.
UKKO: Will it be enough?
KLINE: Too many variables.
UKKO: That's not an answer.
KLINE: The Formics are still an unknown. We don't
    know all their capabilities.
UKKO: My son's life is on the line here.
KLINE: I can't predict the future, sir.
UKKO: Then what the hell am I paying you for?

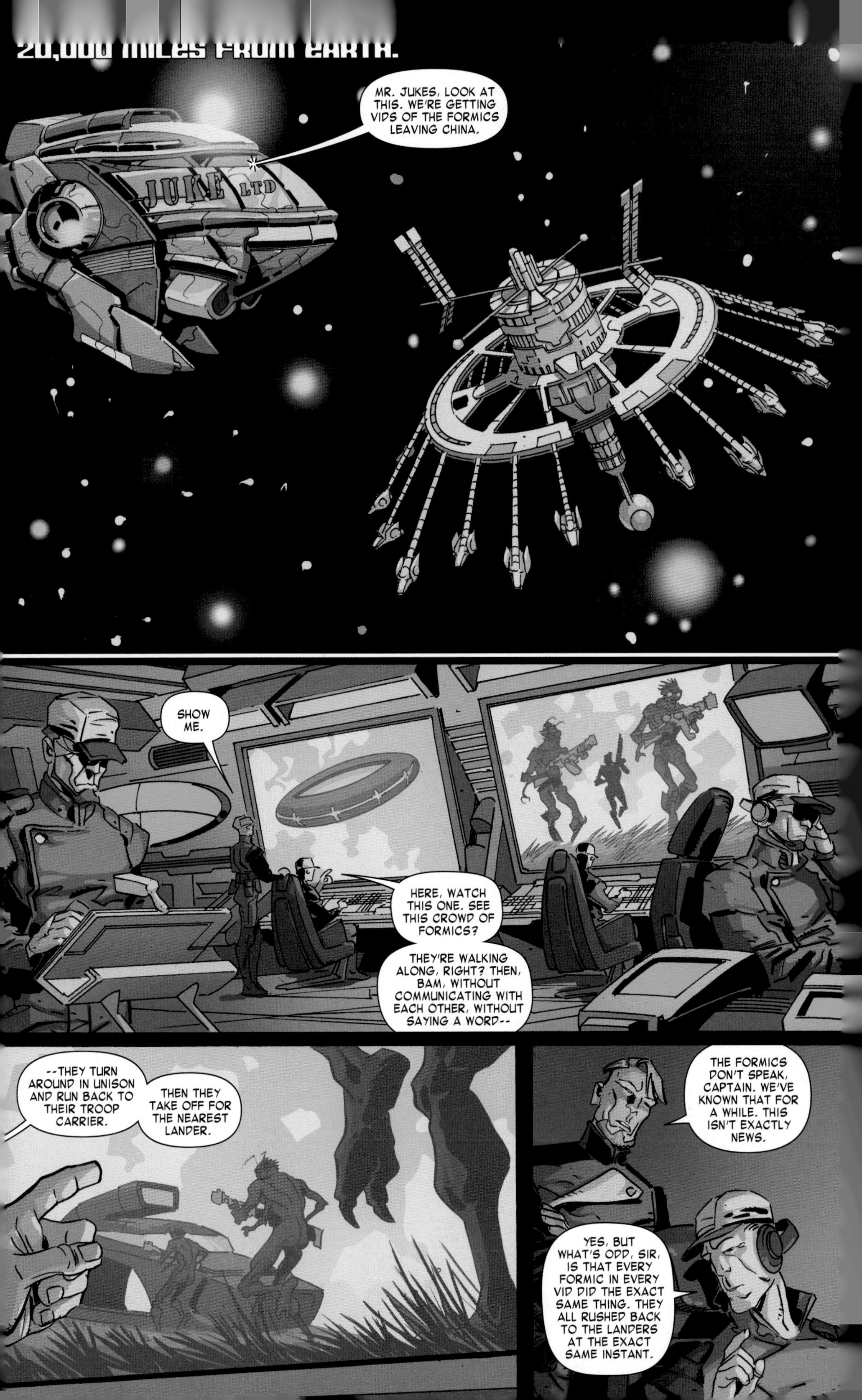
20,000 MILES FROM EARTH.
MR. JUKES, LOOK AT THIS. WE'RE GETTING VIDS OF THE FORMICS LEAVING CHINA.
JUKE LTD
SHOW ME.
HERE, WATCH THIS ONE. SEE THIS CROWD OF FORMICS?
THEY'RE WALKING ALONG, RIGHT? THEN, BAM, WITHOUT COMMUNICATING WITH EACH OTHER, WITHOUT SAYING A WORD--
--THEY TURN AROUND IN UNISON AND RUN BACK TO THEIR TROOP CARRIER.
THEN THEY TAKE OFF FOR THE NEAREST LANDER.
THE FORMICS DON'T SPEAK, CAPTAIN. WE'VE KNOWN THAT FOR A WHILE. THIS ISN'T EXACTLY NEWS.
YES, BUT WHAT'S ODD, SIR, IS THAT EVERY FORMIC IN EVERY VID DID THE EXACT SAME THING. THEY ALL RUSHED BACK TO THE LANDERS AT THE EXACT SAME INSTANT.

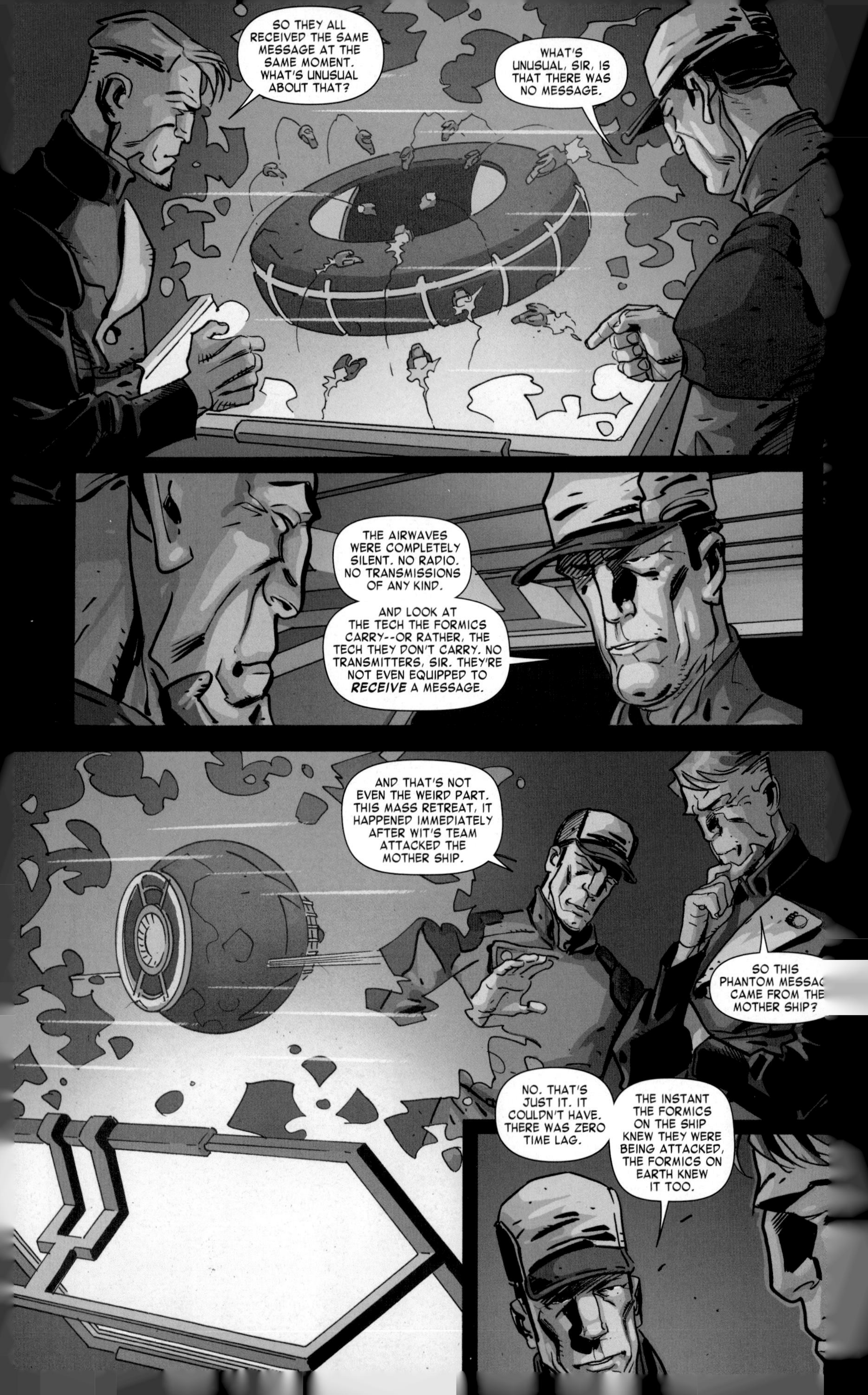
SO THEY ALL RECEIVED THE SAME MESSAGE AT THE SAME MOMENT. WHAT'S UNUSUAL ABOUT THAT?
WHAT'S UNUSUAL, SIR, IS THAT THERE WAS NO MESSAGE.
THE AIRWAVES WERE COMPLETELY SILENT. NO RADIO. NO TRANSMISSIONS OF ANY KIND.
AND LOOK AT THE TECH THE FORMICS CARRY--OR RATHER, THE TECH THEY DON'T CARRY. NO TRANSMITTERS, SIR. THEY'RE NOT EVEN EQUIPPED TO RECEIVE A MESSAGE.
AND THAT'S NOT EVEN THE WEIRD PART. THIS MASS RETREAT, IT HAPPENED IMMEDIATELY AFTER WIT'S TEAM ATTACKED THE MOTHER SHIP.
SO THIS PHANTOM MESSAG CAME FROM THE MOTHER SHIP?
NO. THAT'S JUST IT. IT COULDN'T HAVE. THERE WAS ZERO TIME LAG.
THE INSTANT THE FORMICS ON THE SHIP KNEW THEY WERE BEING ATTACKED, THE FORMICS ON EARTH KNEW IT TOO.

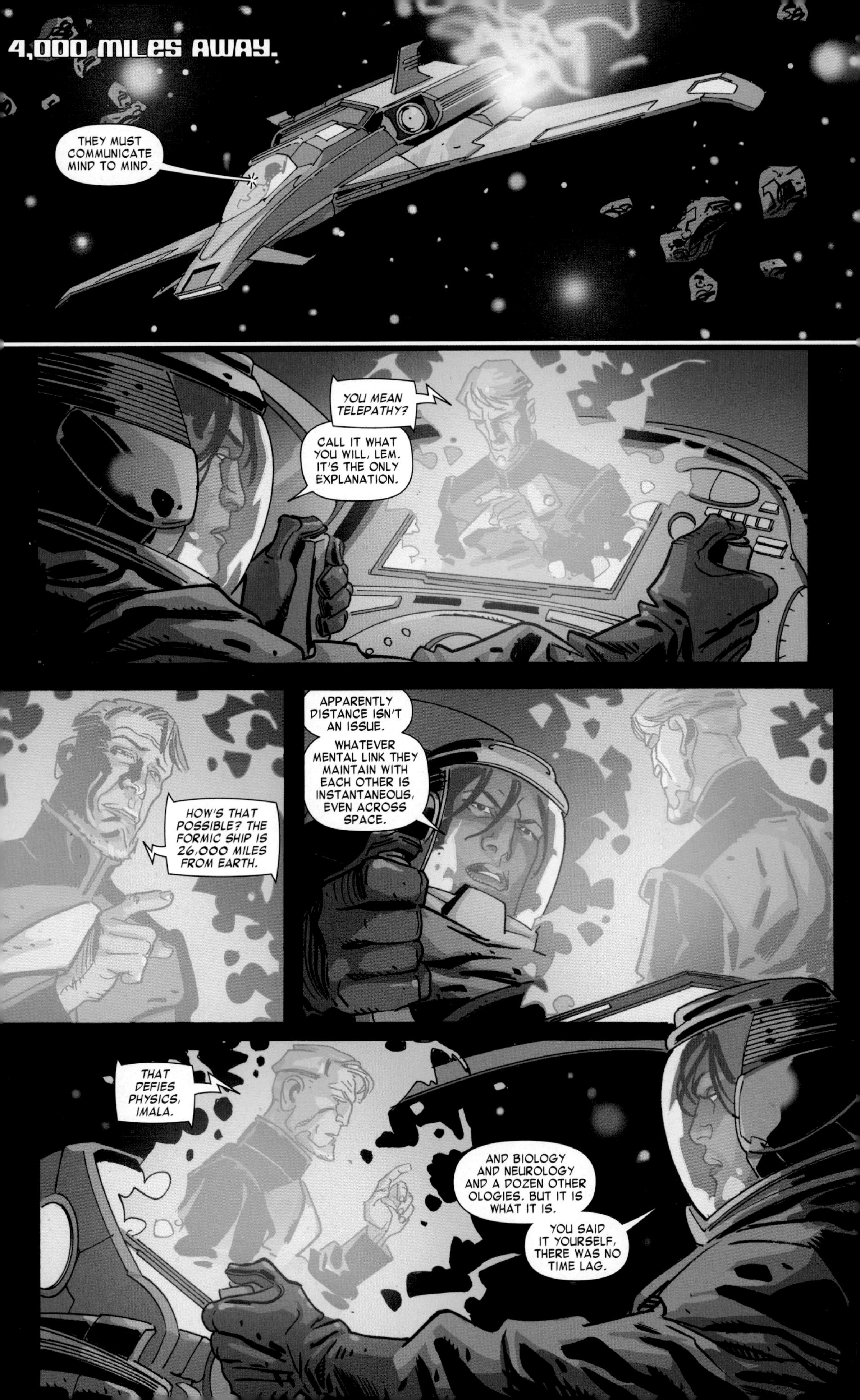
4,000 MILES AWAY.
THEY MUST COMMUNICATE MIND TO MIND.
YOU MEAN TELEPATHY?
CALL IT WHAT YOU WILL, LEM. IT'S THE ONLY EXPLANATION.
HOW'S THAT POSSIBLE? THE FORMIC SHIP IS 26,000 MILES FROM EARTH.
APPARENTLY DISTANCE ISN'T AN ISSUE.
WHATEVER MENTAL LINK THEY MAINTAIN WITH EACH OTHER IS INSTANTANEOUS, EVEN ACROSS SPACE.
THAT DEFIES PHYSICS, IMALA.
AND BIOLOGY AND NEUROLOGY AND A DOZEN OTHER OLOGIES. BUT IT IS WHAT IT IS.
YOU SAID IT YOURSELF, THERE WAS NO TIME LAG.

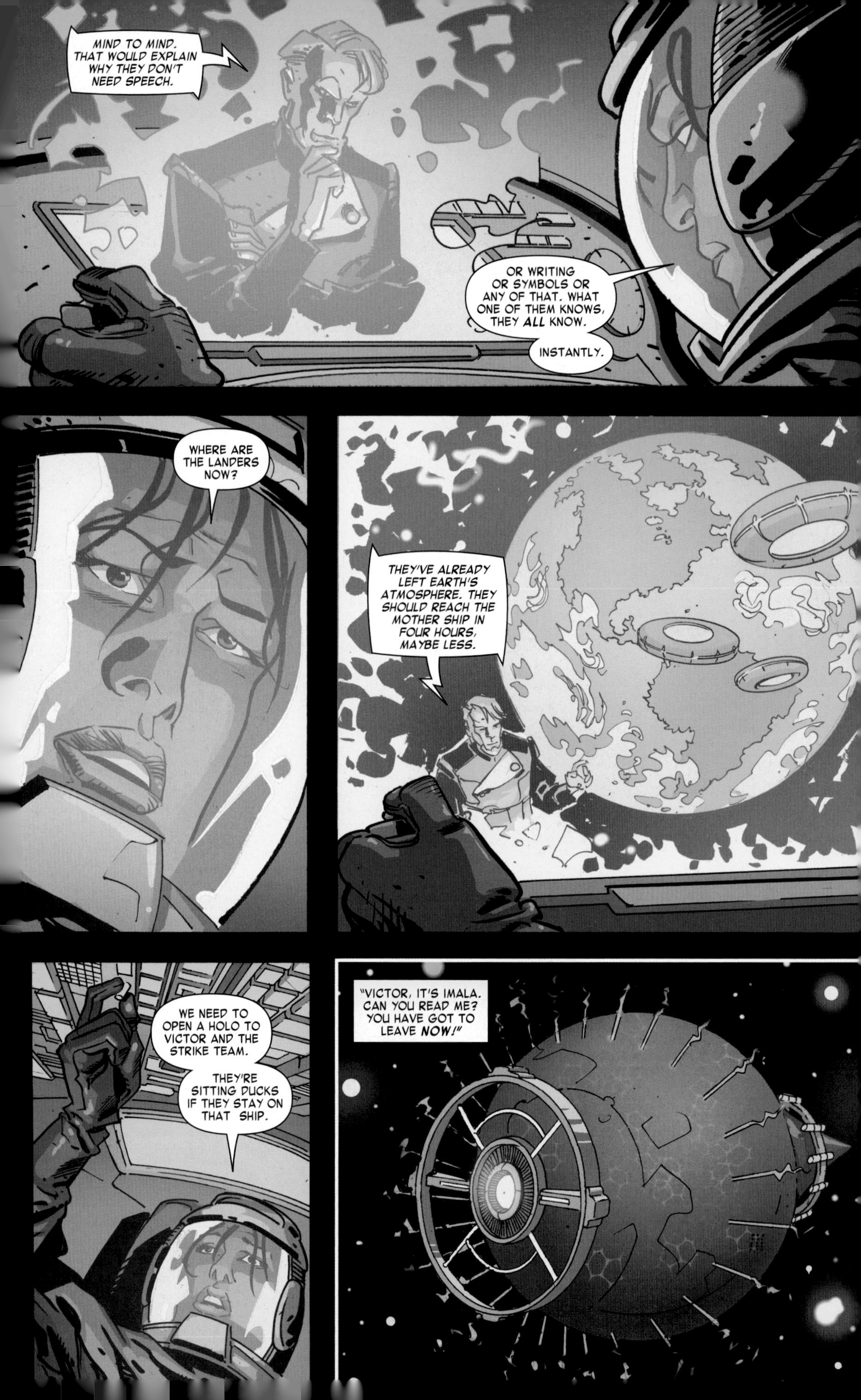
MIND TO MIND. THAT WOULD EXPLAIN WHY THEY DON'T NEED SPEECH.
OR WRITING OR SYMBOLS OR ANY OF THAT. WHAT ONE OF THEM KNOWS, THEY ALL KNOW.
INSTANTLY.
WHERE ARE THE LANDERS NOW?
THEY'VE ALREADY LEFT EARTH'S ATMOSPHERE. THEY SHOULD REACH THE MOTHER SHIP IN FOUR HOURS, MAYBE LESS.
WE NEED TO OPEN A HOLO TO VICTOR AND THE STRIKE TEAM.
THEY'RE SITTING DUCKS IF THEY STAY ON THAT SHIP.
"VICTOR, IT'S IMALA. CAN YOU READ ME? YOU HAVE GOT TO LEAVE NOW!"

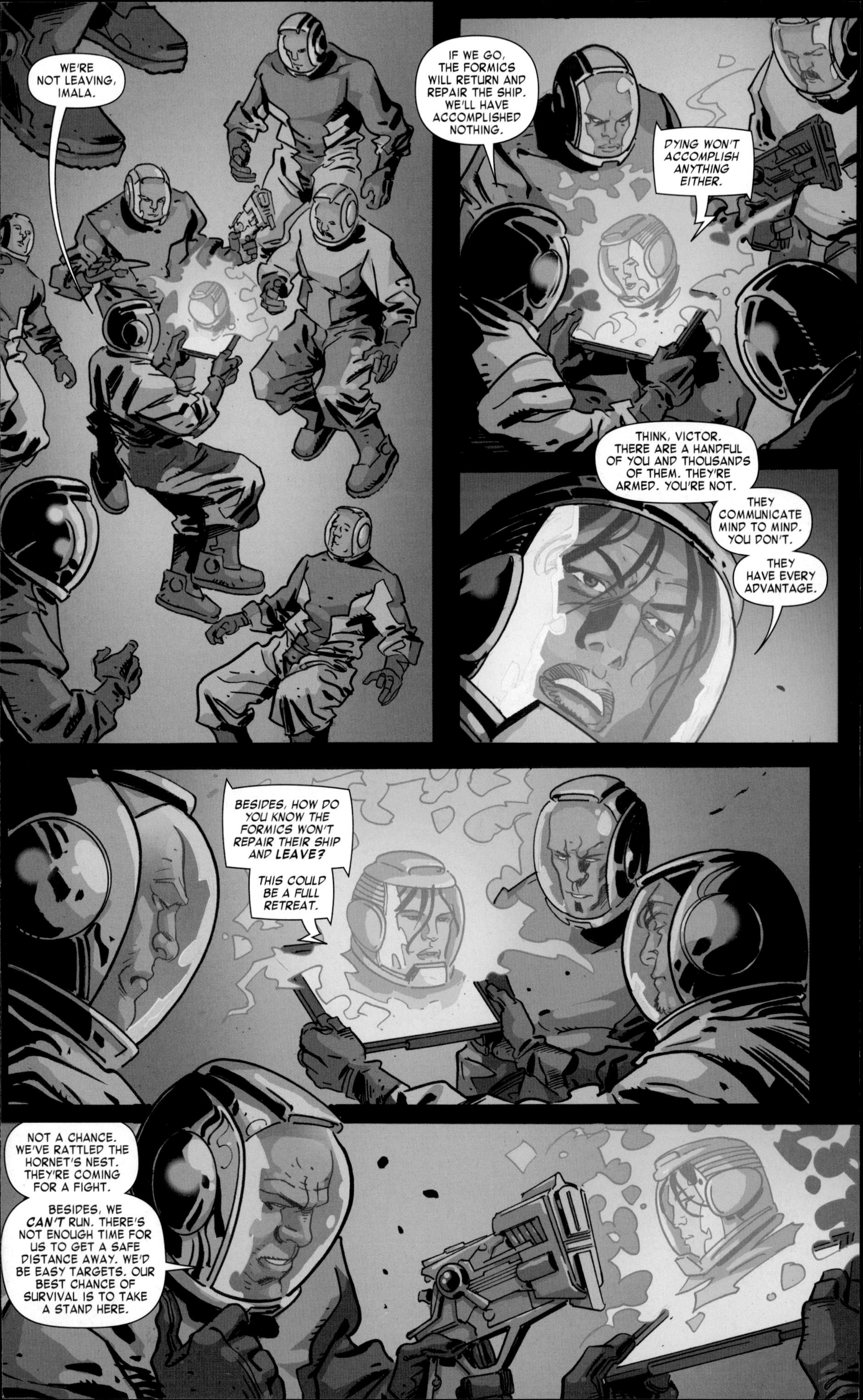
WE'RE NOT LEAVING, IMALA.
IF WE GO, THE FORMICS WILL RETURN AND REPAIR THE SHIP. WE'LL HAVE ACCOMPLISHED NOTHING.
DYING WON'T ACCOMPLISH ANYTHING EITHER.
THINK, VICTOR. THERE ARE A HANDFUL OF YOU AND THOUSANDS OF THEM. THEY'RE ARMED. YOU'RE NOT.
THEY COMMUNICATE MIND TO MIND. YOU DON'T.
THEY HAVE EVERY ADVANTAGE.
BESIDES, HOW DO YOU KNOW THE FORMICS WON'T REPAIR THEIR SHIP AND LEAVE?
THIS COULD BE A FULL RETREAT.
NOT A CHANCE. WE'VE RATTLED THE HORNET'S NEST. THEY'RE COMING FOR A FIGHT.
BESIDES, WE CAN'T RUN. THERE'S NOT ENOUGH TIME FOR US TO GET A SAFE DISTANCE AWAY. WE'D BE EASY TARGETS. OUR BEST CHANCE OF SURVIVAL IS TO TAKE A STAND HERE.

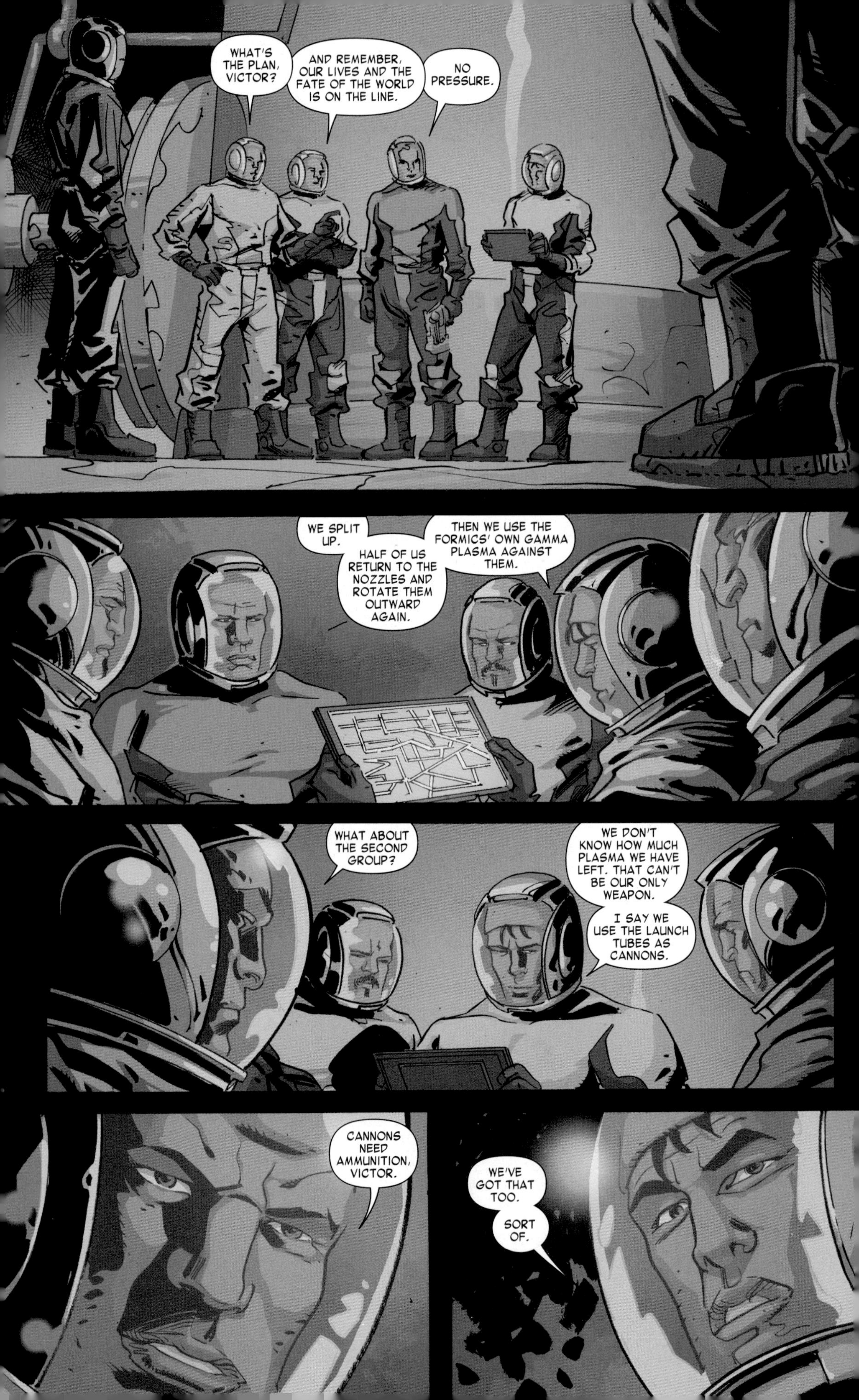
WHAT'S THE PLAN, VICTOR?
AND REMEMBER, OUR LIVES AND THE FATE OF THE WORLD IS ON THE LINE.
NO PRESSURE.
WE SPLIT UP.
HALF OF US RETURN TO THE NOZZLES AND ROTATE THEM OUTWARD AGAIN.
THEN WE USE THE FORMICS' OWN GAMMA PLASMA AGAINST THEM.
WHAT ABOUT THE SECOND GROUP?
WE DON'T KNOW HOW MUCH PLASMA WE HAVE LEFT. THAT CAN'T BE OUR ONLY WEAPON.
I SAY WE USE THE LAUNCH TUBES AS CANNONS.
CANNONS NEED AMMUNITION, VICTOR.
WE'VE GOT THAT TOO.
SORT OF.

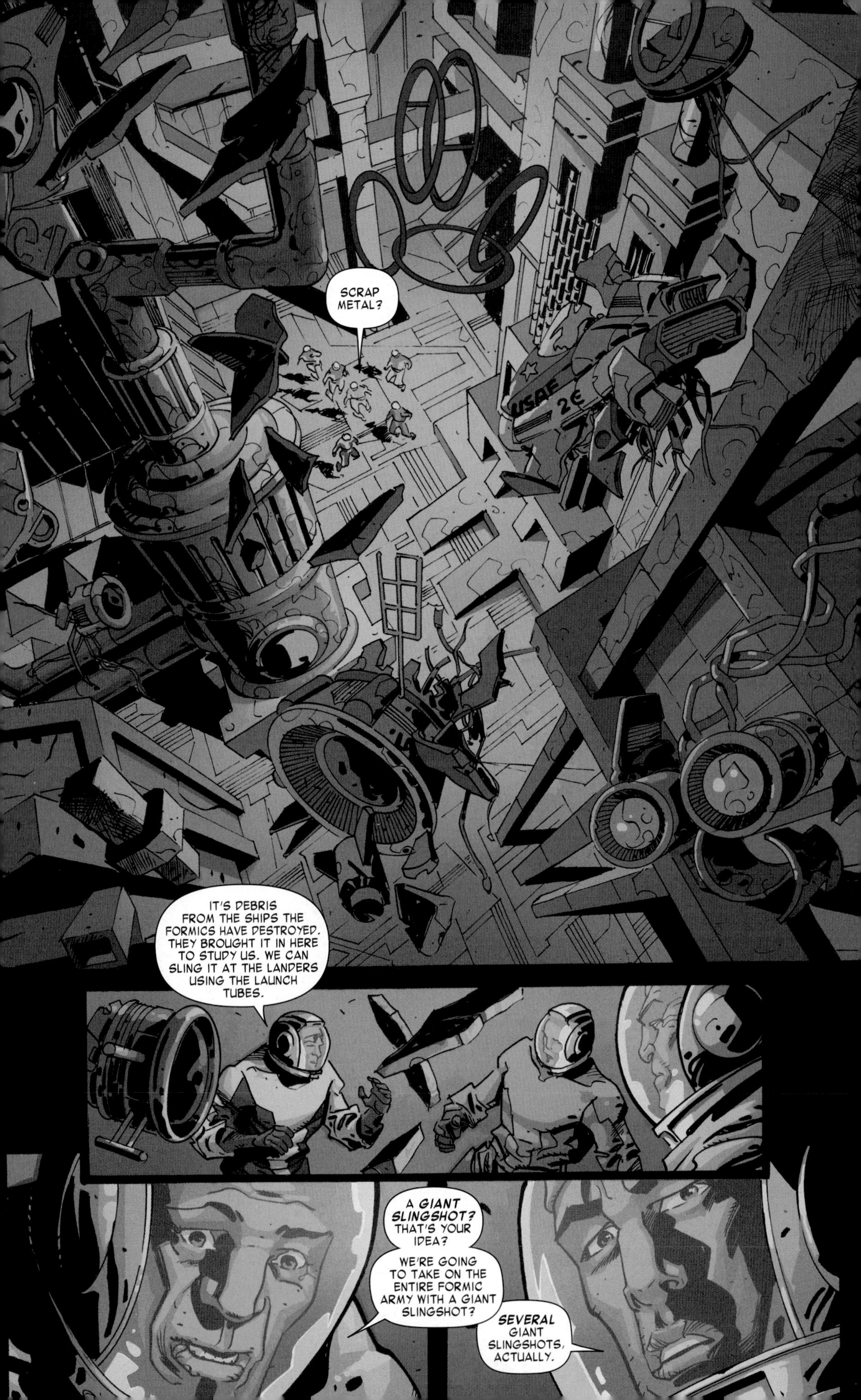
SCRAP METAL?
IT'S DEBRIS FROM THE SHIPS THE FORMICS HAVE DESTROYED. THEY BROUGHT IT IN HERE TO STUDY US. WE CAN SLING IT AT THE LANDERS USING THE LAUNCH TUBES.
A GIANT SLINGSHOT? THAT'S YOUR IDEA?
WE'RE GOING TO TAKE ON THE ENTIRE FORMIC ARMY WITH A GIANT SLINGSHOT?
SEVERAL GIANT SLINGSHOTS, ACTUALLY.
USAF

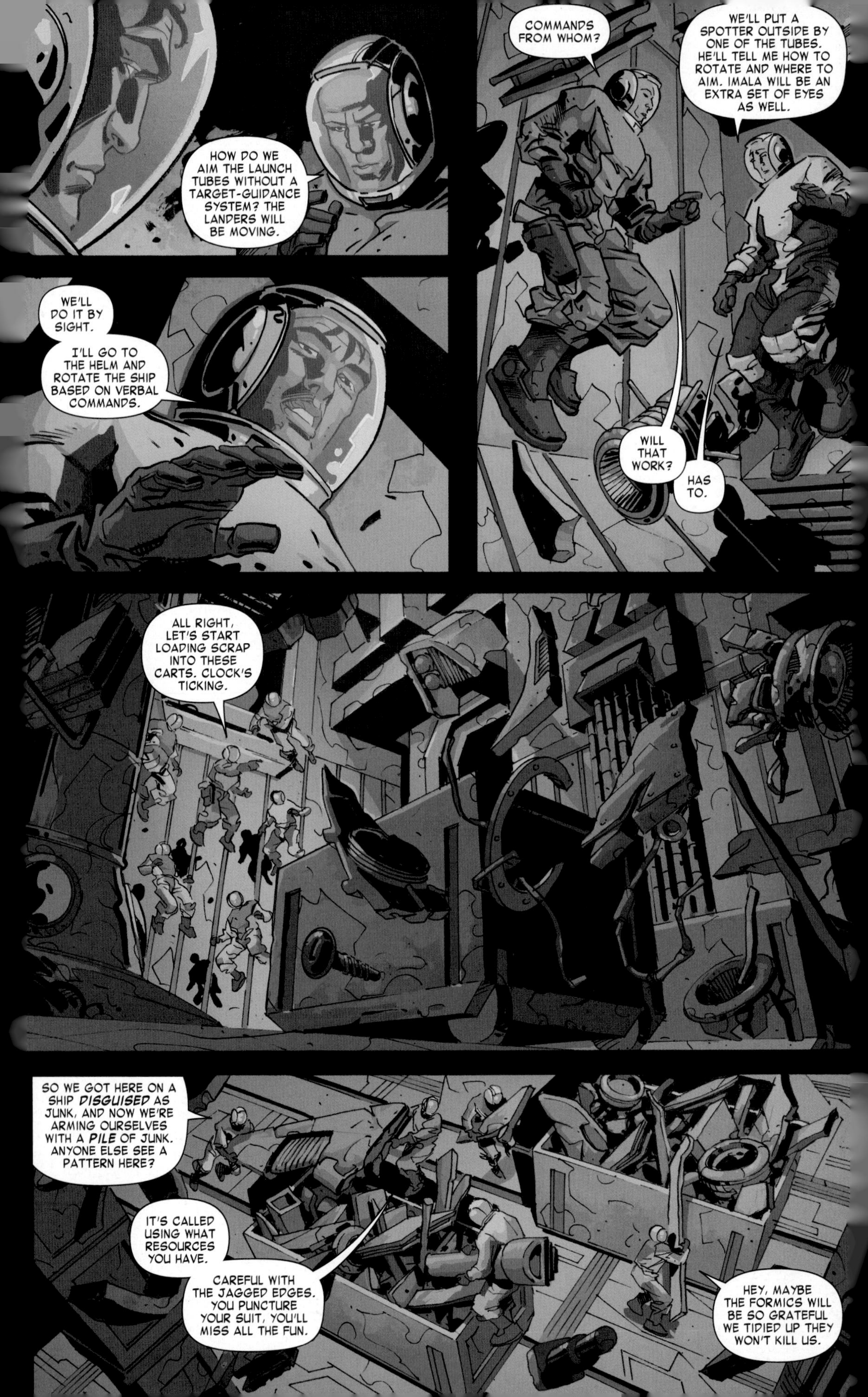
HOW DO WE AIM THE LAUNCH TUBES WITHOUT A TARGET-GUIDANCE SYSTEM? THE LANDERS WILL BE MOVING.
WE'LL DO IT BY SIGHT.
I'LL GO TO THE HELM AND ROTATE THE SHIP BASED ON VERBAL COMMANDS.
COMMANDS FROM WHOM?
WE'LL PUT A SPOTTER OUTSIDE BY ONE OF THE TUBES. HE'LL TELL ME HOW TO ROTATE AND WHERE TO AIM. IMALA WILL BE AN EXTRA SET OF EYES AS WELL.
WILL THAT WORK?
HAS TO.
ALL RIGHT, LET'S START LOADING SCRAP INTO THESE CARTS. CLOCK'S TICKING.
SO WE GOT HERE ON A SHIP *DISGUISED* AS JUNK, AND NOW WE'RE ARMING OURSELVES WITH A *PILE* OF JUNK. ANYONE ELSE SEE A PATTERN HERE?
IT'S CALLED USING WHAT RESOURCES YOU HAVE.
CAREFUL WITH THE JAGGED EDGES. YOU PUNCTURE YOUR SUIT, YOU'LL MISS ALL THE FUN.
HEY, MAYBE THE FORMICS WILL BE SO GRATEFUL WE TIDIED UP THEY WON'T KILL US.

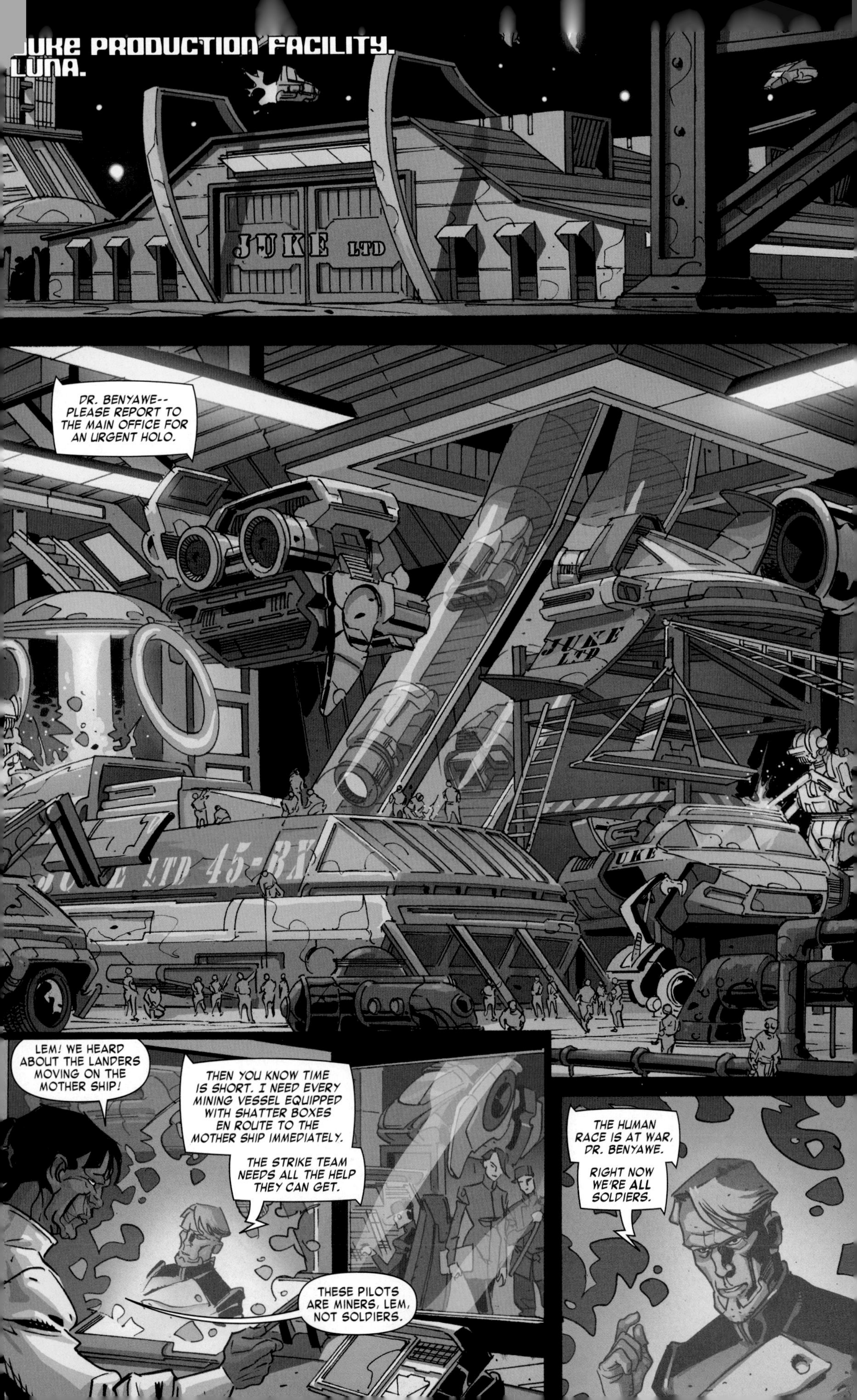
JUKE PRODUCTION FACILITY.
LUNA.
JUKE LTD
DR. BENYAWE-- PLEASE REPORT TO THE MAIN OFFICE FOR AN URGENT HOLO.
JUKE LTD
JUKE LTD 45-BX
JUKE
LEM! WE HEARD ABOUT THE LANDERS MOVING ON THE MOTHER SHIP!
THEN YOU KNOW TIME IS SHORT. I NEED EVERY MINING VESSEL EQUIPPED WITH SHATTER BOXES EN ROUTE TO THE MOTHER SHIP IMMEDIATELY.
THE STRIKE TEAM NEEDS ALL THE HELP THEY CAN GET.
THESE PILOTS ARE MINERS, LEM, NOT SOLDIERS.
THE HUMAN RACE IS AT WAR, DR. BENYAWE.
RIGHT NOW WE'RE ALL SOLDIERS.

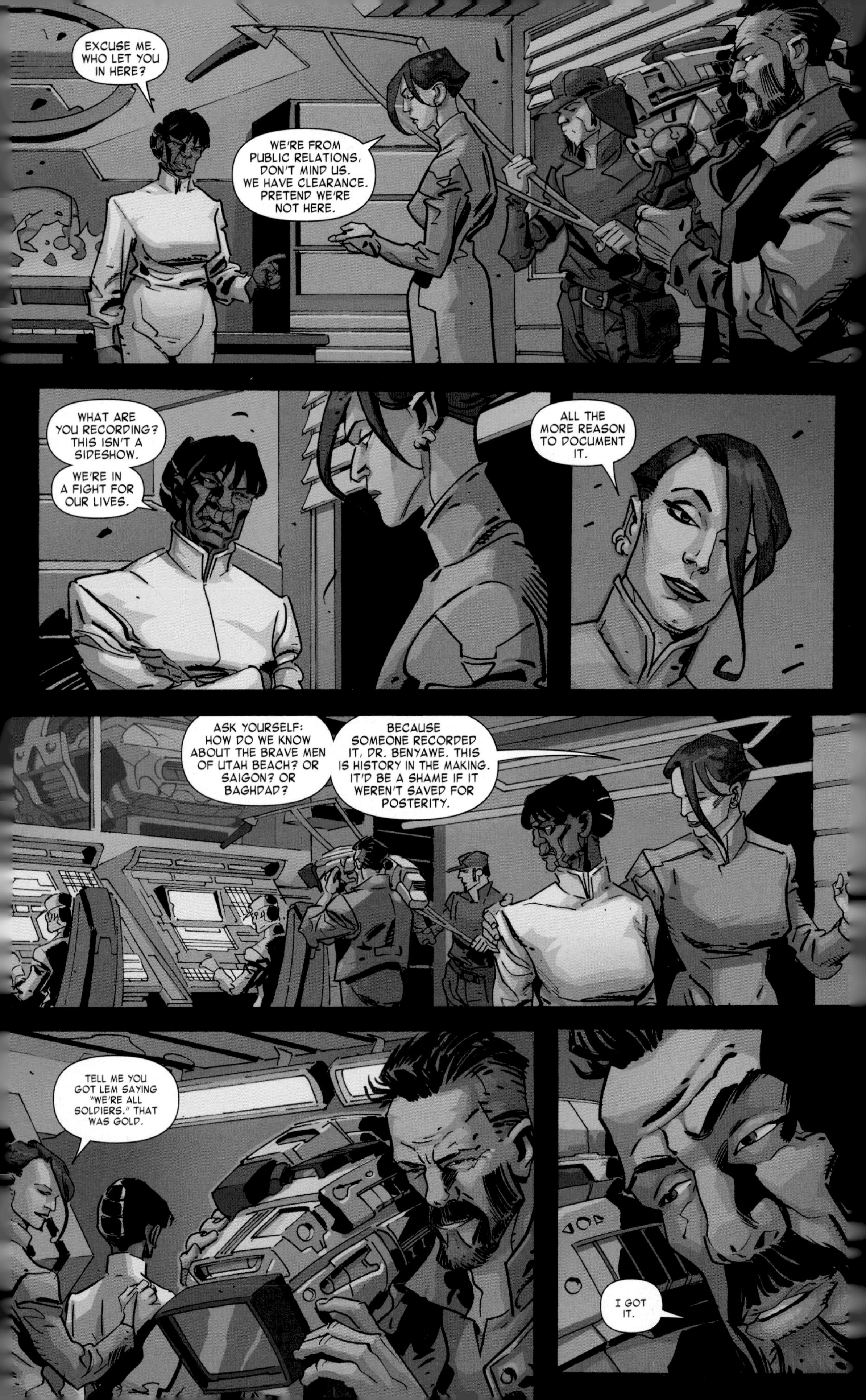
EXCUSE ME. WHO LET YOU IN HERE?
WE'RE FROM PUBLIC RELATIONS, DON'T MIND US. WE HAVE CLEARANCE. PRETEND WE'RE NOT HERE.
WHAT ARE YOU RECORDING? THIS ISN'T A SIDESHOW.
WE'RE IN A FIGHT FOR OUR LIVES.
ALL THE MORE REASON TO DOCUMENT IT.
ASK YOURSELF: HOW DO WE KNOW ABOUT THE BRAVE MEN OF UTAH BEACH? OR SAIGON? OR BAGHDAD?
BECAUSE SOMEONE RECORDED IT, DR. BENYAWE. THIS IS HISTORY IN THE MAKING. IT'D BE A SHAME IF IT WEREN'T SAVED FOR POSTERITY.
TELL ME YOU GOT LEM SAYING "WE'RE ALL SOLDIERS." THAT WAS GOLD.
I GOT IT.

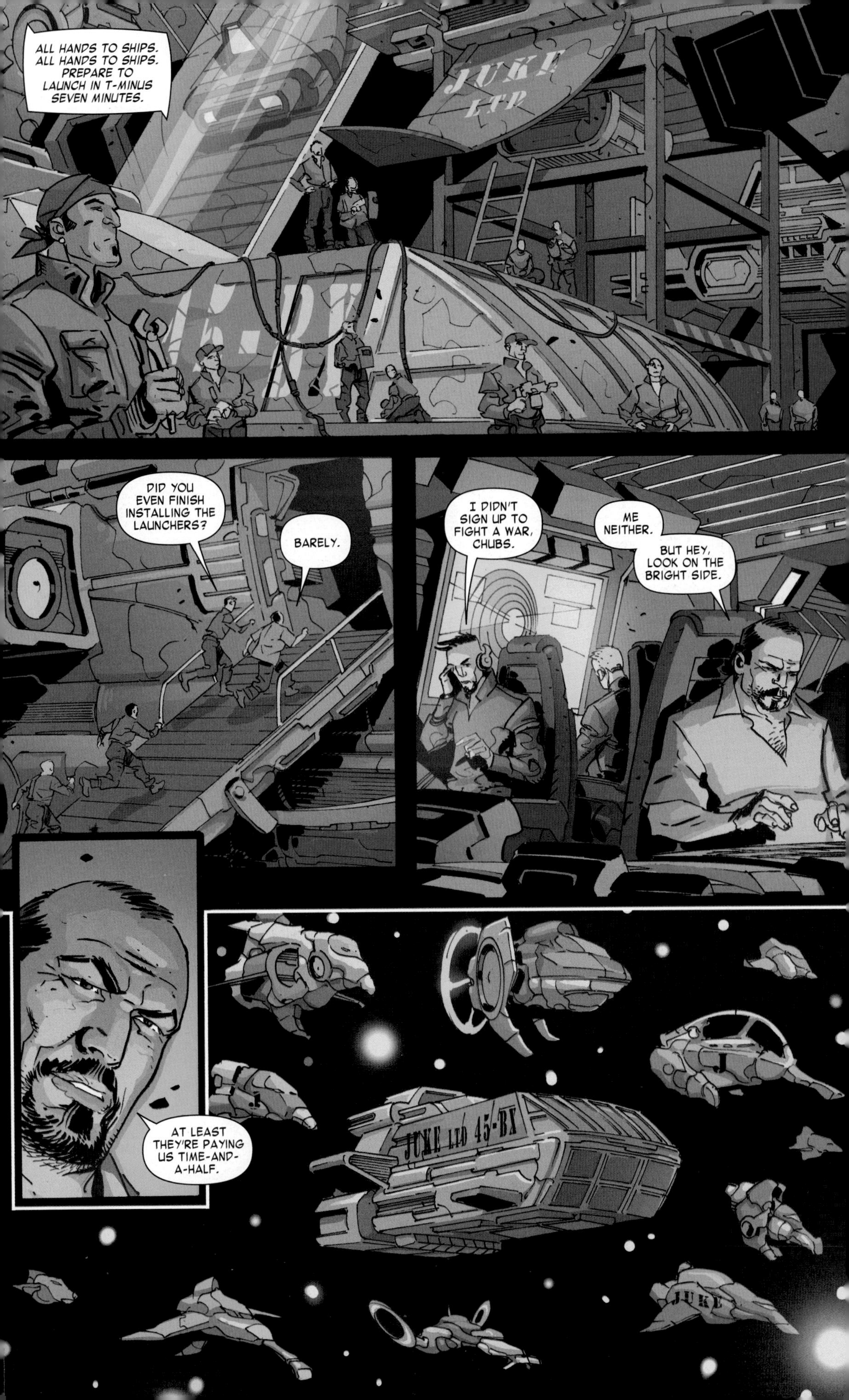
ALL HANDS TO SHIPS. ALL HANDS TO SHIPS. PREPARE TO LAUNCH IN T-MINUS SEVEN MINUTES.
JUKE LTD
DID YOU EVEN FINISH INSTALLING THE LAUNCHERS?
BARELY.
I DIDN'T SIGN UP TO FIGHT A WAR, CHUBS.
ME NEITHER.
BUT HEY, LOOK ON THE BRIGHT SIDE.
AT LEAST THEY'RE PAYING US TIME-AND-A-HALF.
JUKE LTD 45-BX
JUKE

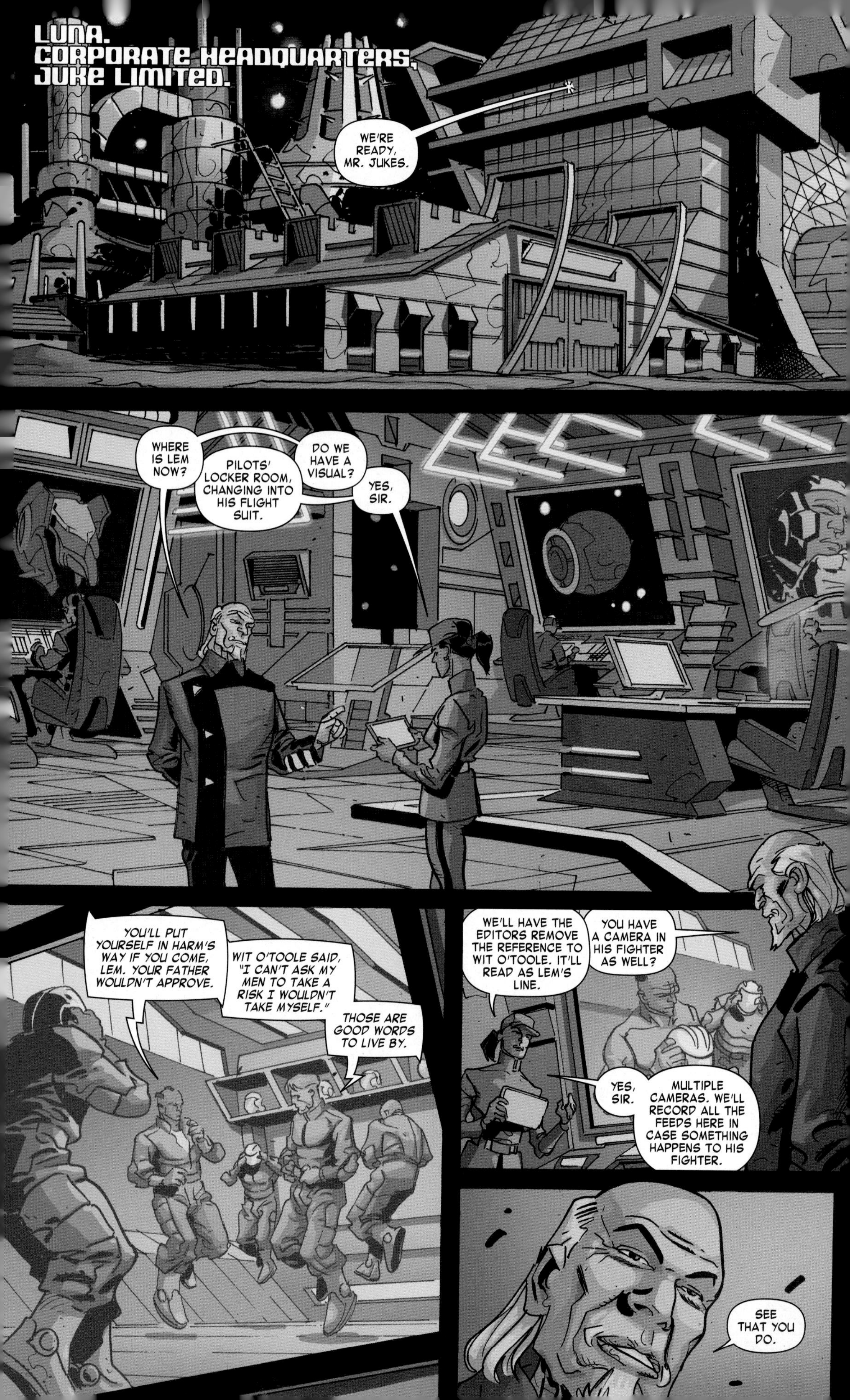
LUNA.
CORPORATE HEADQUARTERS, JUKE LIMITED.
WE'RE READY, MR. JUKES.
WHERE IS LEM NOW?
PILOTS' LOCKER ROOM, CHANGING INTO HIS FLIGHT SUIT.
DO WE HAVE A VISUAL?
YES, SIR.
YOU'LL PUT YOURSELF IN HARM'S WAY IF YOU COME, LEM. YOUR FATHER WOULDN'T APPROVE.
WIT O'TOOLE SAID, "I CAN'T ASK MY MEN TO TAKE A RISK I WOULDN'T TAKE MYSELF."
THOSE ARE GOOD WORDS TO LIVE BY.
WE'LL HAVE THE EDITORS REMOVE THE REFERENCE TO WIT O'TOOLE. IT'LL READ AS LEM'S LINE.
YOU HAVE A CAMERA IN HIS FIGHTER AS WELL?
YES, SIR.
MULTIPLE CAMERAS. WE'LL RECORD ALL THE FEEDS HERE IN CASE SOMETHING HAPPENS TO HIS FIGHTER.
SEE THAT YOU DO.

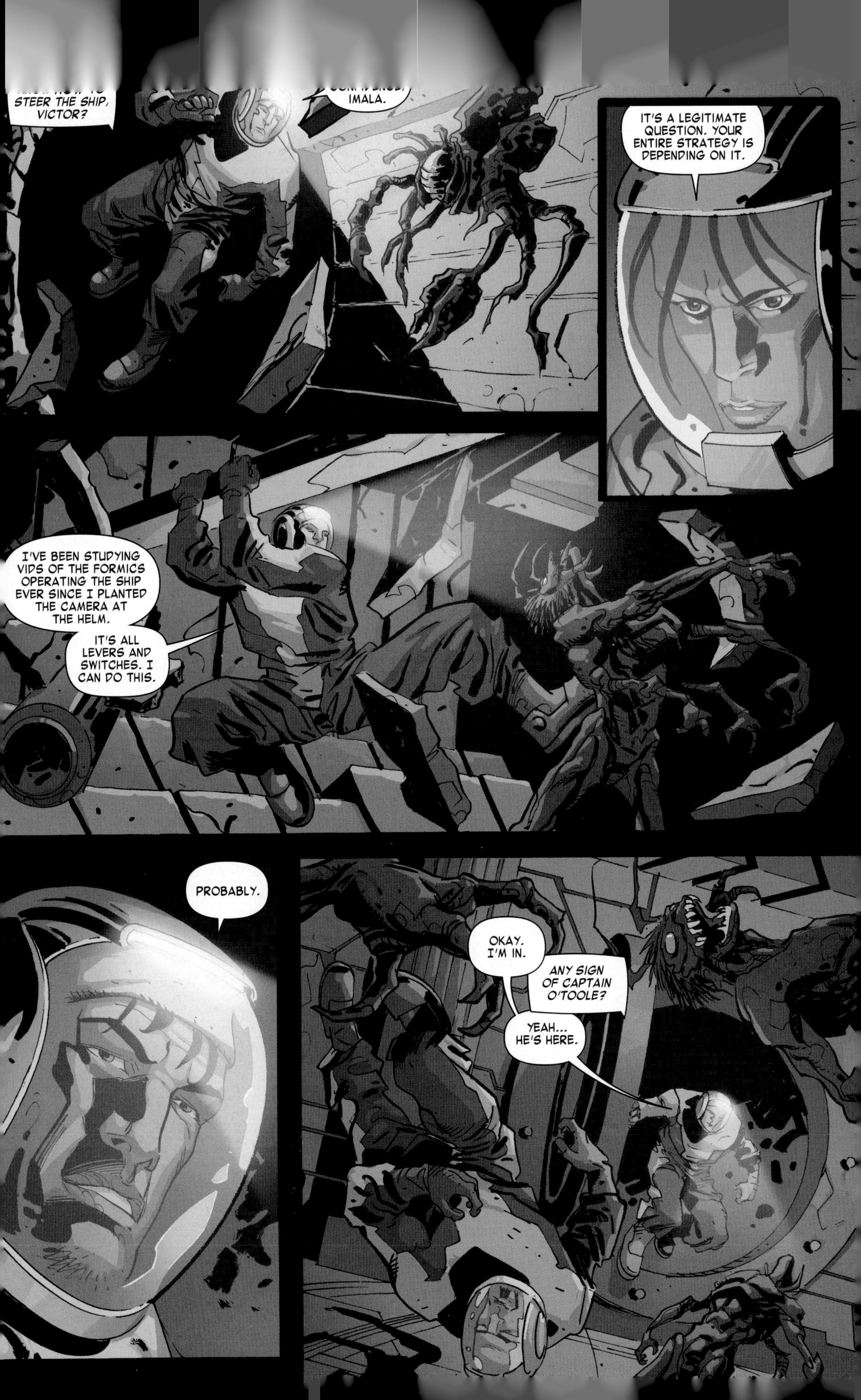
STEER THE SHIP, VICTOR?
IMALA.
IT'S A LEGITIMATE QUESTION. YOUR ENTIRE STRATEGY IS DEPENDING ON IT.
I'VE BEEN STUDYING VIDS OF THE FORMICS OPERATING THE SHIP EVER SINCE I PLANTED THE CAMERA AT THE HELM.
IT'S ALL LEVERS AND SWITCHES. I CAN DO THIS.
PROBABLY.
OKAY. I'M IN.
ANY SIGN OF CAPTAIN O'TOOLE?
YEAH... HE'S HERE.

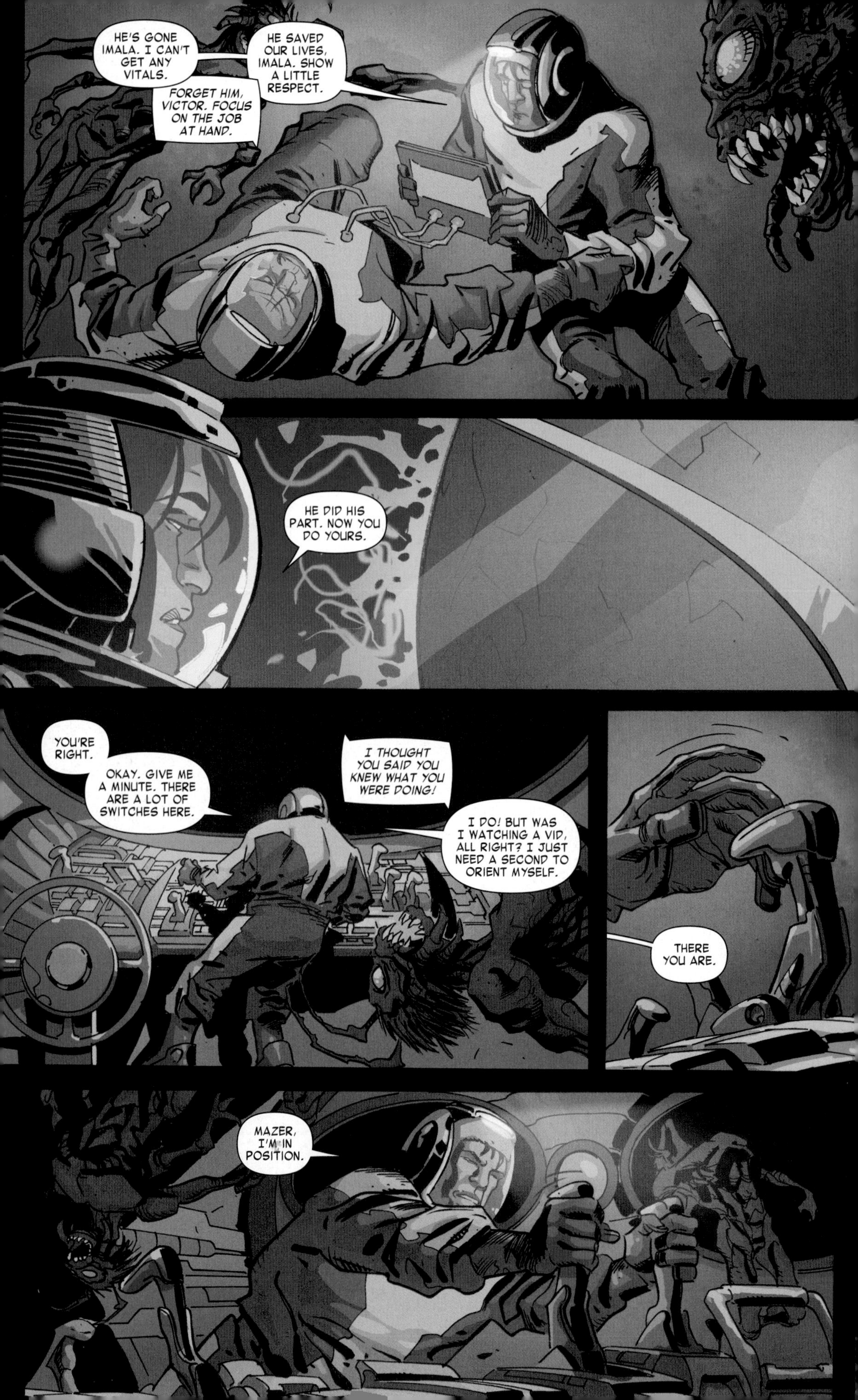
HE'S GONE IMALA. I CAN'T GET ANY VITALS.
HE SAVED OUR LIVES, IMALA. SHOW A LITTLE RESPECT.
FORGET HIM, VICTOR. FOCUS ON THE JOB AT HAND.
HE DID HIS PART. NOW YOU DO YOURS.
YOU'RE RIGHT.
OKAY. GIVE ME A MINUTE. THERE ARE A LOT OF SWITCHES HERE.
I THOUGHT YOU SAID YOU KNEW WHAT YOU WERE DOING!
I DO! BUT WAS I WATCHING A VID, ALL RIGHT? I JUST NEED A SECOND TO ORIENT MYSELF.
THERE YOU ARE.
MAZER, I'M IN POSITION.

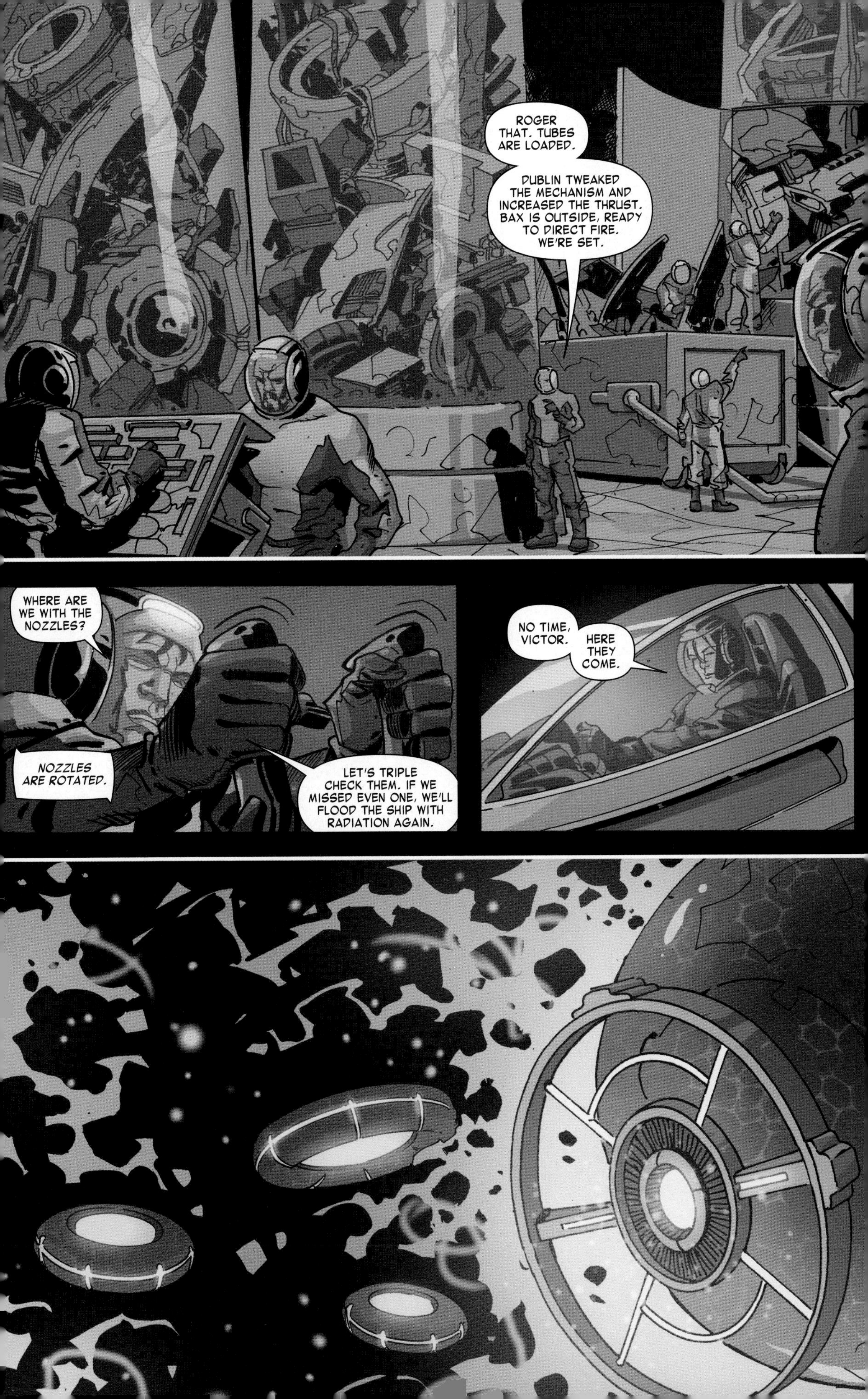
ROGER THAT. TUBES ARE LOADED.
DUBLIN TWEAKED THE MECHANISM AND INCREASED THE THRUST. BAX IS OUTSIDE, READY TO DIRECT FIRE. WE'RE SET.
WHERE ARE WE WITH THE NOZZLES?
NOZZLES ARE ROTATED.
LET'S TRIPLE CHECK THEM. IF WE MISSED EVEN ONE, WE'LL FLOOD THE SHIP WITH RADIATION AGAIN.
NO TIME, VICTOR.
HERE THEY COME.

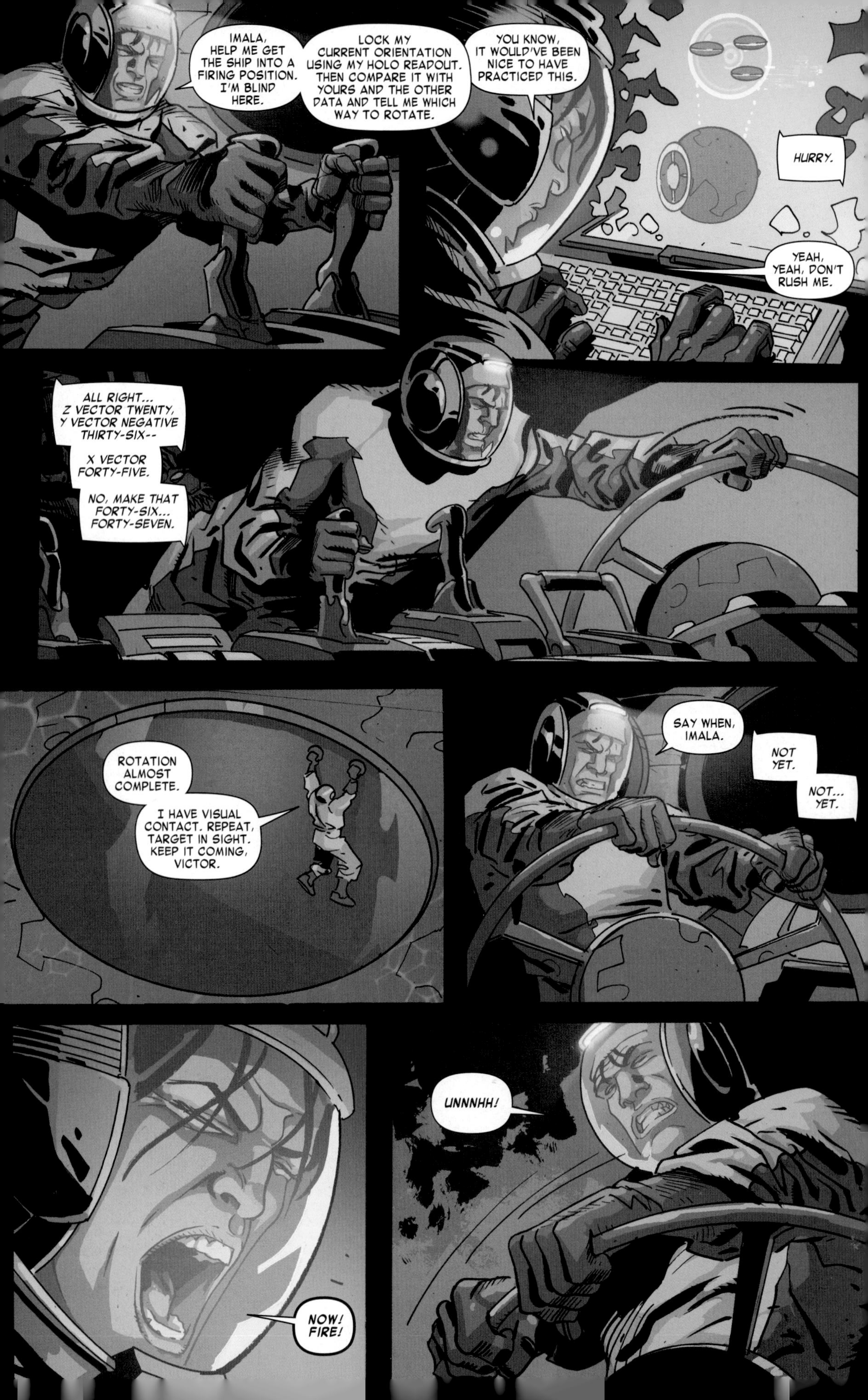
IMALA, HELP ME GET THE SHIP INTO A FIRING POSITION. I'M BLIND HERE.
LOCK MY CURRENT ORIENTATION USING MY HOLO READOUT. THEN COMPARE IT WITH YOURS AND THE OTHER DATA AND TELL ME WHICH WAY TO ROTATE.
YOU KNOW, IT WOULD'VE BEEN NICE TO HAVE PRACTICED THIS.
HURRY.
YEAH, YEAH, DON'T RUSH ME.
ALL RIGHT... Z VECTOR TWENTY, Y VECTOR NEGATIVE THIRTY-SIX--
X VECTOR FORTY-FIVE.
NO, MAKE THAT FORTY-SIX... FORTY-SEVEN.
ROTATION ALMOST COMPLETE.
I HAVE VISUAL CONTACT. REPEAT, TARGET IN SIGHT. KEEP IT COMING, VICTOR.
SAY WHEN, IMALA.
NOT YET.
NOT... YET.
NOW! FIRE!
UNNNHH!

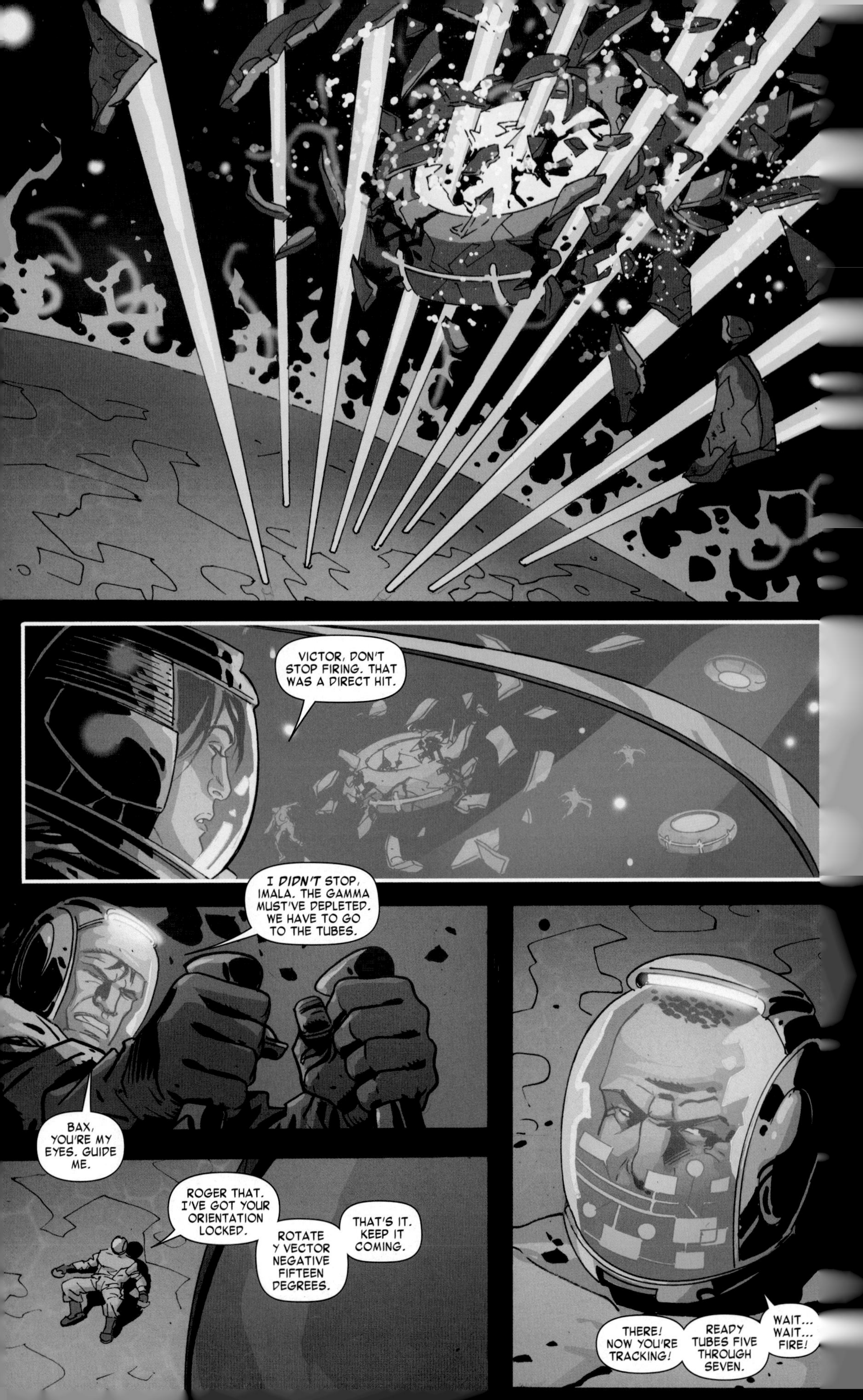
VICTOR, DON'T STOP FIRING. THAT WAS A DIRECT HIT.
I *DIDN'T* STOP, IMALA. THE GAMMA MUST'VE DEPLETED. WE HAVE TO GO TO THE TUBES.
BAX, YOU'RE MY EYES. GUIDE ME.
ROGER THAT. I'VE GOT YOUR ORIENTATION LOCKED.
ROTATE Y VECTOR NEGATIVE FIFTEEN DEGREES.
THAT'S IT. KEEP IT COMING.
THERE! NOW YOU'RE TRACKING!
READY TUBES FIVE THROUGH SEVEN.
WAIT... WAIT... FIRE!

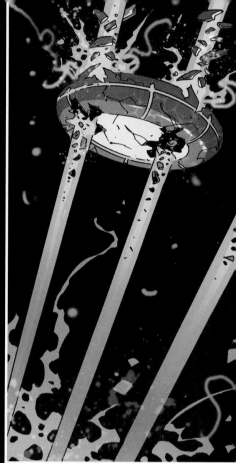

CONTACT! BREACHED HULL AND STRUCTURAL DAMAGE!

LANDER THREE IS ON APPROACH. STANDBY TUBES ONE AND TWO.

WAIT...IT'S OPENING UP!

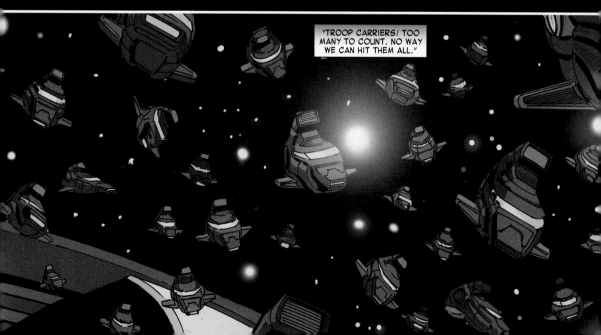

"TROOP CARRIERS! TOO MANY TO COUNT. NO WAY WE CAN HIT THEM ALL."

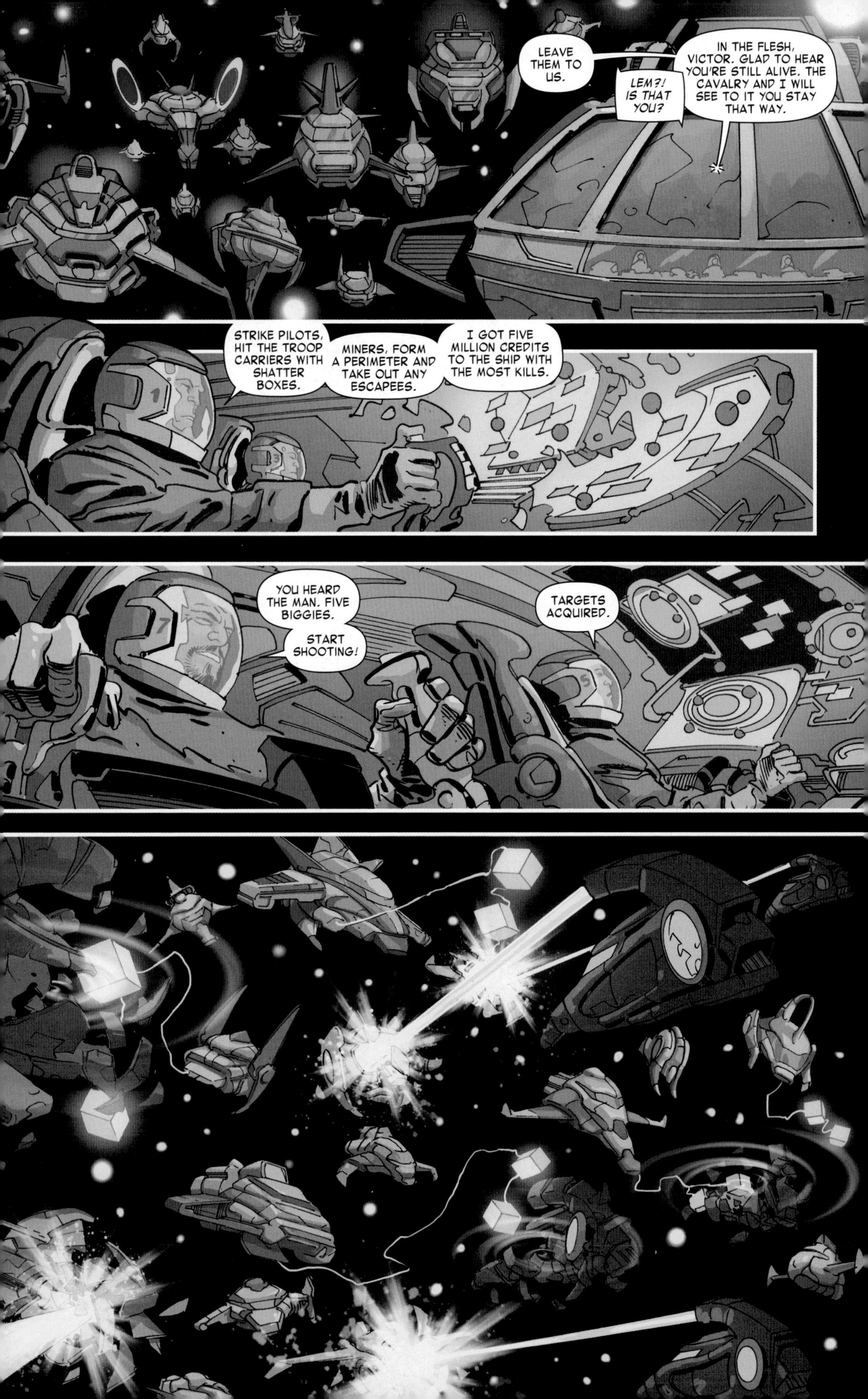
LEAVE THEM TO US.
LEM?! IS THAT YOU?
IN THE FLESH, VICTOR. GLAD TO HEAR YOU'RE STILL ALIVE. THE CAVALRY AND I WILL SEE TO IT YOU STAY THAT WAY.
STRIKE PILOTS, HIT THE TROOP CARRIERS WITH SHATTER BOXES.
MINERS, FORM A PERIMETER AND TAKE OUT ANY ESCAPEES.
I GOT FIVE MILLION CREDITS TO THE SHIP WITH THE MOST KILLS.
YOU HEARD THE MAN. FIVE BIGGIES.
START SHOOTING!
TARGETS ACQUIRED.

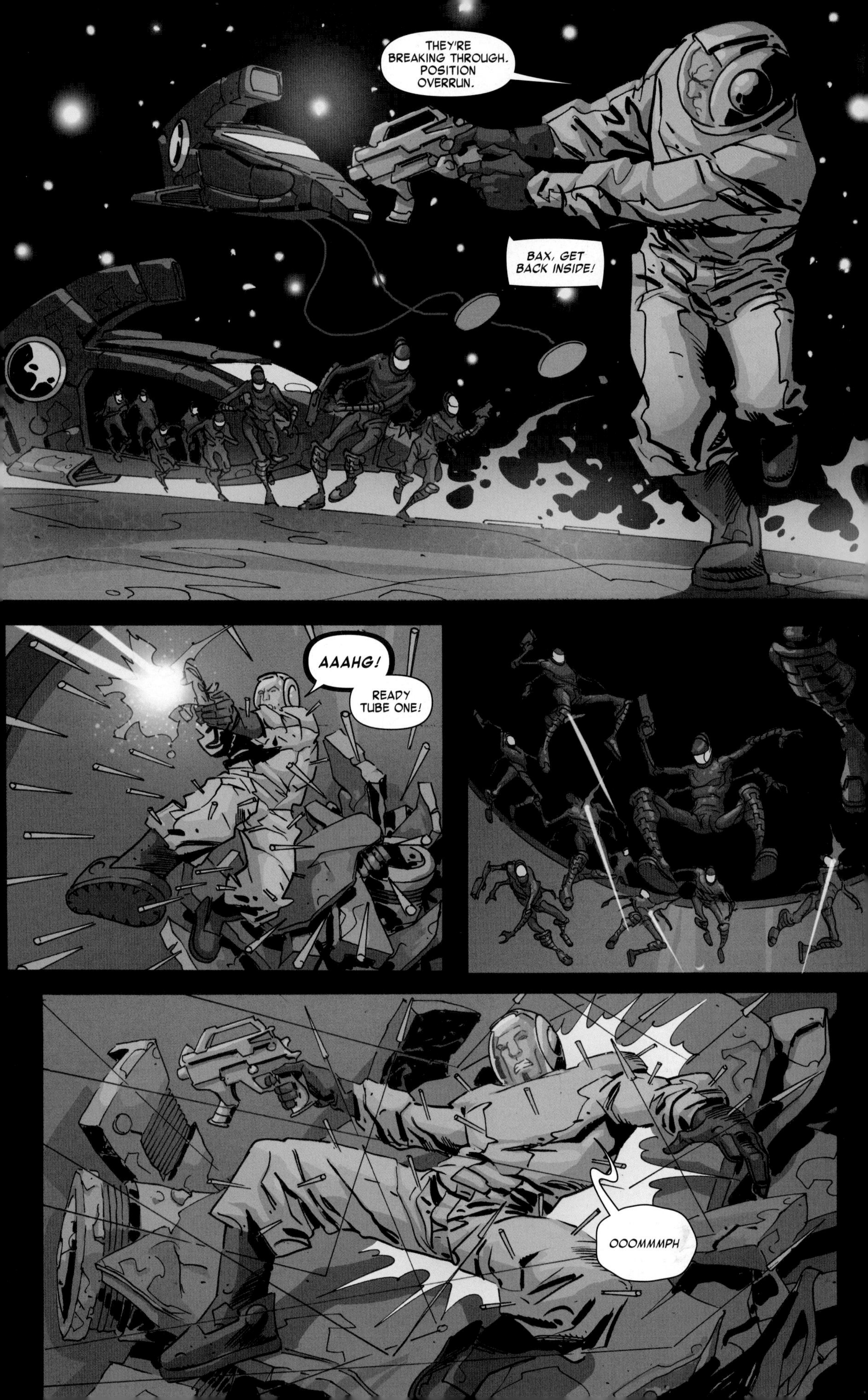
THEY'RE BREAKING THROUGH. POSITION OVERRUN.
BAX, GET BACK INSIDE!
AAAHG!
READY TUBE ONE!
OOOMMMPH

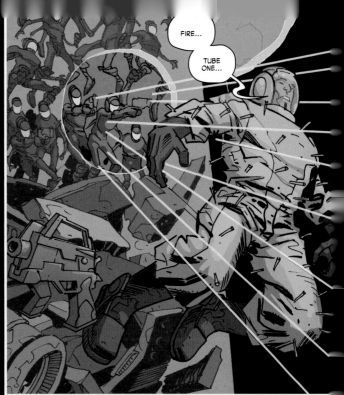

FIRE...

TUBE ONE...

HIS SUIT'S PUNCTURED. HE'S LOSING AIR.

AND BLEEDING.

DUBLIN, GIVE US A HAND HERE.

THE TUBES.

HSSSSSHSSSSSHSSSSS

FORGET THE TUBES FOR A SECOND! WE NEED TO--

OH.

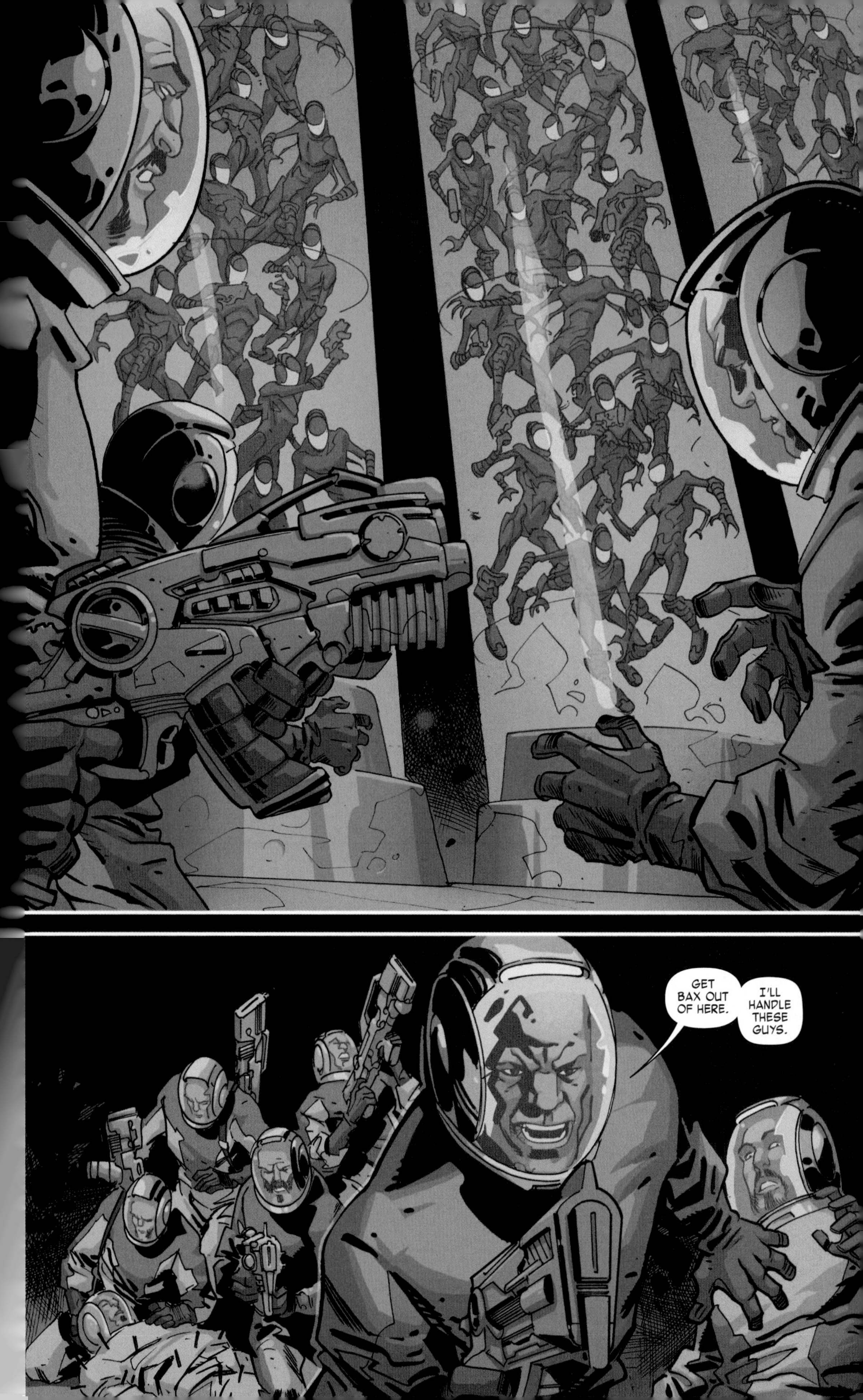
GET BAX OUT OF HERE.
I'LL HANDLE THESE GUYS.

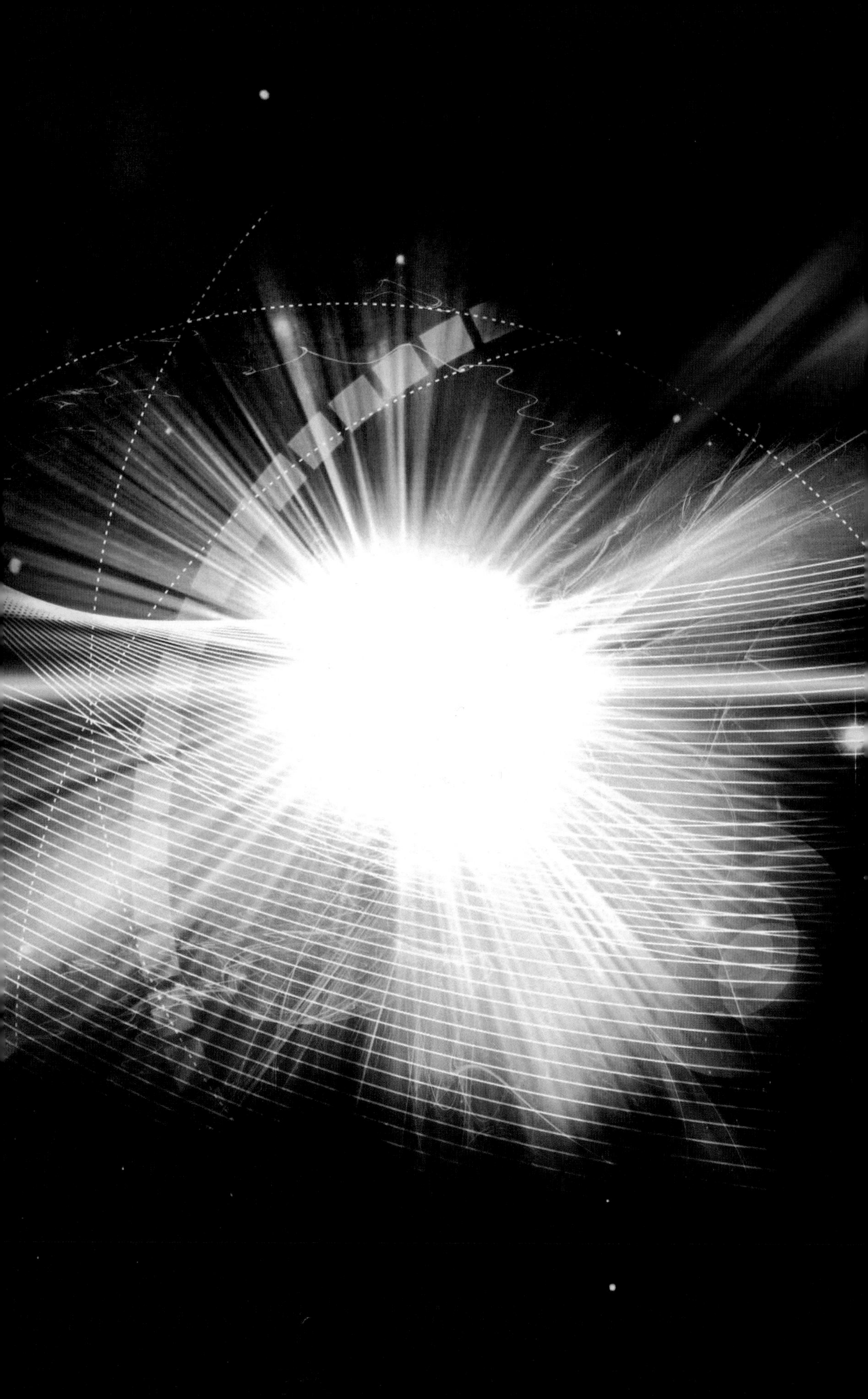

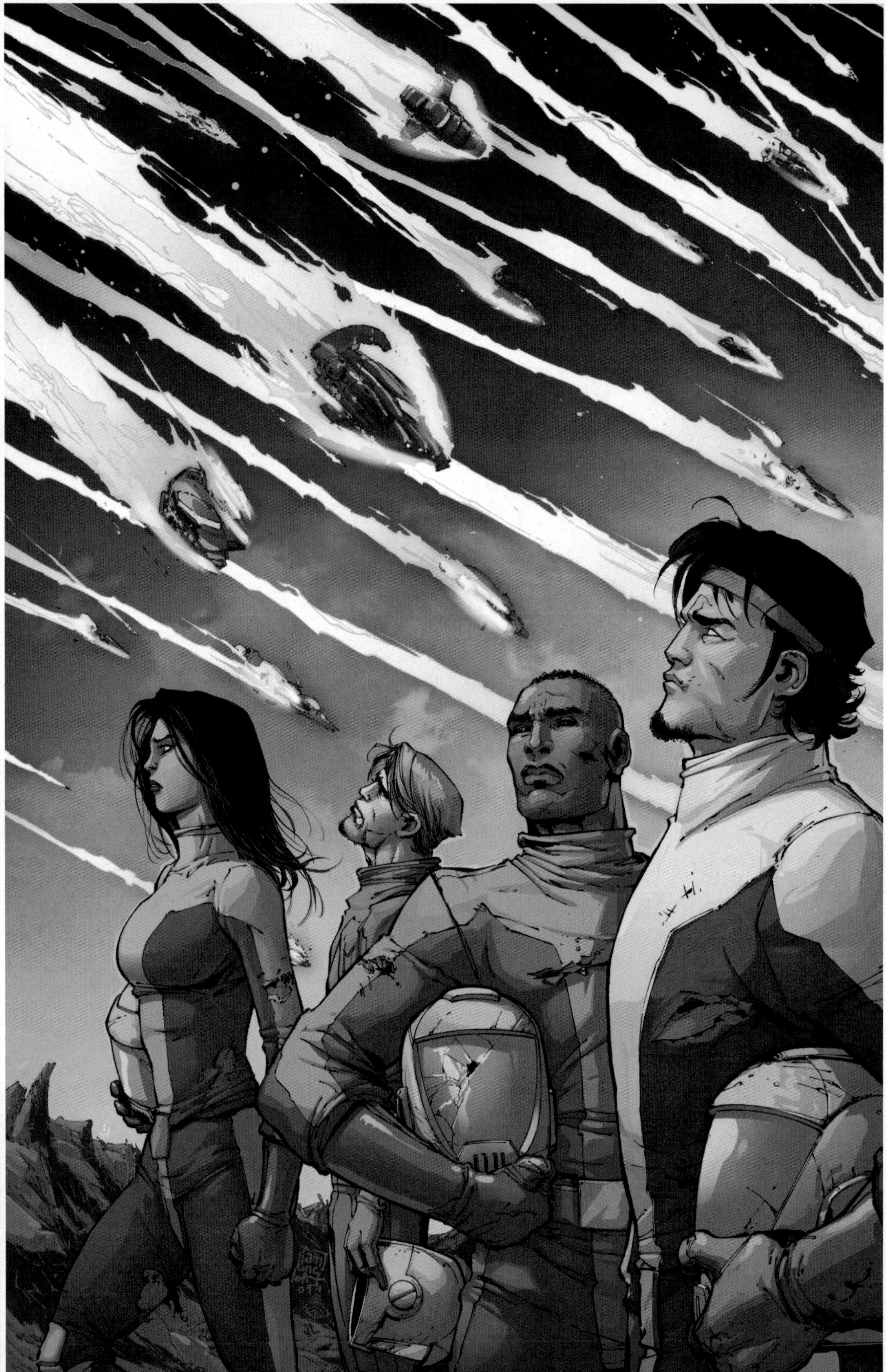

F I V E

Department of the Army
Army Special Operations Command
Fifth Special Forces Group
Second Battalion
Fort Campbell, Kentucky

Mr. and Mrs. Clinton O'Toole
PO BOX 6618
Chittenango, New York 13037

Dear Mr. and Mrs. O'Toole,
Please accept my deepest sympathy on the recent death of your son, Captain DeWitt Clinton O'Toole, who died in the service of his country and the human race while battling the Formics aboard their ship.

Your son, as a member of the Mobile Operations Police, was no longer under my command at the time of his death, but his impact on me and on those of his unit with whom he served while a member of the U.S. Special Forces was profound and enduring. I have never met a more exemplary soldier and servant of freedom.

News of your son's death came as a shock to us all, but we were not surprised to learn that he gave his life to save his fellow soldiers. Wit was always the first to rush to anyone's aid. Many of his operations while under my command are still classified, but suffice it to say that I owe your son my life. If all parents instilled in their children such a love of country and duty and moral principles as you clearly instilled in Wit, I suspect that no alien army, however great, could ever take us.

Sincerely,
Patrick Caneer
Lieutenant Colonel
U.S. Special Forces

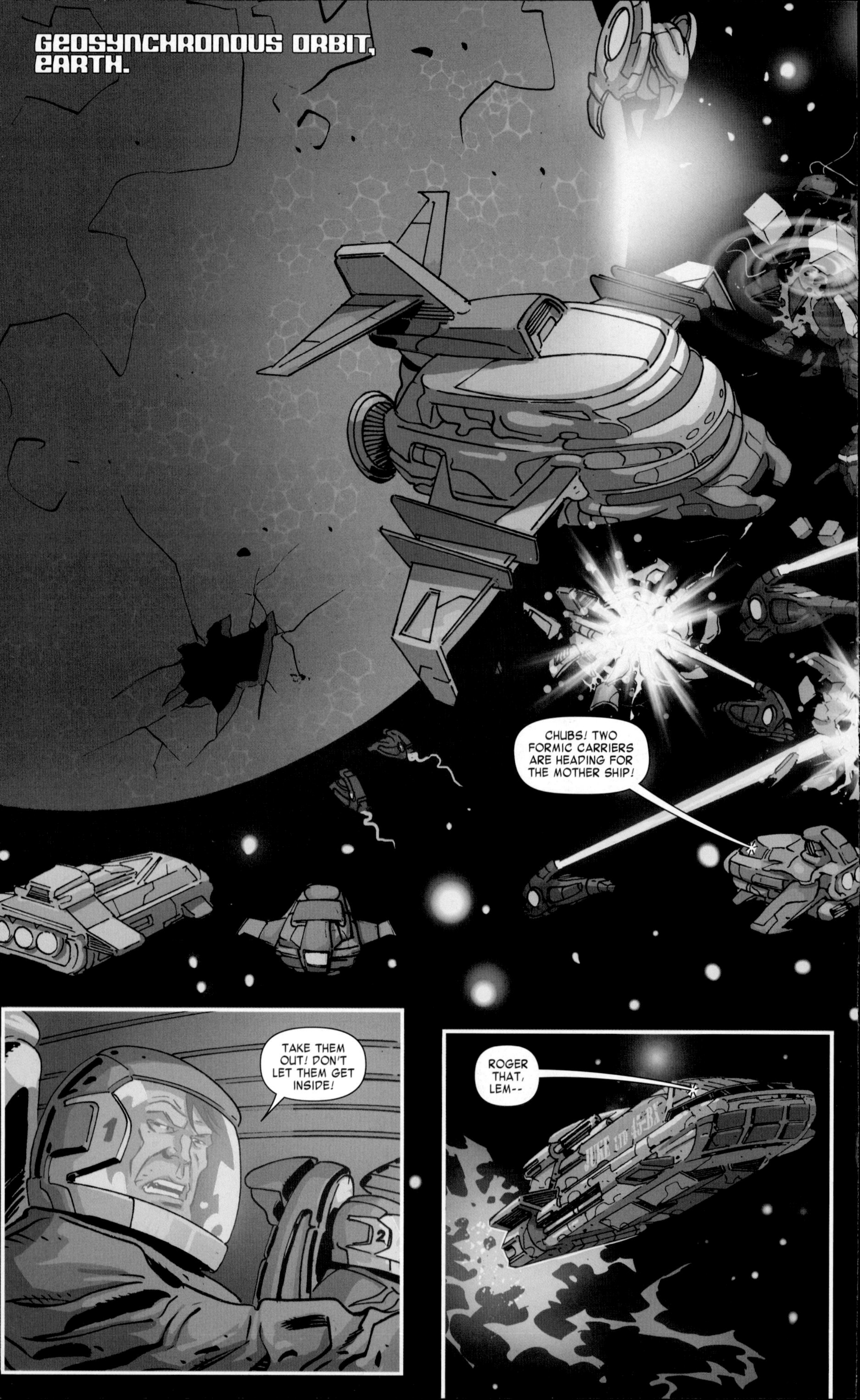
GEOSYNCHRONOUS ORBIT, EARTH.
CHUBS! TWO FORMIC CARRIERS ARE HEADING FOR THE MOTHER SHIP!
TAKE THEM OUT! DON'T LET THEM GET INSIDE!
ROGER THAT, LEM--

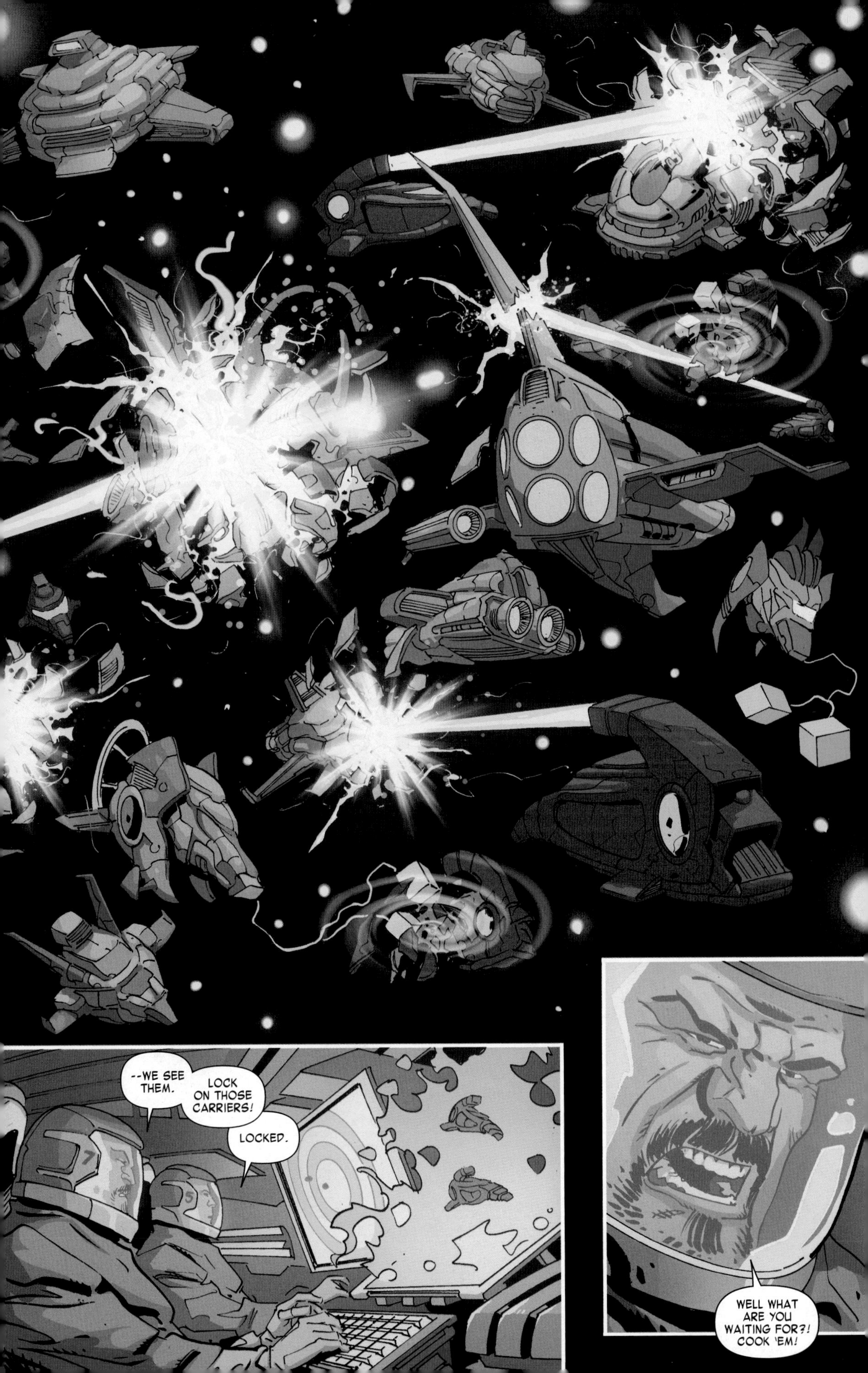
--WE SEE THEM.
LOCK ON THOSE CARRIERS!
LOCKED.
WELL WHAT ARE YOU WAITING FOR?! COOK 'EM!

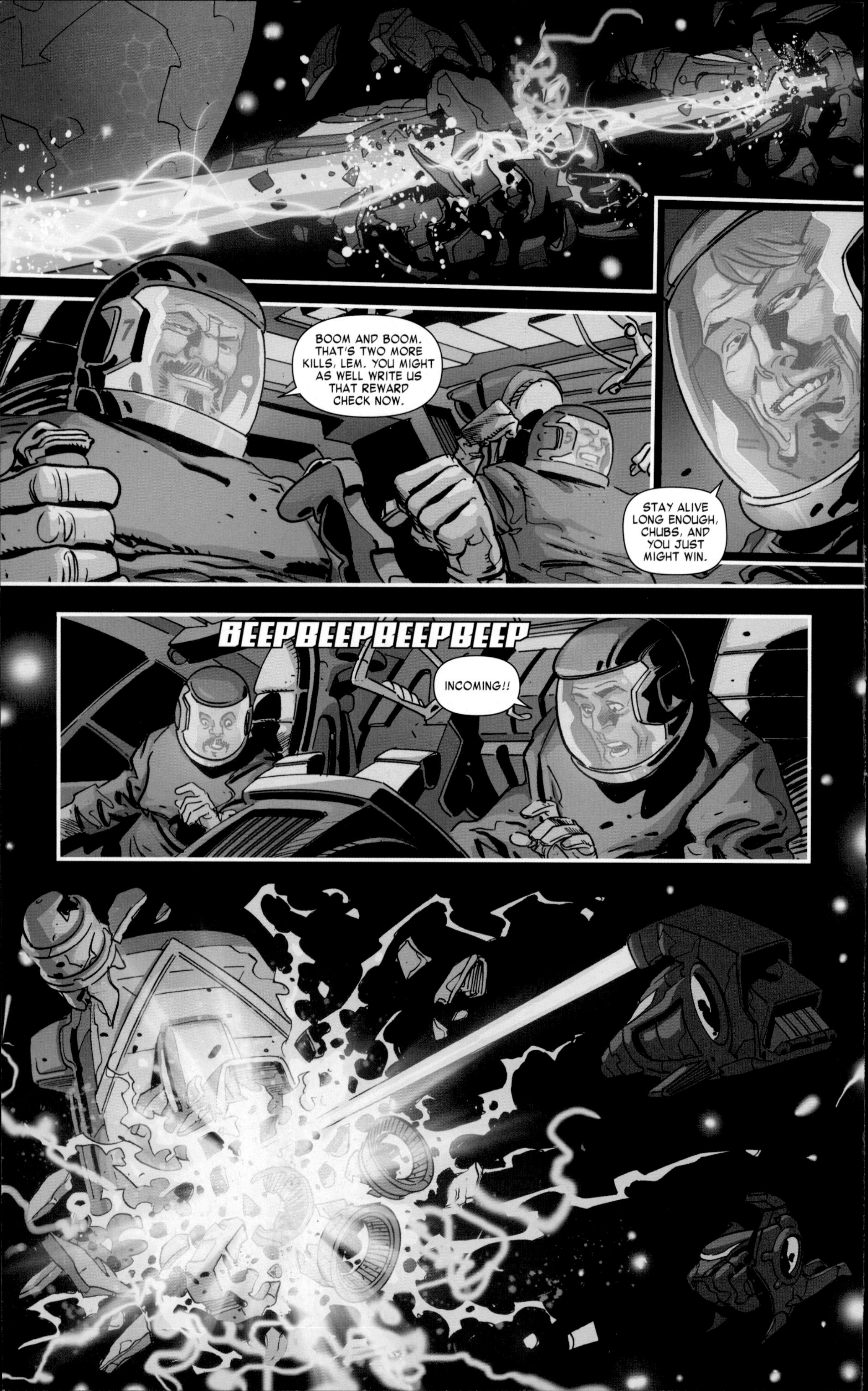
BOOM AND BOOM. THAT'S TWO MORE KILLS, LEM. YOU MIGHT AS WELL WRITE US THAT REWARD CHECK NOW.
STAY ALIVE LONG ENOUGH, CHUBS, AND YOU JUST MIGHT WIN.
BEEPBEEPBEEPBEEP
INCOMING!!

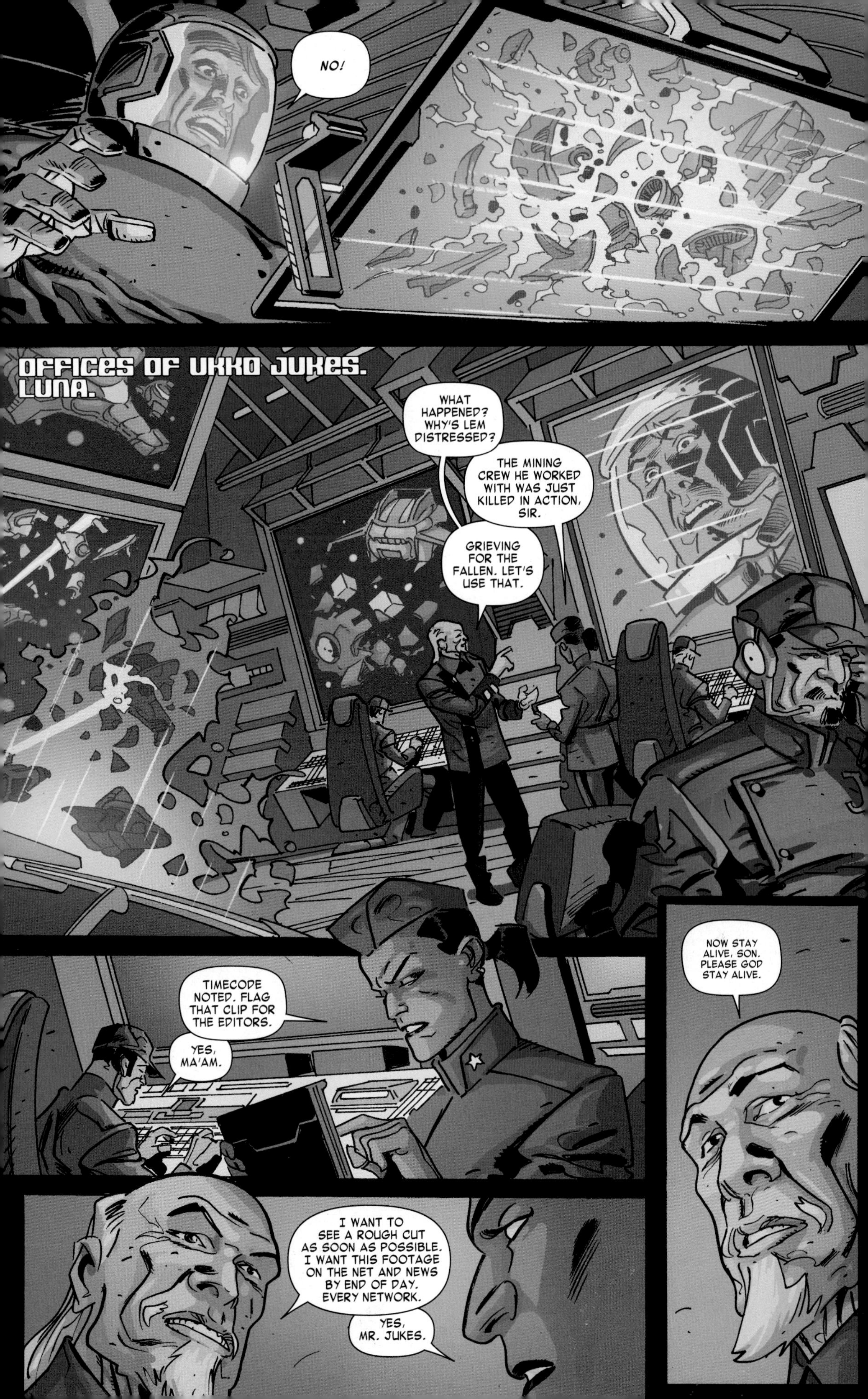
NO!
OFFICES OF UKKO JUKES. LUNA.
WHAT HAPPENED? WHY'S LEM DISTRESSED?
THE MINING CREW HE WORKED WITH WAS JUST KILLED IN ACTION, SIR.
GRIEVING FOR THE FALLEN. LET'S USE THAT.
TIMECODE NOTED. FLAG THAT CLIP FOR THE EDITORS.
YES, MA'AM.
NOW STAY ALIVE, SON. PLEASE GOD STAY ALIVE.
I WANT TO SEE A ROUGH CUT AS SOON AS POSSIBLE. I WANT THIS FOOTAGE ON THE NET AND NEWS BY END OF DAY. EVERY NETWORK.
YES, MR. JUKES.

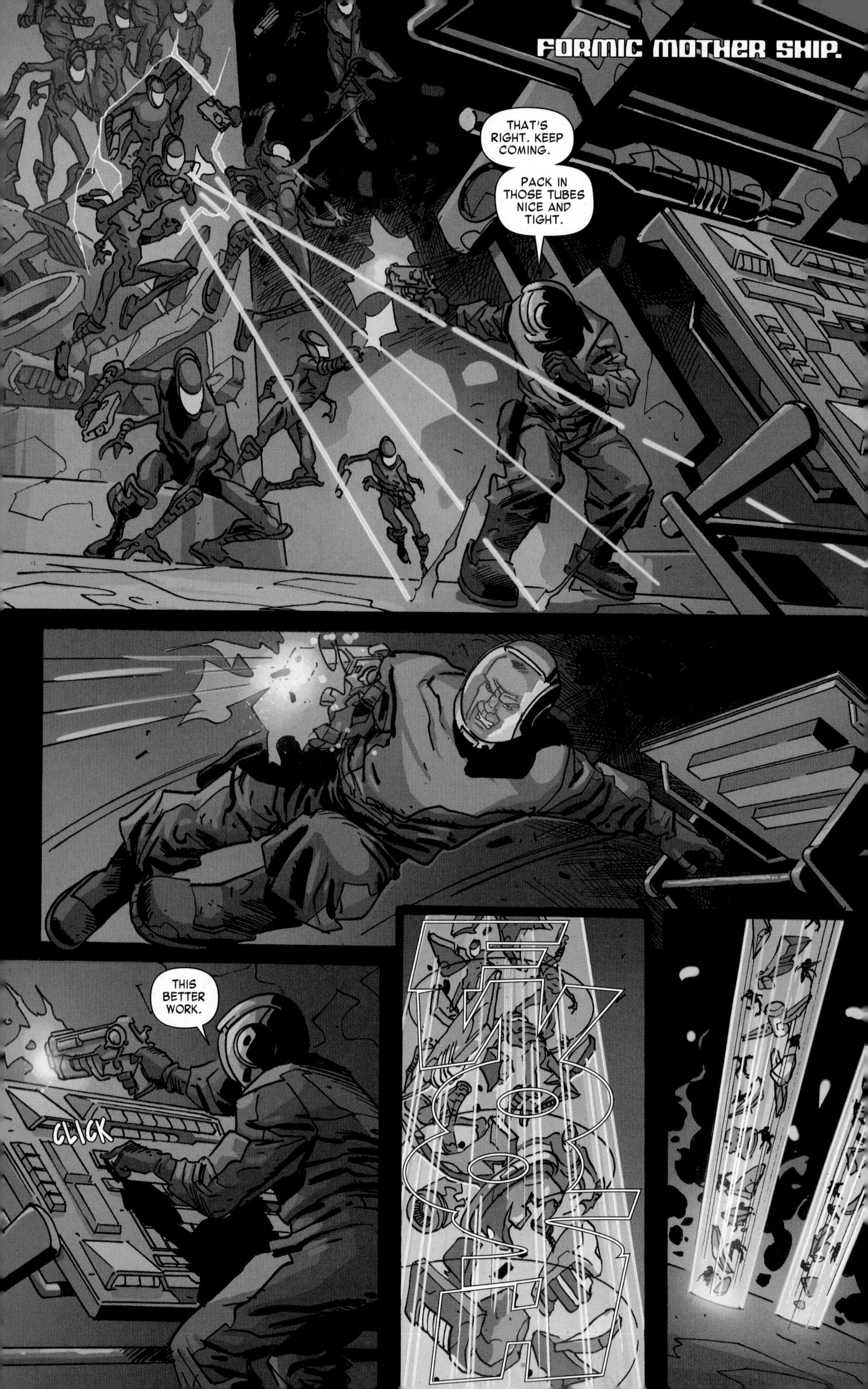
FORMIC MOTHER SHIP.
THAT'S RIGHT. KEEP COMING.
PACK IN THOSE TUBES NICE AND TIGHT.
THIS BETTER WORK.
CLICK

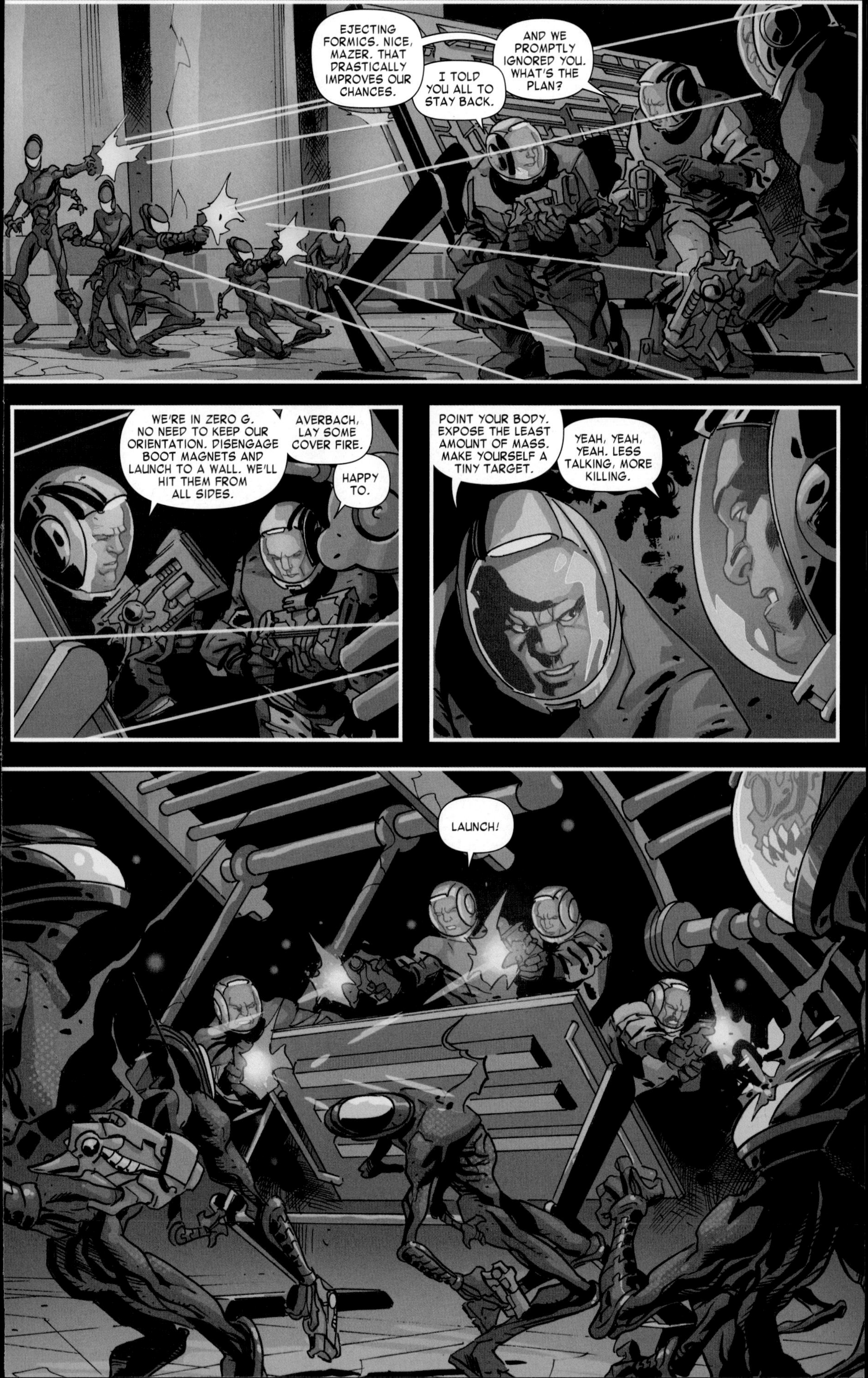
EJECTING FORMICS. NICE, MAZER. THAT DRASTICALLY IMPROVES OUR CHANCES.
I TOLD YOU ALL TO STAY BACK.
AND WE PROMPTLY IGNORED YOU. WHAT'S THE PLAN?
WE'RE IN ZERO G. NO NEED TO KEEP OUR ORIENTATION. DISENGAGE BOOT MAGNETS AND LAUNCH TO A WALL. WE'LL HIT THEM FROM ALL SIDES.
AVERBACH, LAY SOME COVER FIRE.
HAPPY TO.
POINT YOUR BODY. EXPOSE THE LEAST AMOUNT OF MASS. MAKE YOURSELF A TINY TARGET.
YEAH, YEAH, YEAH. LESS TALKING, MORE KILLING.
LAUNCH!

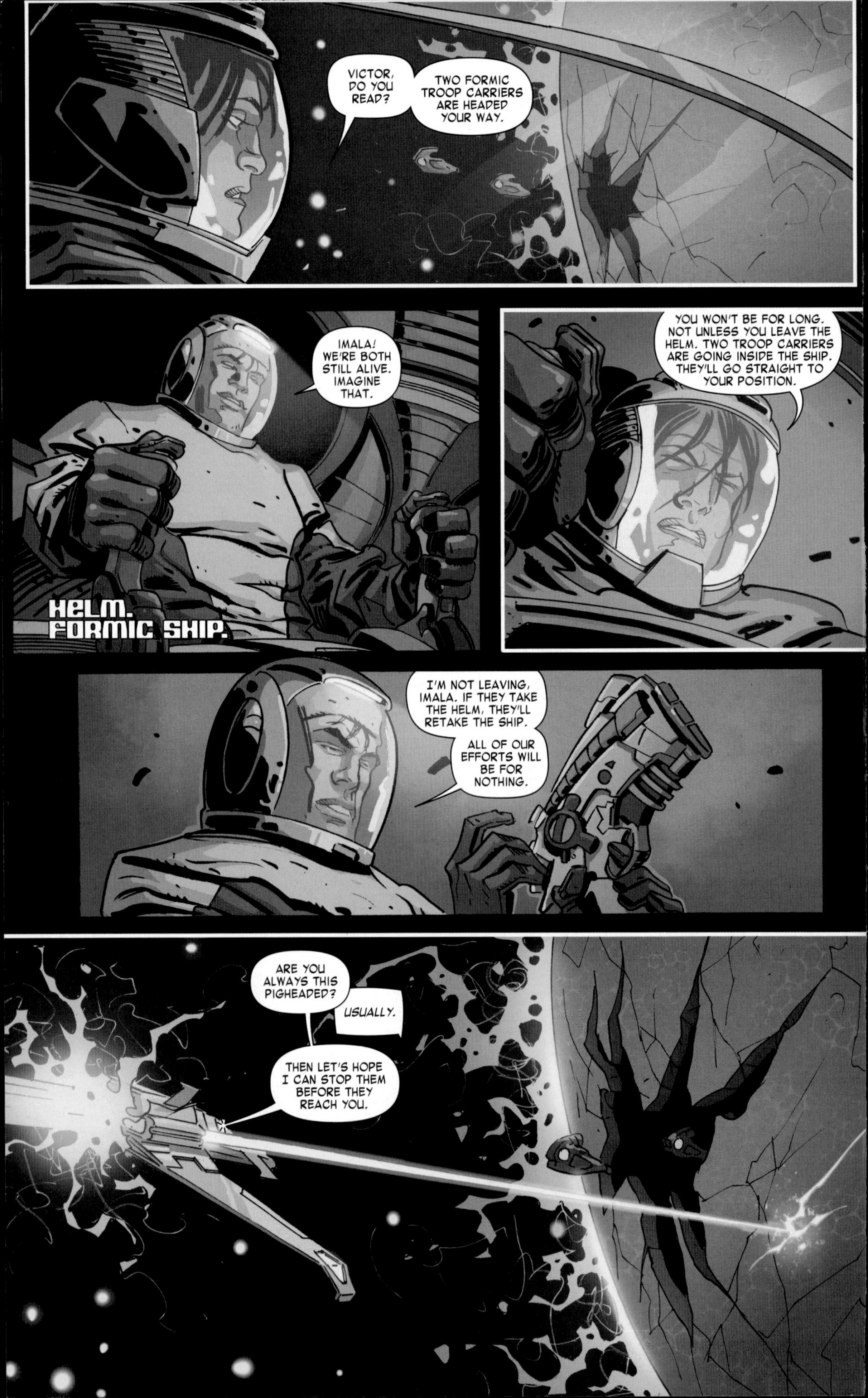
VICTOR, DO YOU READ?
TWO FORMIC TROOP CARRIERS ARE HEADED YOUR WAY.
IMALA! WE'RE BOTH STILL ALIVE. IMAGINE THAT.
HELM. FORMIC SHIP.
YOU WON'T BE FOR LONG. NOT UNLESS YOU LEAVE THE HELM. TWO TROOP CARRIERS ARE GOING INSIDE THE SHIP. THEY'LL GO STRAIGHT TO YOUR POSITION.
I'M NOT LEAVING, IMALA. IF THEY TAKE THE HELM, THEY'LL RETAKE THE SHIP.
ALL OF OUR EFFORTS WILL BE FOR NOTHING.
ARE YOU ALWAYS THIS PIGHEADED?
USUALLY.
THEN LET'S HOPE I CAN STOP THEM BEFORE THEY REACH YOU.

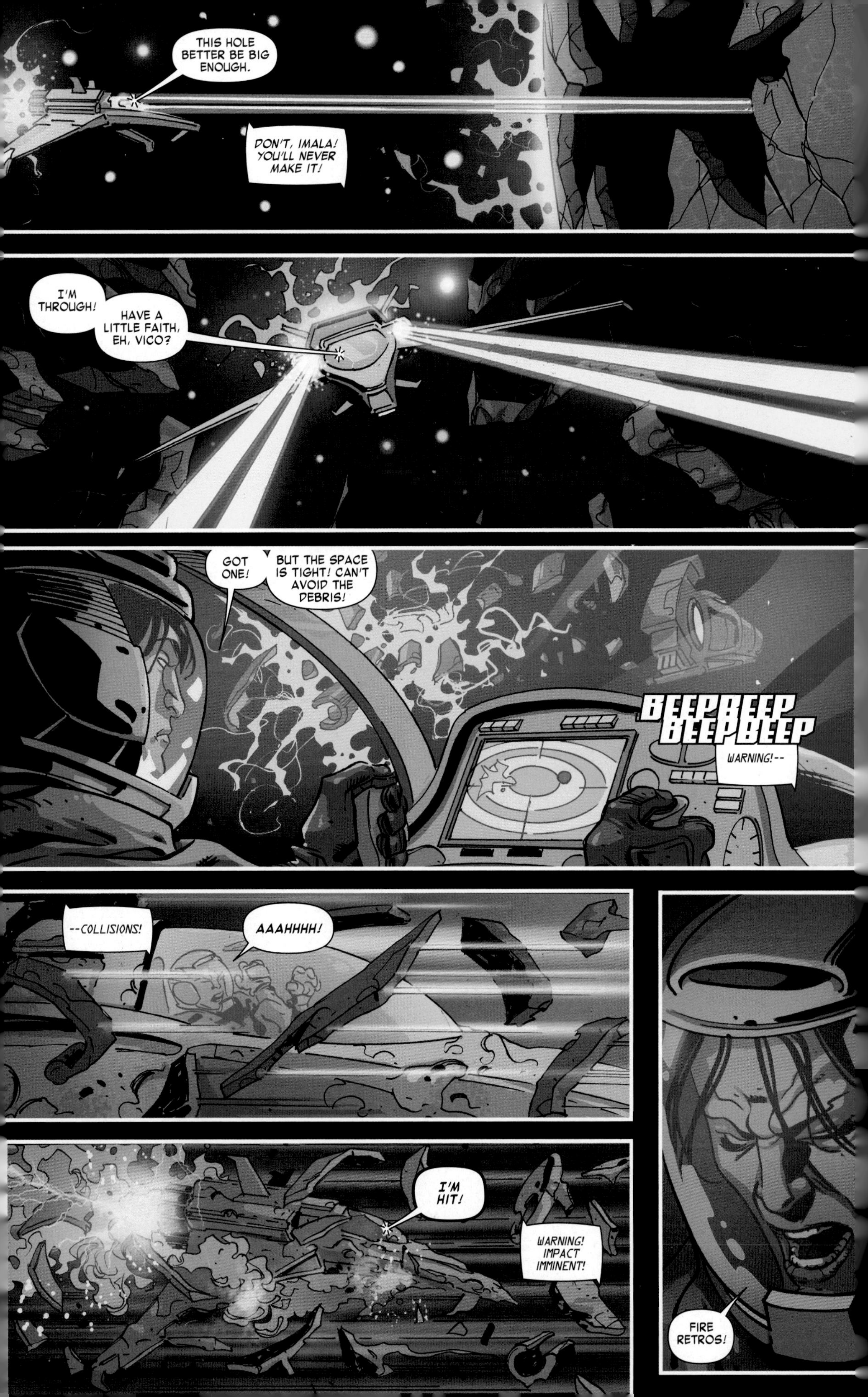

THIS HOLE BETTER BE BIG ENOUGH.
DON'T, IMALA! YOU'LL NEVER MAKE IT!
I'M THROUGH!
HAVE A LITTLE FAITH, EH, VICO?
GOT ONE!
BUT THE SPACE IS TIGHT! CAN'T AVOID THE DEBRIS!
BEEPBEEP BEEPBEEP
WARNING!--
--COLLISIONS!
AAAHHHH!
I'M HIT!
WARNING! IMPACT IMMINENT!
FIRE RETROS!

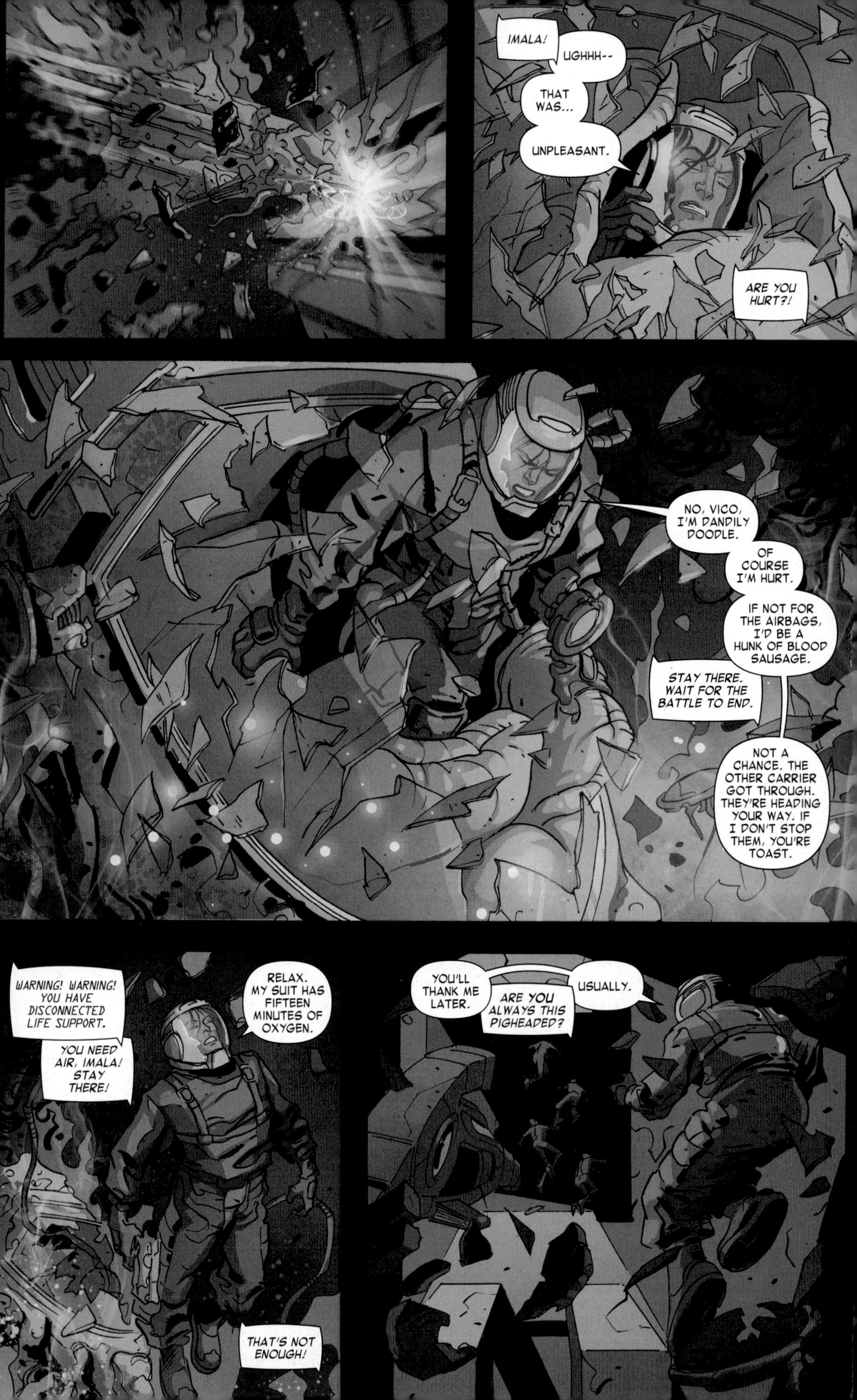
IMALA!
UGHHH--
THAT WAS...
UNPLEASANT.
ARE YOU HURT?!
NO, VICO, I'M DANDILY DOODLE.
OF COURSE I'M HURT.
IF NOT FOR THE AIRBAGS, I'D BE A HUNK OF BLOOD SAUSAGE.
STAY THERE. WAIT FOR THE BATTLE TO END.
NOT A CHANCE. THE OTHER CARRIER GOT THROUGH. THEY'RE HEADING YOUR WAY. IF I DON'T STOP THEM, YOU'RE TOAST.
WARNING! WARNING! YOU HAVE DISCONNECTED LIFE SUPPORT.
YOU NEED AIR, IMALA! STAY THERE!
RELAX. MY SUIT HAS FIFTEEN MINUTES OF OXYGEN.
THAT'S NOT ENOUGH!
YOU'LL THANK ME LATER.
ARE YOU ALWAYS THIS PIGHEADED?
USUALLY.

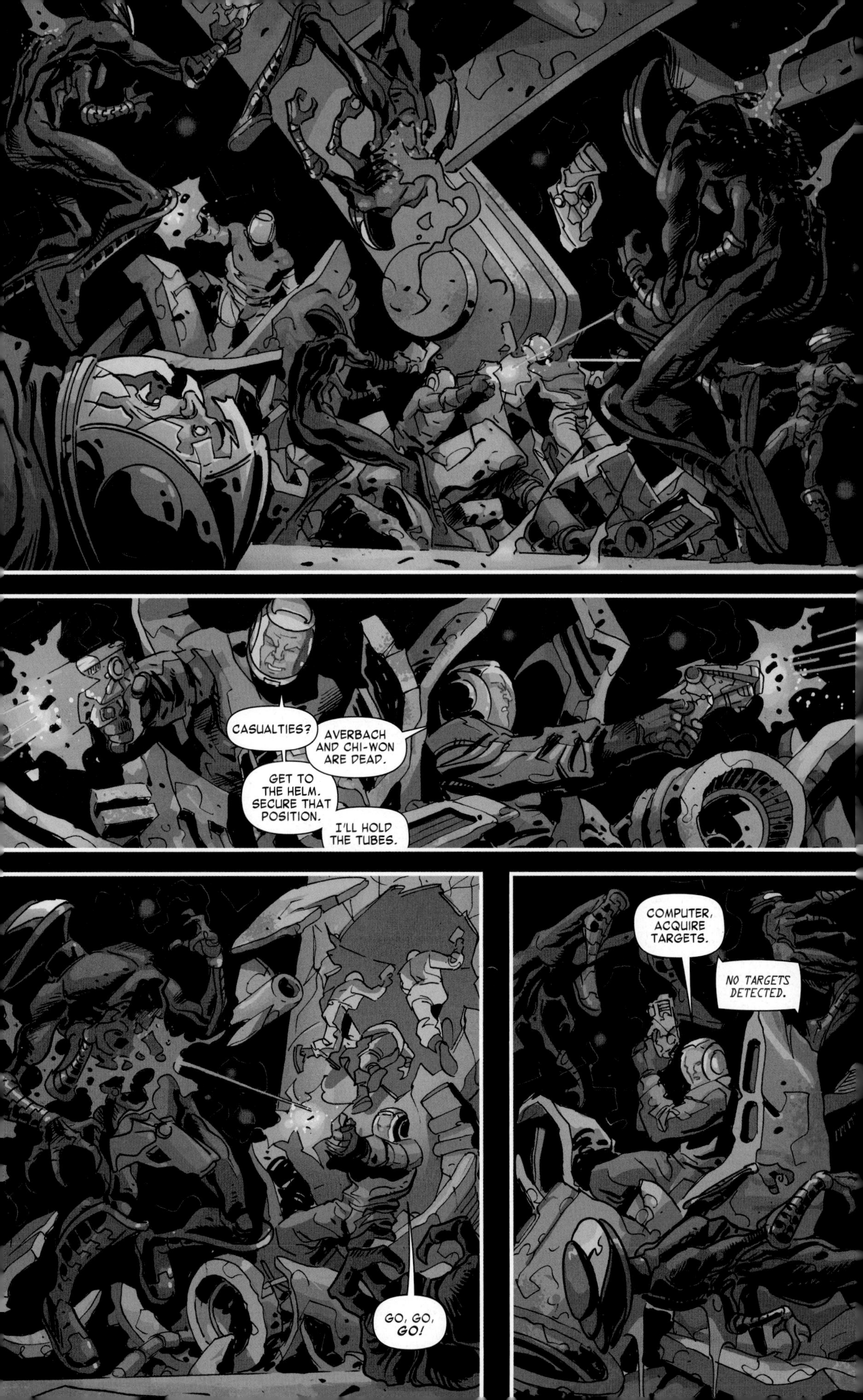
CASUALTIES?
AVERBACH AND CHI-WON ARE DEAD.
GET TO THE HELM. SECURE THAT POSITION.
I'LL HOLD THE TUBES.
GO, GO, GO!
COMPUTER, ACQUIRE TARGETS.
NO TARGETS DETECTED.

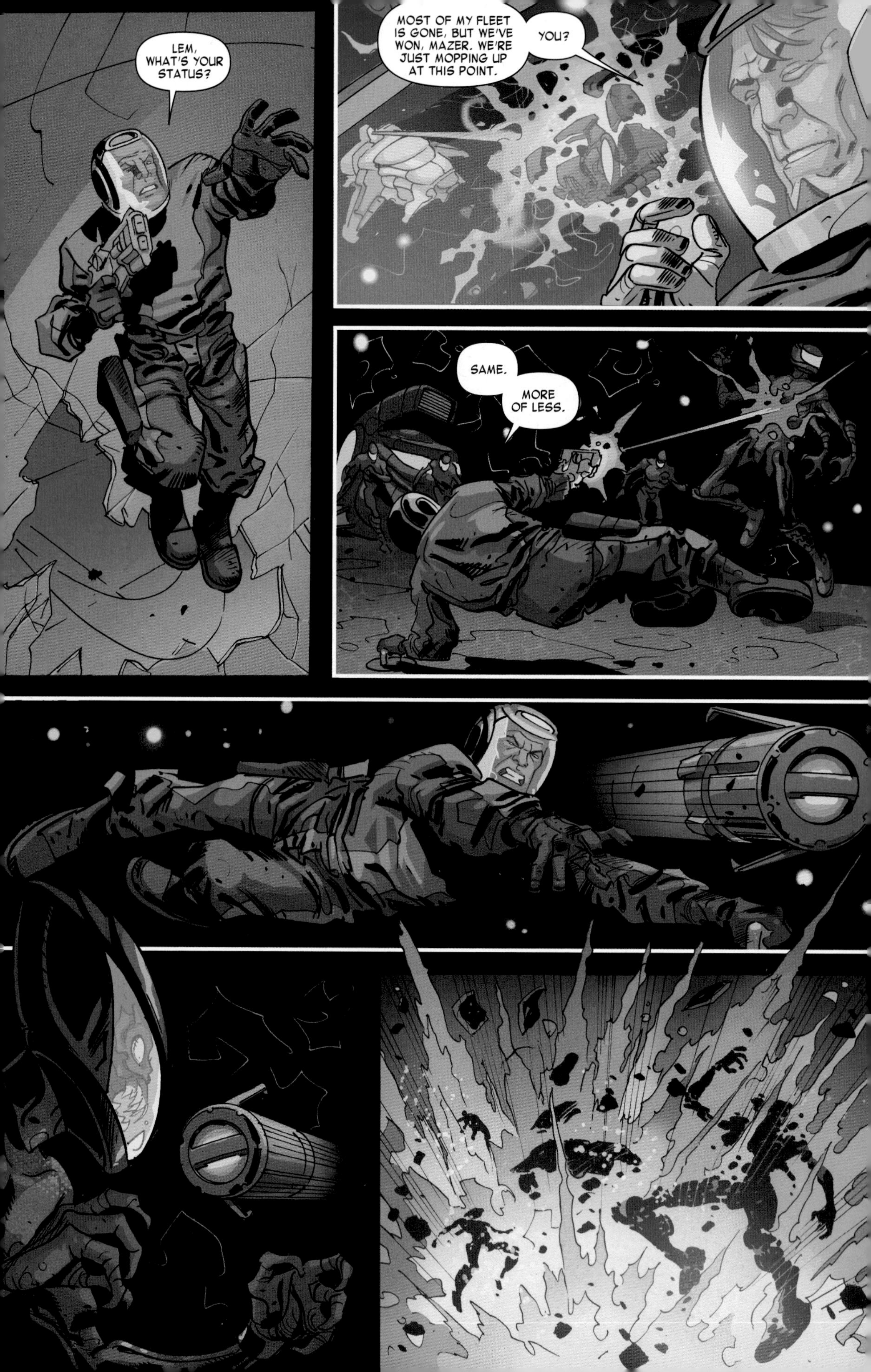
LEM, WHAT'S YOUR STATUS?
MOST OF MY FLEET IS GONE, BUT WE'VE WON, MAZER. WE'RE JUST MOPPING UP AT THIS POINT.
YOU?
SAME.
MORE OF LESS.

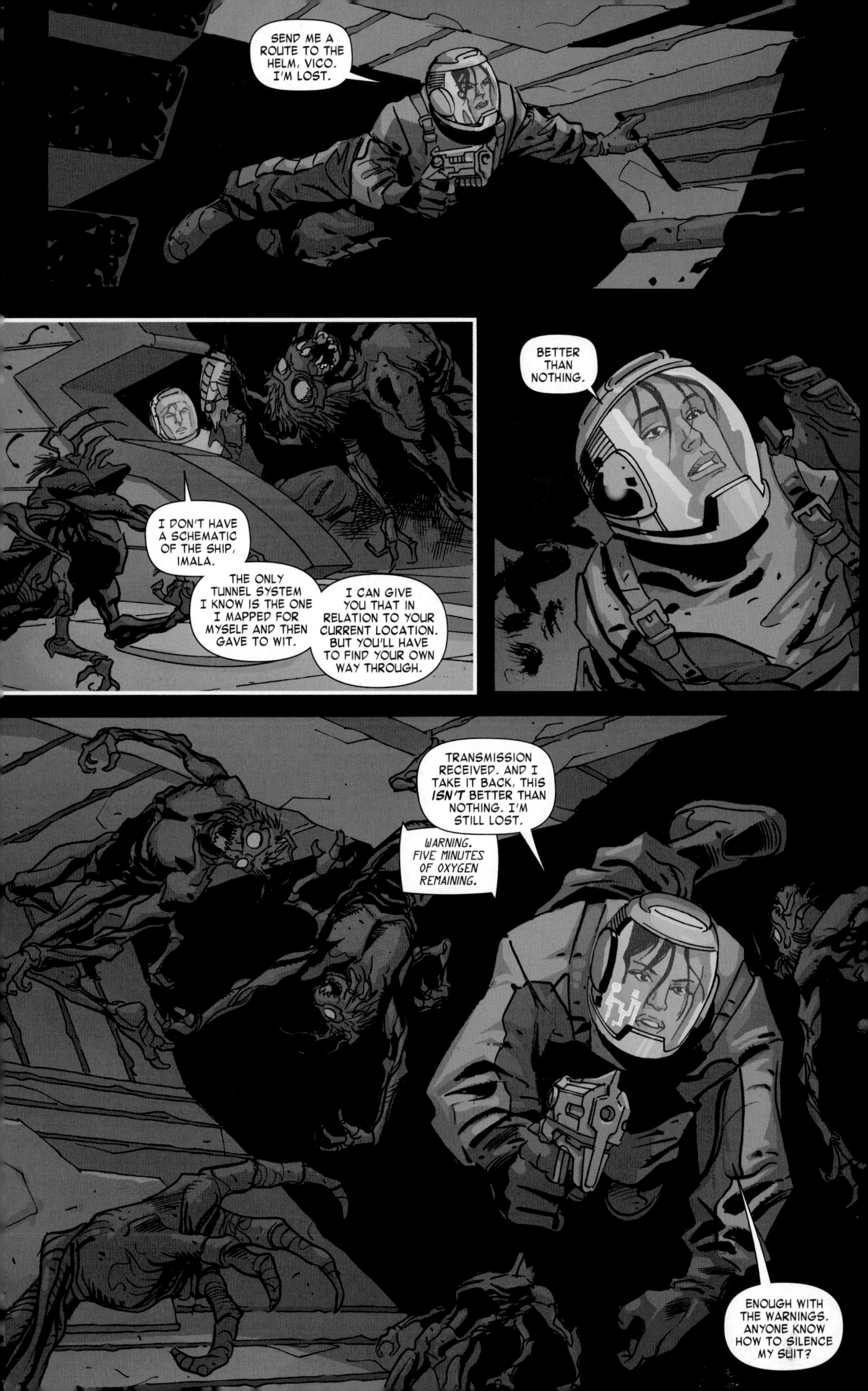
SEND ME A ROUTE TO THE HELM, VICO. I'M LOST.
I DON'T HAVE A SCHEMATIC OF THE SHIP, IMALA.
THE ONLY TUNNEL SYSTEM I KNOW IS THE ONE I MAPPED FOR MYSELF AND THEN GAVE TO WIT.
I CAN GIVE YOU THAT IN RELATION TO YOUR CURRENT LOCATION. BUT YOU'LL HAVE TO FIND YOUR OWN WAY THROUGH.
BETTER THAN NOTHING.
TRANSMISSION RECEIVED. AND I TAKE IT BACK, THIS ISN'T BETTER THAN NOTHING. I'M STILL LOST.
WARNING. FIVE MINUTES OF OXYGEN REMAINING.
ENOUGH WITH THE WARNINGS. ANYONE KNOW HOW TO SILENCE MY SUIT?

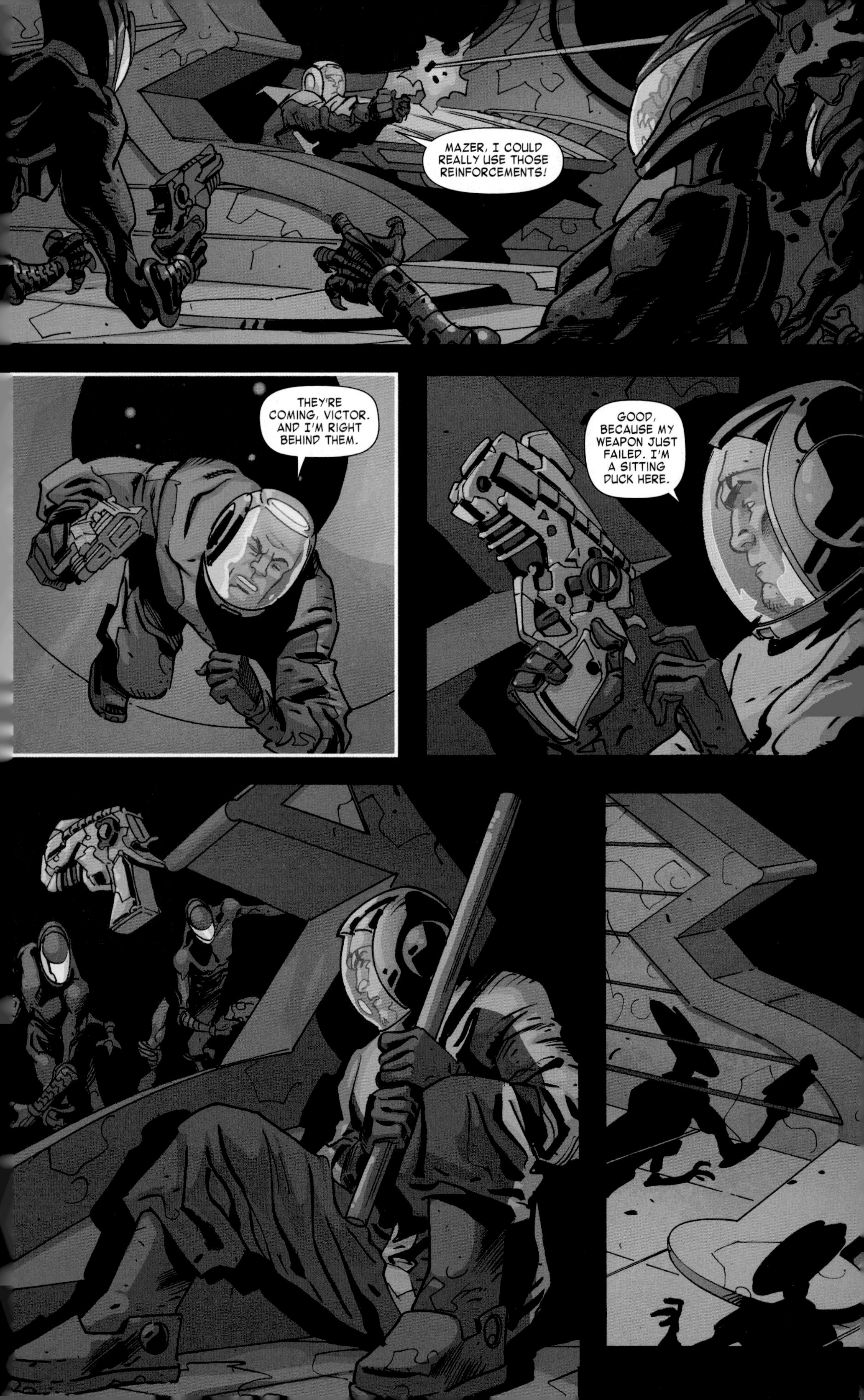
MAZER, I COULD REALLY USE THOSE REINFORCEMENTS!
THEY'RE COMING, VICTOR. AND I'M RIGHT BEHIND THEM.
GOOD, BECAUSE MY WEAPON JUST FAILED. I'M A SITTING DUCK HERE.

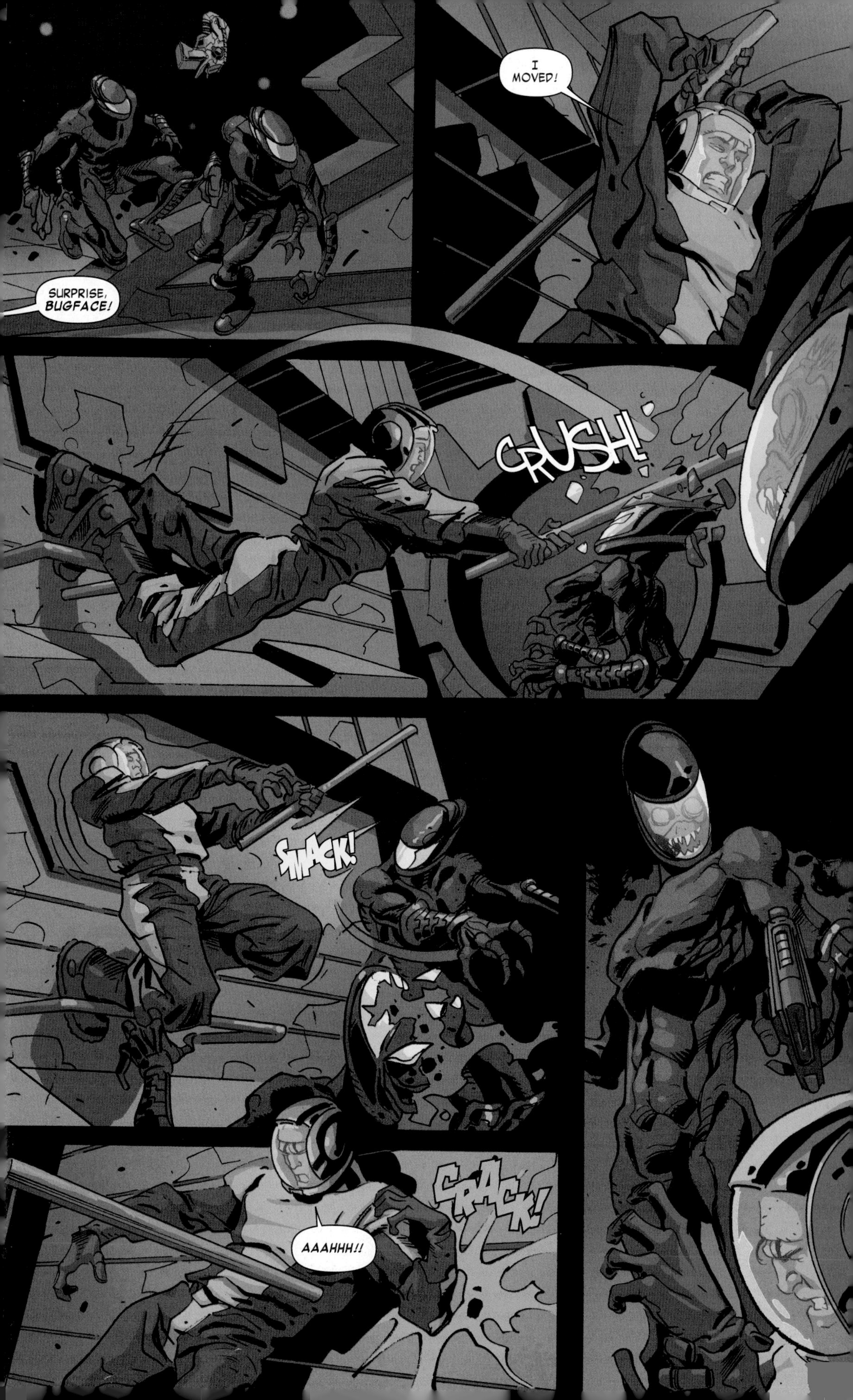
SURPRISE, BUGFACE!
I MOVED!
CRUSH!
SMACK!
CRACK!
AAAHHH!!

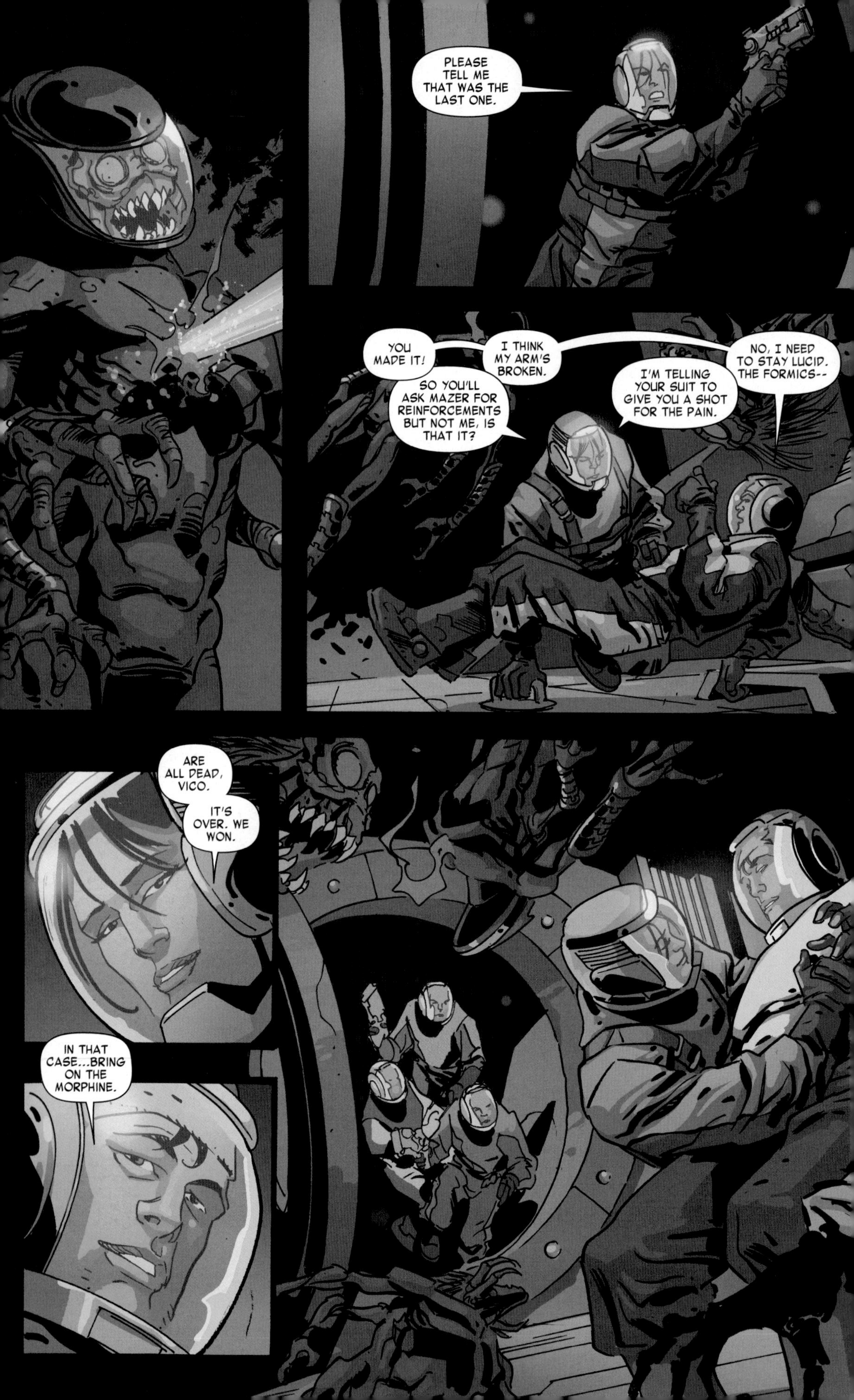
PLEASE TELL ME THAT WAS THE LAST ONE.
YOU MADE IT!
I THINK MY ARM'S BROKEN.
SO YOU'LL ASK MAZER FOR REINFORCEMENTS BUT NOT ME, IS THAT IT?
I'M TELLING YOUR SUIT TO GIVE YOU A SHOT FOR THE PAIN.
NO, I NEED TO STAY LUCID. THE FORMICS--
ARE ALL DEAD, VICO.
IT'S OVER. WE WON.
IN THAT CASE...BRING ON THE MORPHINE.

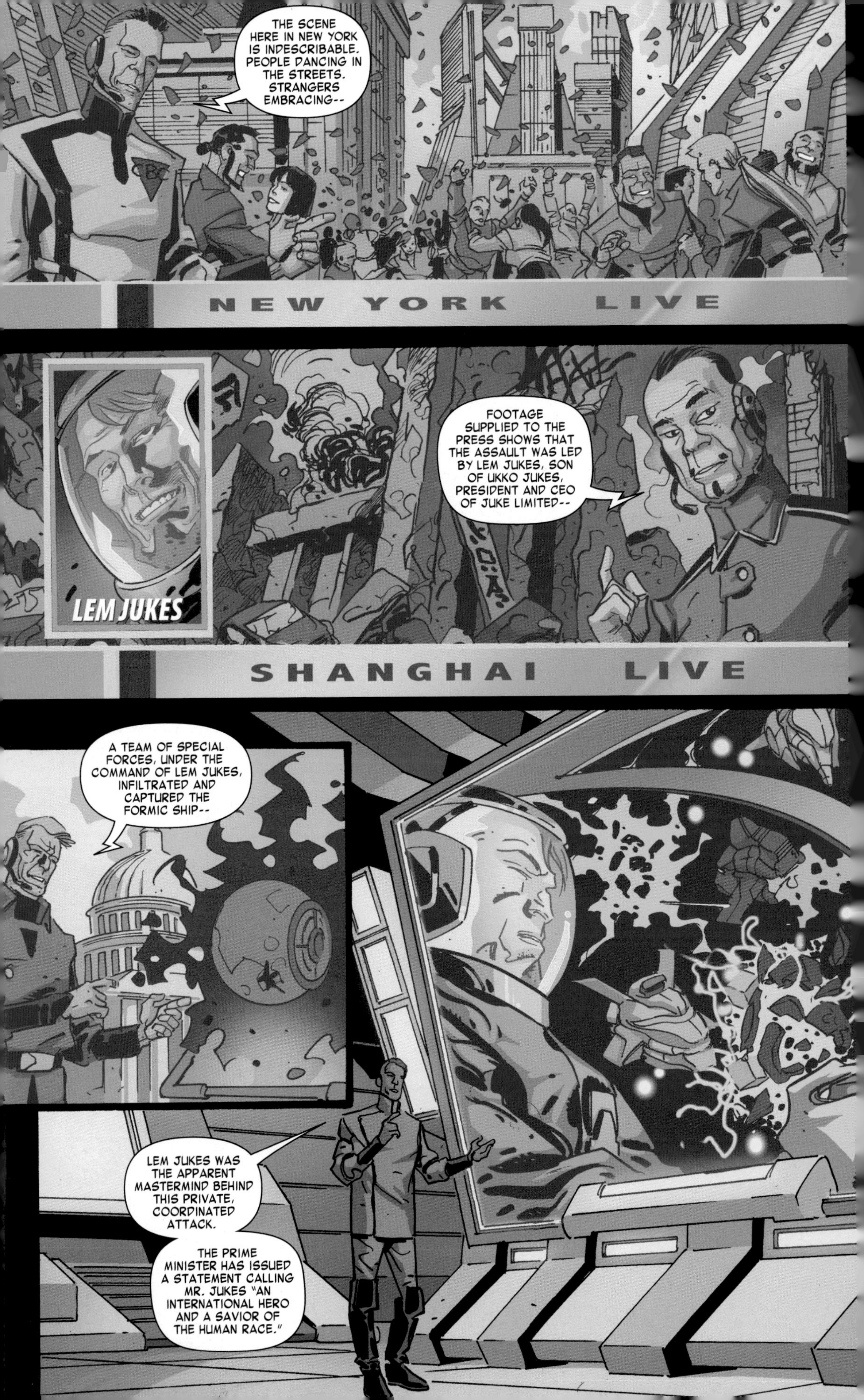
THE SCENE HERE IN NEW YORK IS INDESCRIBABLE. PEOPLE DANCING IN THE STREETS. STRANGERS EMBRACING--
NEW YORK LIVE
LEM JUKES
FOOTAGE SUPPLIED TO THE PRESS SHOWS THAT THE ASSAULT WAS LED BY LEM JUKES, SON OF UKKO JUKES, PRESIDENT AND CEO OF JUKE LIMITED--
SHANGHAI LIVE
A TEAM OF SPECIAL FORCES, UNDER THE COMMAND OF LEM JUKES, INFILTRATED AND CAPTURED THE FORMIC SHIP--
LEM JUKES WAS THE APPARENT MASTERMIND BEHIND THIS PRIVATE, COORDINATED ATTACK.
THE PRIME MINISTER HAS ISSUED A STATEMENT CALLING MR. JUKES "AN INTERNATIONAL HERO AND A SAVIOR OF THE HUMAN RACE."

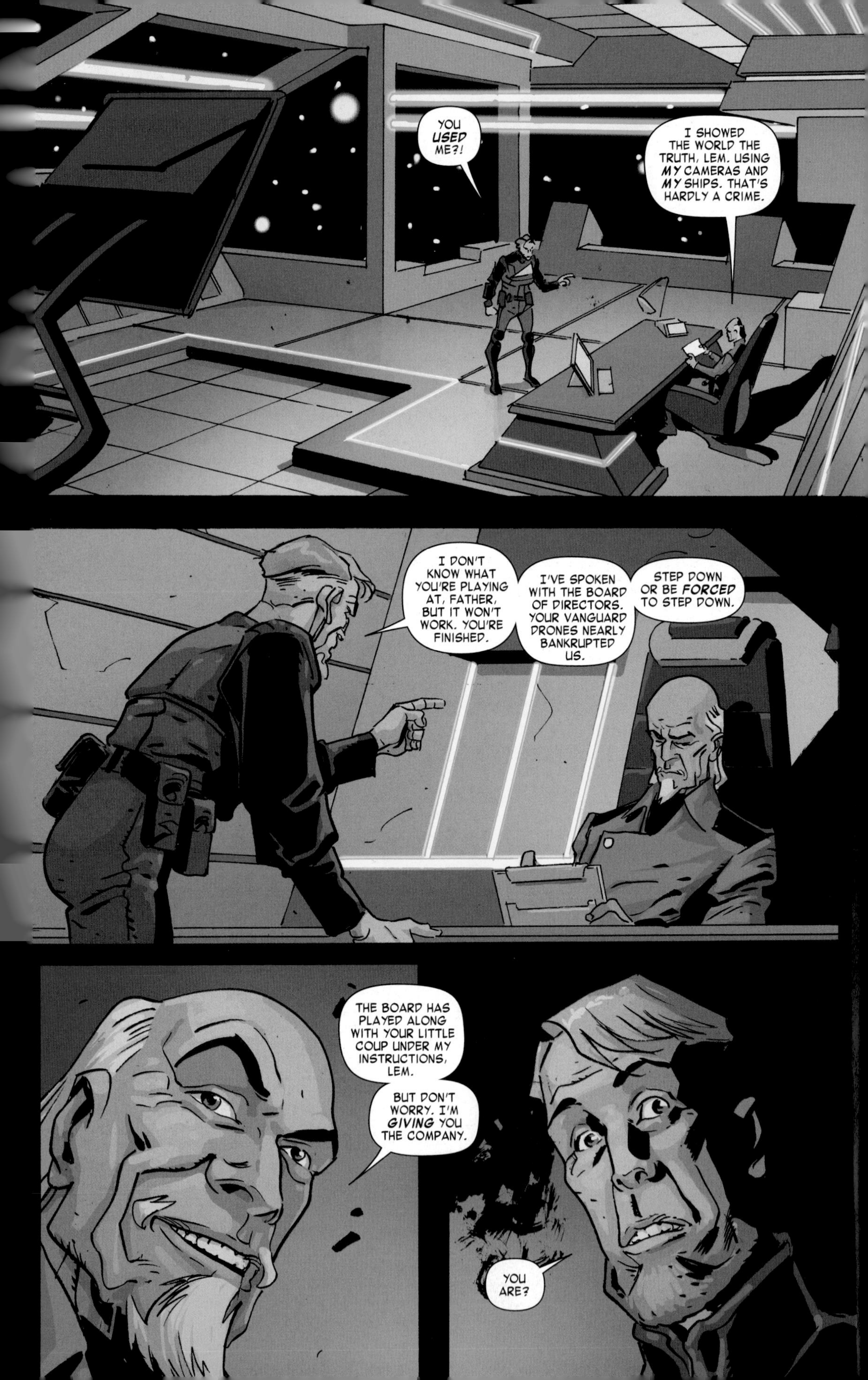
YOU USED ME?!
I SHOWED THE WORLD THE TRUTH, LEM. USING MY CAMERAS AND MY SHIPS. THAT'S HARDLY A CRIME.
I DON'T KNOW WHAT YOU'RE PLAYING AT, FATHER, BUT IT WON'T WORK. YOU'RE FINISHED.
I'VE SPOKEN WITH THE BOARD OF DIRECTORS. YOUR VANGUARD DRONES NEARLY BANKRUPTED US.
STEP DOWN OR BE FORCED TO STEP DOWN.
THE BOARD HAS PLAYED ALONG WITH YOUR LITTLE COUP UNDER MY INSTRUCTIONS, LEM.
BUT DON'T WORRY. I'M GIVING YOU THE COMPANY.
YOU ARE?

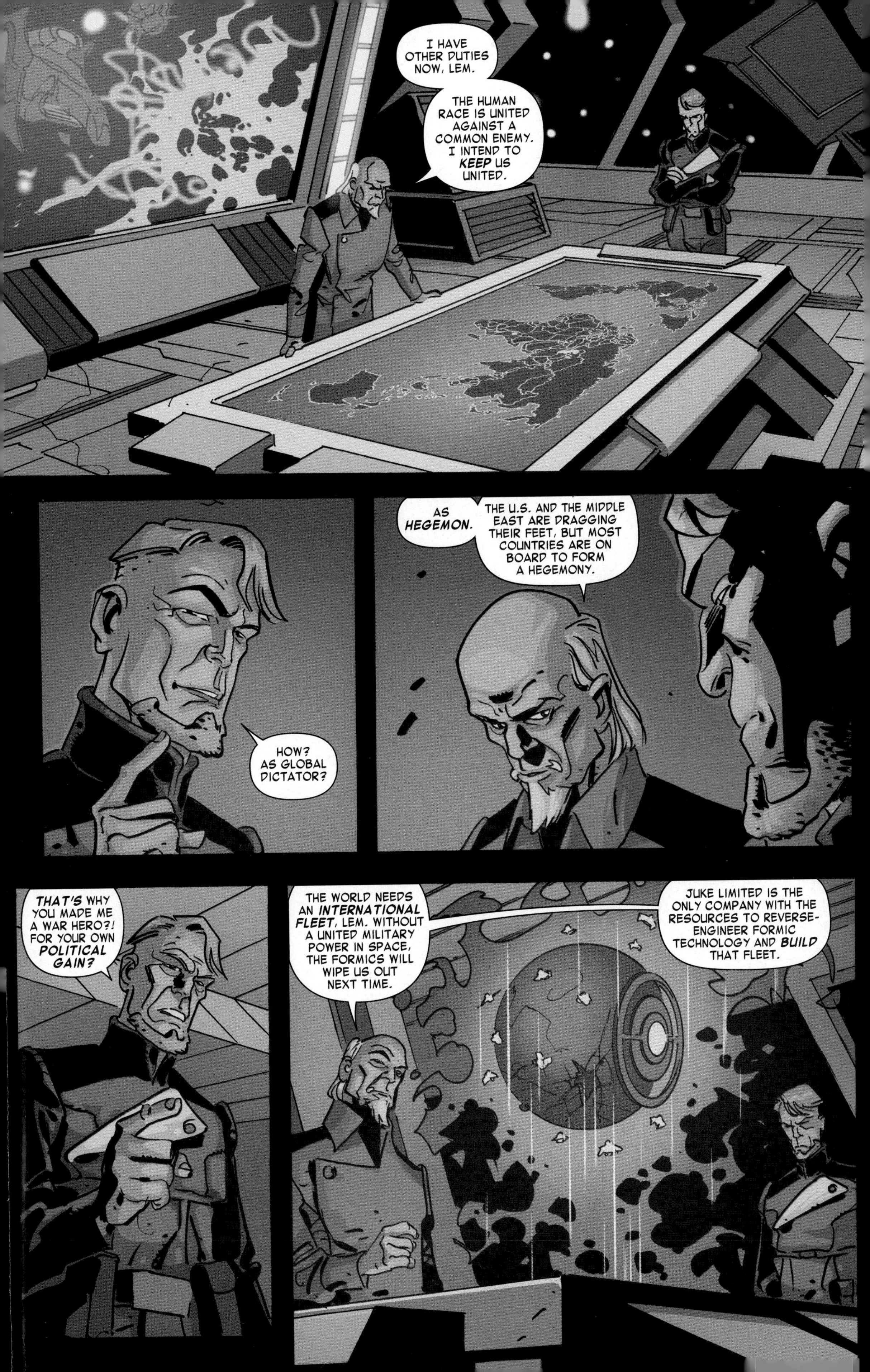
I HAVE OTHER DUTIES NOW, LEM.
THE HUMAN RACE IS UNITED AGAINST A COMMON ENEMY. I INTEND TO *KEEP* US UNITED.
HOW? AS GLOBAL DICTATOR?
AS *HEGEMON.*
THE U.S. AND THE MIDDLE EAST ARE DRAGGING THEIR FEET, BUT MOST COUNTRIES ARE ON BOARD TO FORM A HEGEMONY.
THAT'S WHY YOU MADE ME A WAR HERO?! FOR YOUR OWN *POLITICAL GAIN?*
THE WORLD NEEDS AN *INTERNATIONAL FLEET*, LEM. WITHOUT A UNITED MILITARY POWER IN SPACE, THE FORMICS WILL WIPE US OUT NEXT TIME.
JUKE LIMITED IS THE ONLY COMPANY WITH THE RESOURCES TO REVERSE-ENGINEER FORMIC TECHNOLOGY AND *BUILD* THAT FLEET.

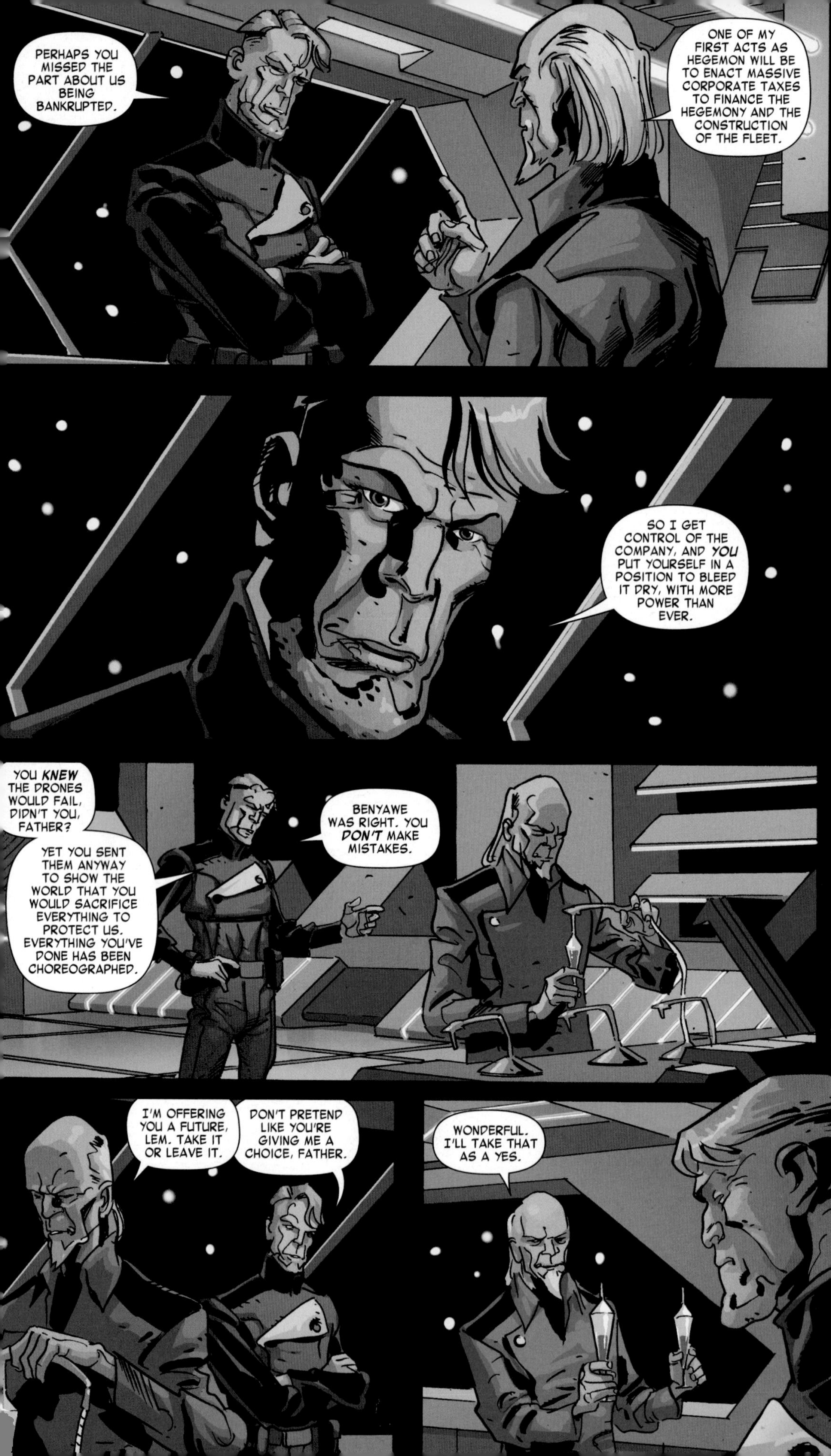
PERHAPS YOU MISSED THE PART ABOUT US BEING BANKRUPTED.
ONE OF MY FIRST ACTS AS HEGEMON WILL BE TO ENACT MASSIVE CORPORATE TAXES TO FINANCE THE HEGEMONY AND THE CONSTRUCTION OF THE FLEET.
SO I GET CONTROL OF THE COMPANY, AND YOU PUT YOURSELF IN A POSITION TO BLEED IT DRY, WITH MORE POWER THAN EVER.
YOU KNEW THE DRONES WOULD FAIL, DIDN'T YOU, FATHER?
YET YOU SENT THEM ANYWAY TO SHOW THE WORLD THAT YOU WOULD SACRIFICE EVERYTHING TO PROTECT US. EVERYTHING YOU'VE DONE HAS BEEN CHOREOGRAPHED.
BENYAWE WAS RIGHT. YOU DON'T MAKE MISTAKES.
I'M OFFERING YOU A FUTURE, LEM. TAKE IT OR LEAVE IT.
DON'T PRETEND LIKE YOU'RE GIVING ME A CHOICE, FATHER.
WONDERFUL. I'LL TAKE THAT AS A YES.

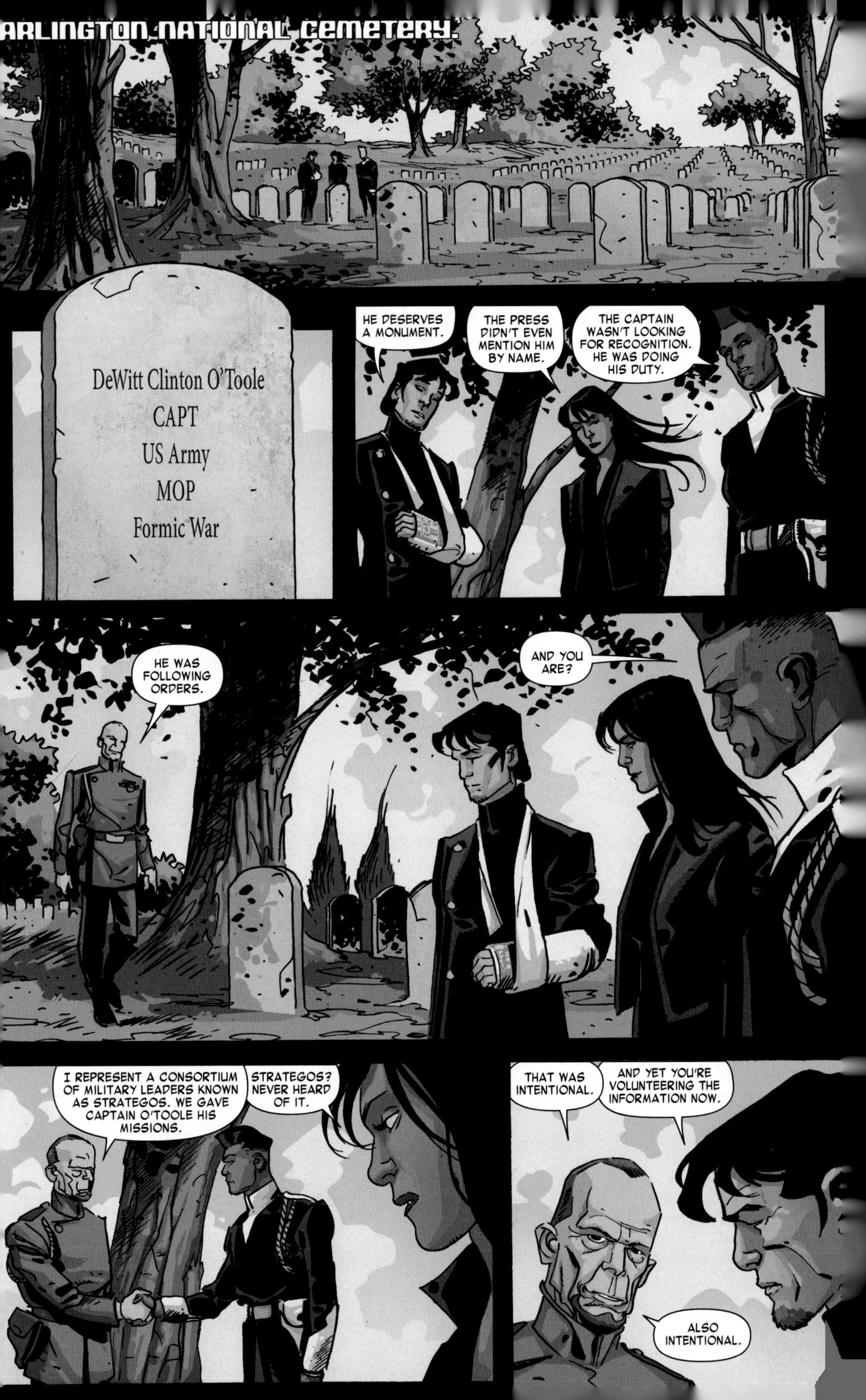
ARLINGTON NATIONAL CEMETERY.
DeWitt Clinton O'Toole
CAPT
US Army
MOP
Formic War
HE DESERVES A MONUMENT.
THE PRESS DIDN'T EVEN MENTION HIM BY NAME.
THE CAPTAIN WASN'T LOOKING FOR RECOGNITION. HE WAS DOING HIS DUTY.
HE WAS FOLLOWING ORDERS.
AND YOU ARE?
I REPRESENT A CONSORTIUM OF MILITARY LEADERS KNOWN AS STRATEGOS. WE GAVE CAPTAIN O'TOOLE HIS MISSIONS.
STRATEGOS? NEVER HEARD OF IT.
THAT WAS INTENTIONAL.
AND YET YOU'RE VOLUNTEERING THE INFORMATION NOW.
ALSO INTENTIONAL.

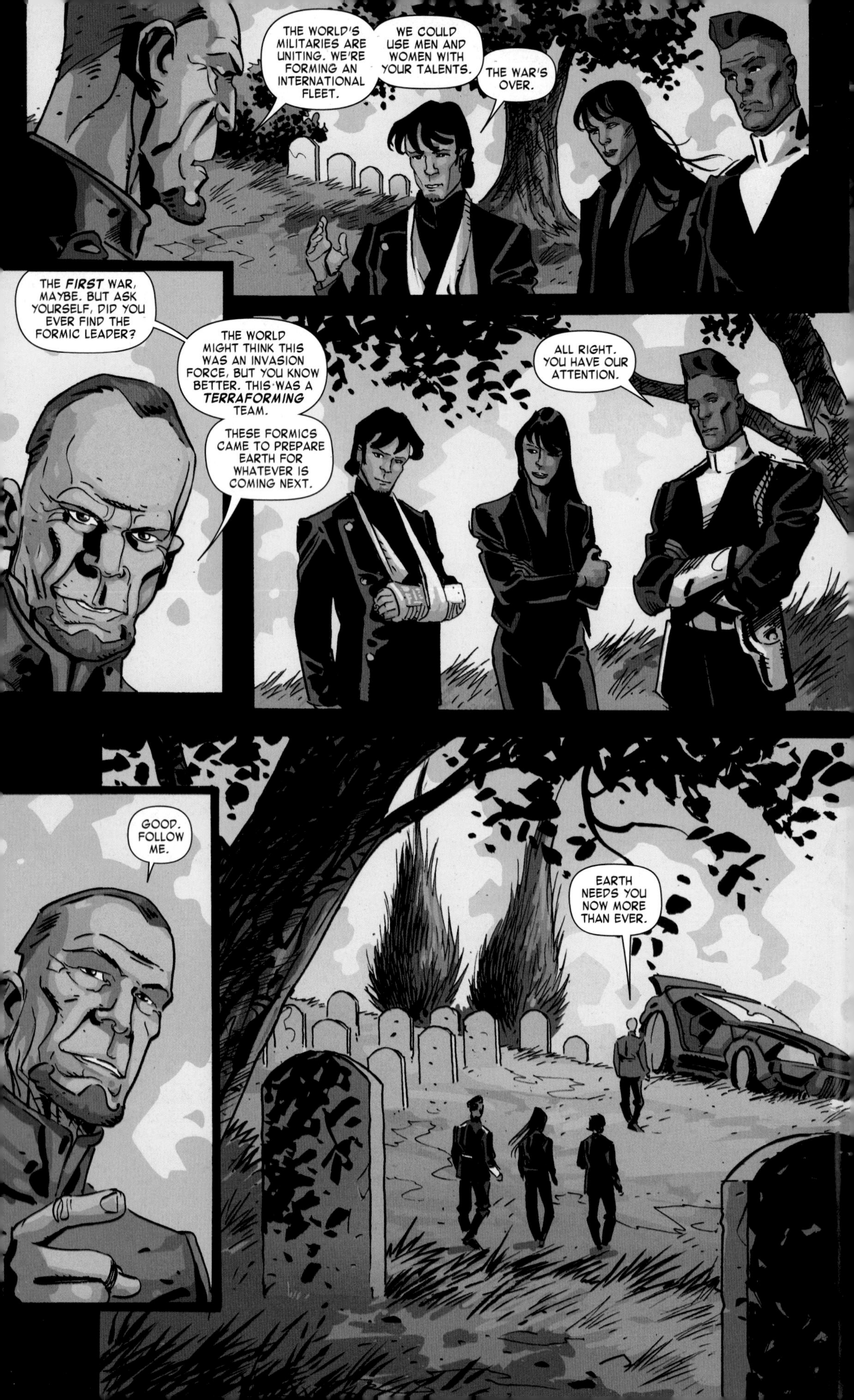
THE WORLD'S MILITARIES ARE UNITING. WE'RE FORMING AN INTERNATIONAL FLEET.
WE COULD USE MEN AND WOMEN WITH YOUR TALENTS.
THE WAR'S OVER.
THE *FIRST* WAR, MAYBE. BUT ASK YOURSELF, DID YOU EVER FIND THE FORMIC LEADER?
THE WORLD MIGHT THINK THIS WAS AN INVASION FORCE, BUT YOU KNOW BETTER. THIS WAS A *TERRAFORMING* TEAM.
THESE FORMICS CAME TO PREPARE EARTH FOR WHATEVER IS COMING NEXT.
ALL RIGHT. YOU HAVE OUR ATTENTION.
GOOD. FOLLOW ME.
EARTH NEEDS YOU NOW MORE THAN EVER.

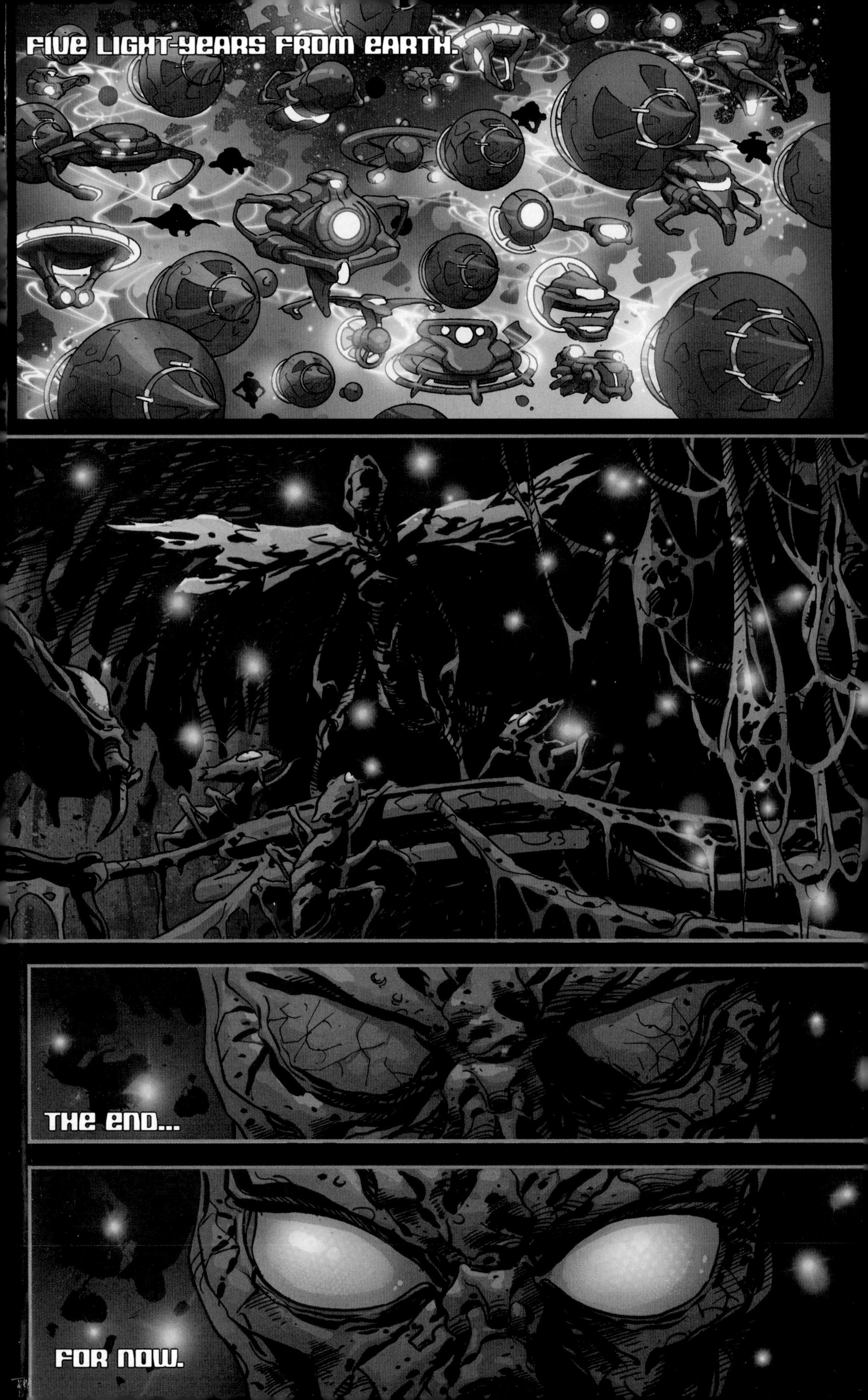
FIVE LIGHT-YEARS FROM EARTH.
THE END...
FOR NOW.

COVER PROCESS

#1

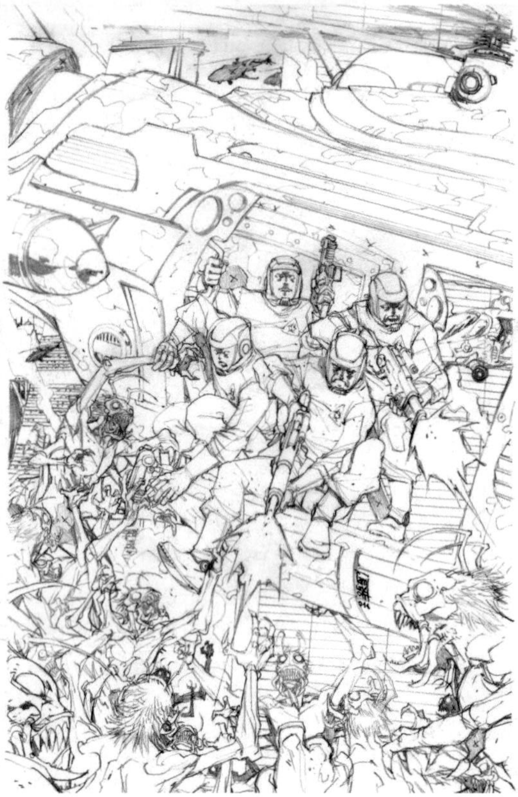

#3

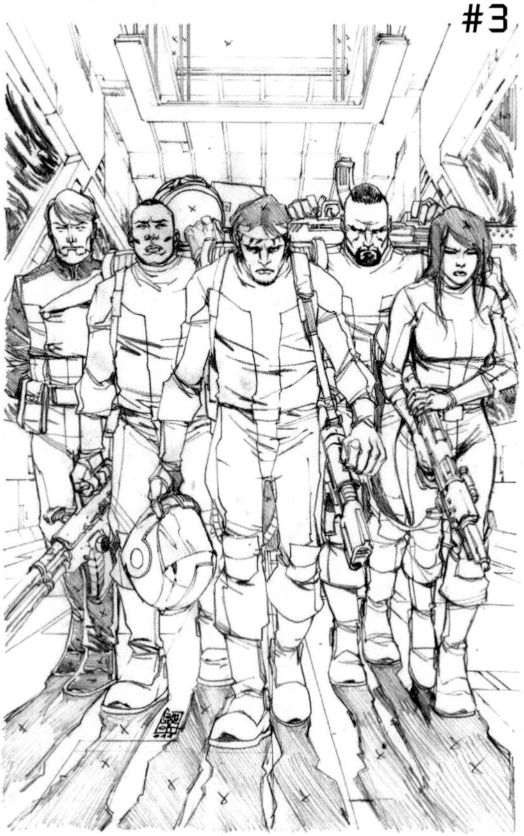

#2

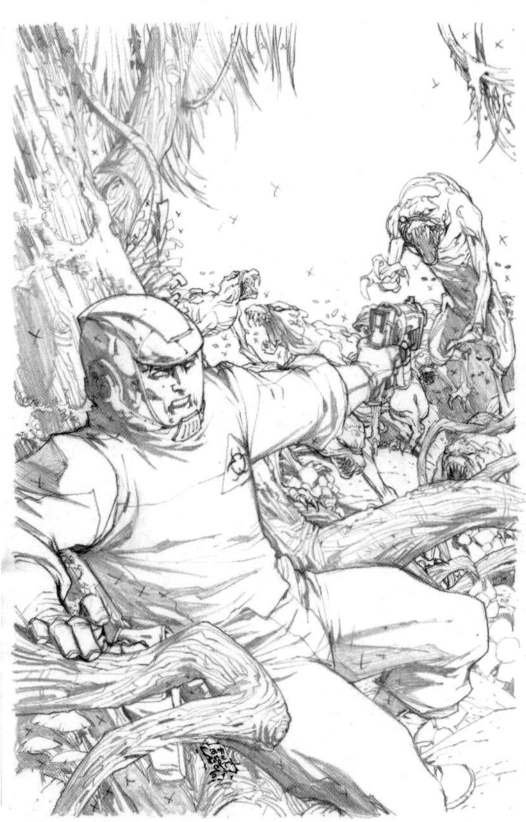

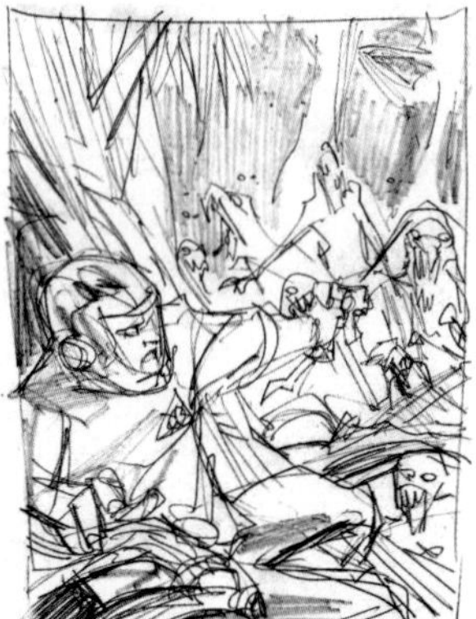

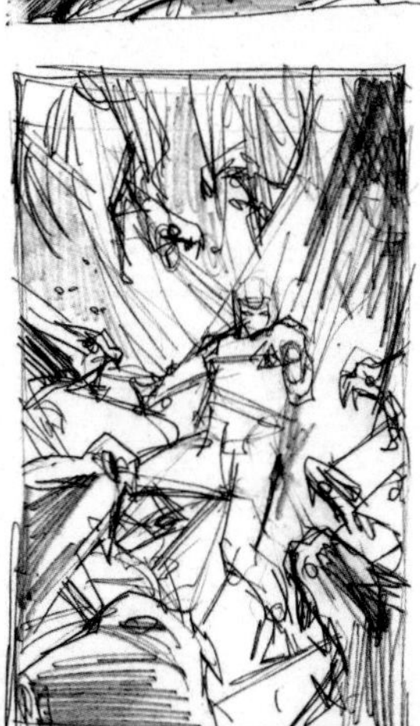

#4

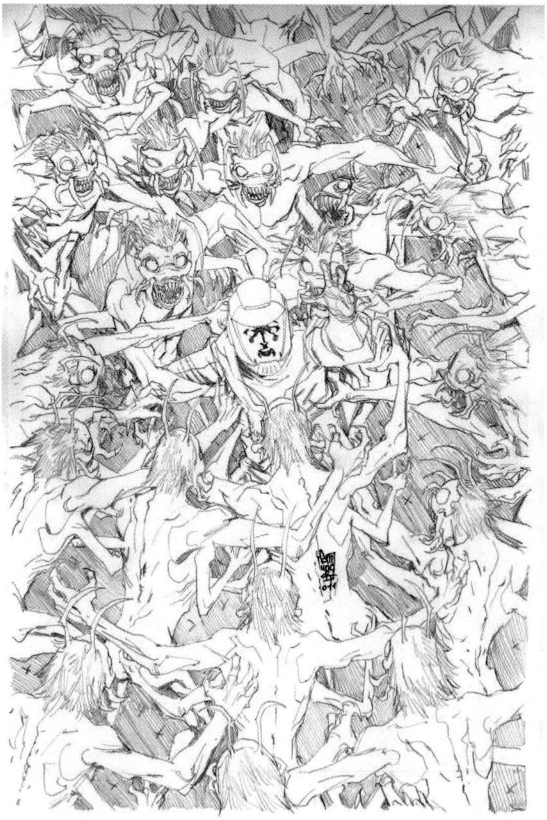

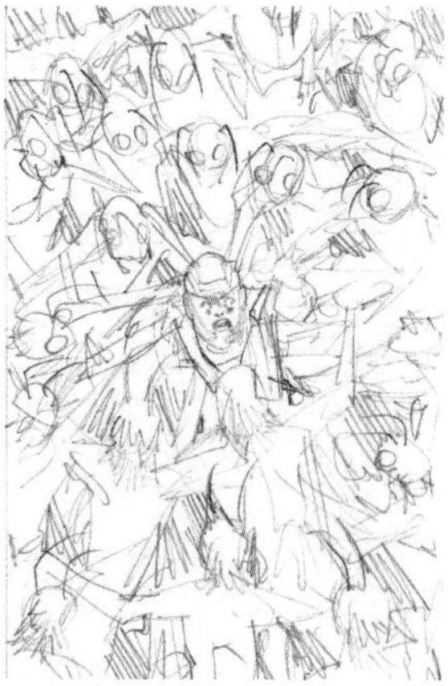

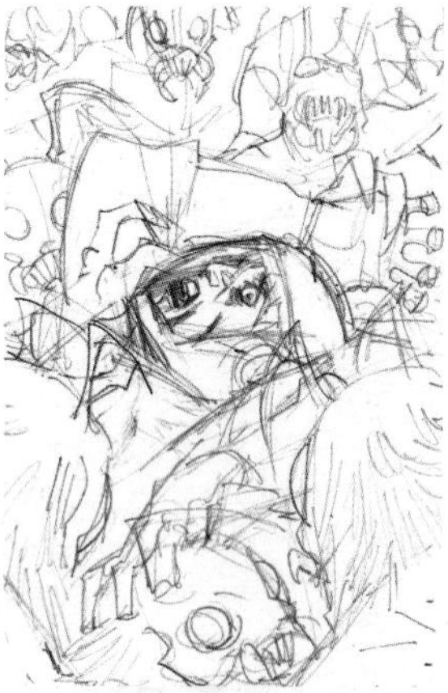

#5

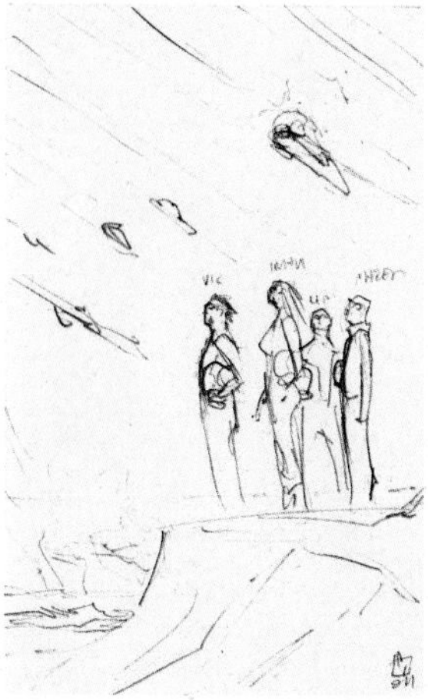

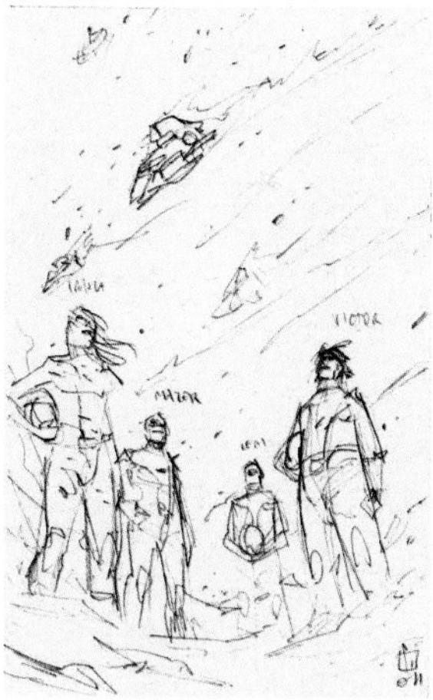

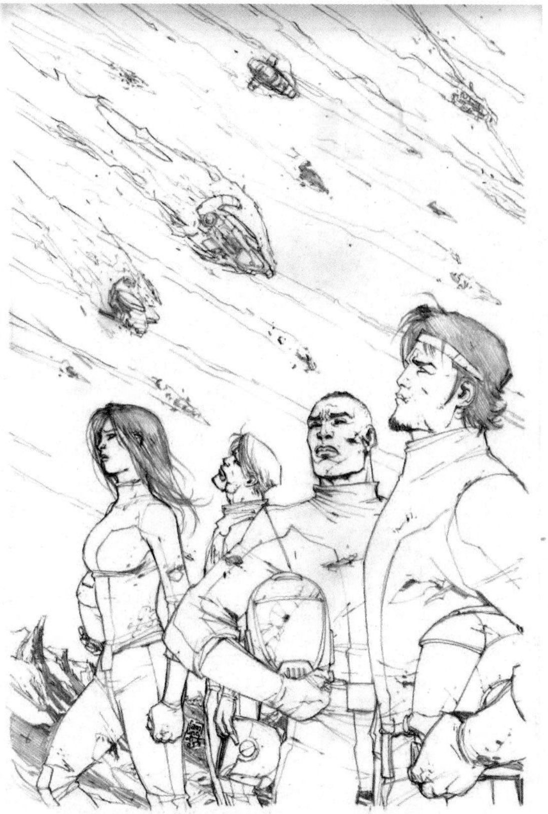

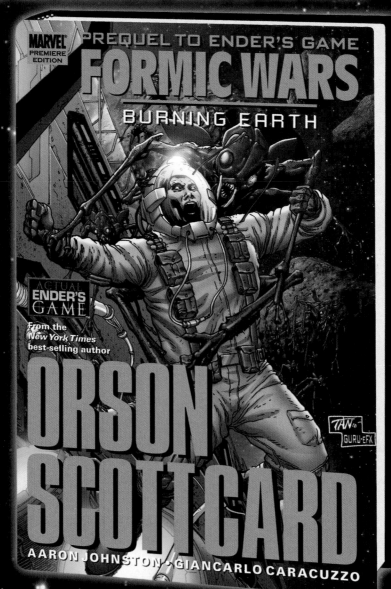

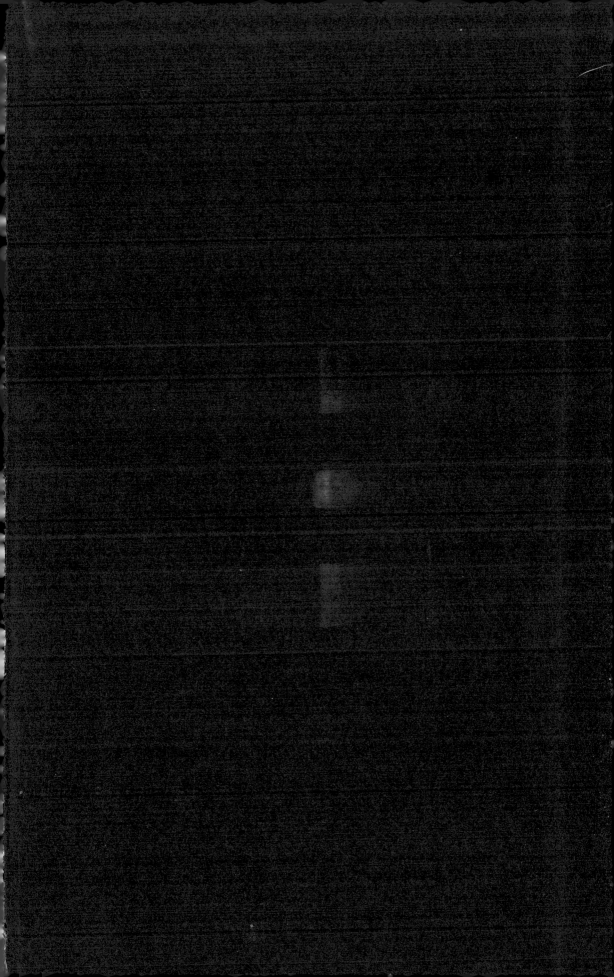